高职高专旅游专业"互联网+"创新规划教材

酒店情景英语(第2版)

主　编　高文知
副主编　李淑君　程　逆　肖　凯
参　编　吕天春

U0369890

北京大学出版社
PEKING UNIVERSITY PRESS

内 容 简 介

　　本书从酒店从业人员的实际工作需要出发进行设计、构思和编写，主要以酒店 6 个主要部门为依托，分为 6 个场景单元，每个场景单元又分为若干个子场景单元。每个单元包含了听力、场景对话、基本知识、课堂场景对话、补充阅读等部分。在加强学生的英语沟通能力之外，重在培养学生在酒店若干场景中的听、说能力，并拓展视野和眼界。本书还配有 3 套试题，供教学之用。

　　本书主要作为高职高专旅游管理类和酒店管理类专业的教材，也可作为职大、夜大、函授和中职旅游类专业的教材，还可作为酒店管理人员、服务人员的培训和工作参考书。

图书在版编目(CIP)数据

酒店情景英语/高文知主编. —2 版. —北京：北京大学出版社，2017.1
（高职高专旅游专业"互联网+"创新规划教材）
ISBN 978-7-301-27841-3

Ⅰ．①酒…　Ⅱ．①高…　Ⅲ．①饭店—英语—高等职业教育—教材　Ⅳ．①F719.3

中国版本图书馆 CIP 数据核字（2016）第 307116 号

书　　　名	酒店情景英语（第 2 版）	
	JIUDIAN QINGJING YINGYU	
著作责任者	高文知　主编	
策 划 编 辑	刘国明	
责 任 编 辑	翟　源	
数 字 编 辑	陈颖颖	
标 准 书 号	ISBN 978-7-301-27841-3	
出 版 发 行	北京大学出版社	
地　　　址	北京市海淀区成府路 205 号　100871	
网　　　址	http://www.pup.cn　新浪微博：@北京大学出版社	
电 子 信 箱	pup_6@163.com	
电　　　话	邮购部 62752015　发行部 62750672　编辑部 62750667	
印 刷 者	北京鑫海金澳胶印有限公司	
经 销 者	新华书店	
	787 毫米×1092 毫米　16 开本　15.75 印张　363 千字	
	2013 年 3 月第 1 版	
	2017 年 1 月第 2 版　　2021 年 8 月第 4 次印刷	
定　　　价	34.00 元	

前言

21 世纪的酒店业正在蓬勃发展，随着中国逐步成为旅游强国，酒店业具有丰富的客源市场。而随着酒店市场的国际化，以及我国国际旅游市场的扩大，要求酒店从业人员必须具备一定的英语应对能力。

我国高职高专院校旅游管理类、酒店管理类相关专业是培养酒店业人才的摇篮。酒店情景英语是此类专业的必修课程之一。目前，在英语课堂中运用情景教学法已经得到许多教师的认同，并且有相当数量的教师已经在实际教学中应用了情景教学模式。但是，高职院校如何开展酒店英语课程的情景教学，仍然是酒店管理专业教师面临的课题。本书再版时仍以酒店实训为依托，以酒店前台、客房部、餐饮部、健身中心、商务中心、酒店商品部六个部门为六个主要场景来进行编排。六个场景又分为若干个子场景，以教学单元的形式体现，侧重于提高学生的英语综合服务技能，加强本书的实用性，让师生如置身在酒店的真实场景中。

本书以任务导向，情景教学为指导思想，每个子场景及教学单元包括"听力""场景对话""基本知识""课堂场景对话""补充阅读"等部分，让学生在加强基本知识的同时，在听、说、读、写方面均有所提高。"基本知识"部分不仅包含本单元场景必须掌握的知识，还进行了知识拓展。编排上注意图文并茂，让学生加深对岗位场景的认识。书后还配有习题，贯彻从难到易的原则，既有利于学生对知识的巩固，也便于教师的教学。再版对部分场景对话、基本知识、补充阅读进行了增订，同时体现了信息化和网络化的教育发展趋势。

本书主要作为高职高专旅游管理类和酒店管理类专业的教材，也可作为职大、夜大、函授和中职旅游类专业的教材，还可作为酒店管理人员、服务人员的培训和工作参考书。

本书由高文知(武汉铁路职业技术学院、武汉大学历史学院)任主编，李淑君(武汉铁路职业技术学院)、程逆(武汉铁路职业技术学院)、肖凯(武汉铁路职业技术学院)任副主编。编写分工如下：高文知负责第一、第四单元，李淑君负责第二、第三单元，肖凯负责第五单元，程逆负责第六单元，吕天春(长春职业技术学院)负责资料的收集与整理。全书由高文知担任审稿和整理工作。高文知完成本书二维码资料的搜集和整理工作。

在本书再版过程中，编者参考了大量的相关文献，在此向原文献的作者表示诚挚的谢意。同时，本书再版得到了北京大学出版社的大力支持，在此感谢出版社为本书的编写工作提出的建议和意见。

由于时间仓促，编者水平有限，书中不妥之处在所难免，欢迎广大读者对本书提出宝贵意见，以便今后改进。

高文知

2016 年 5 月

目录
Contents

【资源索引】

2 Chapter
Housekeeping — 54

3 Chapter
Food & Beverage — 97

6 Chapter
At the Hotel Store ■ 211

The Front Office

Unit 1　Room Reservation (I)

Listening Practice

【听力音频】

1. Listen to the dialogue and fill in the blanks.

A: Room Reservations. Good afternoon.

B: Good afternoon. I'd like to book a _____ room for _____.

A: That's fine, sir. A double room for Tuesday, September 12th, with _____ or _____?

B: What's the difference of price?

A: A double room with a front view is _____ dollars per night, one with a rear view is _____ dollars per night.

B: I think I'll take the one with _____ then.

A: How long will you stay?

B: We'll leave _____.

A: That will be five nights, sir. Thank you very much, and we look forward to seeing you next Tuesday.

B: Good. That's all settled then. Goodbye.

A: Goodbye.

2. Listen and fill in the missing information.

Room type: _____　　Arriving Date: _____

Dep. Date: _____　　Quoted Rate: _____

Room Service: _____　　Guest's Name: _____

Guest's Address: _____

Phone Number: _____

Confirming Way: _____

Situational Dialogues

1. Making Rooms Arrangements with a Hotel

(Scene: David Johnson from the Summer Travel Agency telephones Leslie of Room Reservations of Claude Hotel to arrange rooms from 22nd July to 26th July for a meeting group from Australia.)

(L: Leslie, D: David Johnson)

L: Claude Hotel. Reservations. Leslie speaking. How can I help you?

D: This is David Johnson from Summer Travel Agency.

L: Oh, Mr. Johnson, what can we do for you this time?

D: We'll have a meeting group from Australia, and I'm calling to arrange the accommodations in your place.

L: How many members, please?

D: There'll be 30 members.

L: OK. And their arrival and departure dates?

D: They will be arriving on Friday, 22nd July and leaving on Tuesday, 26th July.

L: That'll be four nights. What type of rooms would they like?

D: Fifteen twin-bed rooms, please.

L: How will they be arriving? Do you want us to offer pick-up service?

D: No, thanks. They will arrive by air. Our tour escort will meet the group at the airport.

L: OK. The contracted room rate for twin-bed rooms is 680 yuan per night, including breakfast.

D: That's right.

L: Do you pay everything?

D: No. We'll give our guests vouchers and we only pay the value on the voucher. Other expenses must be settled by the guests themselves.

L: I see. We'll send you a fax confirmation about reservation later.

D: Thank you for your help. Goodbye.

L: Thanks for calling，Mr. Johnson. We hope to be of any help to you again. Goodbye.

2. Making a Fit Room Reservation

(Scene: A clerk named Zhang Li of Claude Hotel is answering a call from Mostaq Missouri who would like to book hotel rooms in the Claude Hotel.)

【拓展音频】

(Z: Zhang Li, M: Mostaq Missouri)

Z: Good morning. Claude Hotel. Can I help you?

M: Good morning. Have you got any vacancies for the nights of 22nd and 23rd? I'd like to make a reservation for the two nights.

Z: All right. Single or double room?

M: Double room, please.

Z: Let me check… Yes, there is a double room available.

M: Is that with or without bath?

Z: It's a room with shower and toilet.

M: That sounds fine. Is there air-conditioning?

Z: Certainly, sir.

M: How much will it be for one night?

Z: Let me see. A double room is 600 yuan per night.

M: With breakfast?

Z: Yes, that includes a Chinese or American breakfast and a morning newspaper.

M: Do you accept VISA?

Z: Yes, we do. What time will you be arriving?

M: I will be there around 5:30 p.m. on 22nd.

Z: OK, sir. May I have your name and contact number, please?

M: Yes, my name's Mostaq Missouri. It's India 567-998.

Z: Could you spell that, please?

M: M—O—S—T—A—Q, M—I—S—S—O—U—R—I.

Z: Mr. Mostaq Missouri. A double-room with bath and air-conditioning for the nights of 22nd and 23rd. Is that right?

M: Yes. Thank you.

Z: You're welcome, sir. We look forward to your coming. Goodbye.

3. A Corporate Room Reservation

【拓展音频】

(Scene: Mr. West of Beijing Foreign Trade Company is calling the Reservations of New Garden Hotel to reserve a suite for seventeen to twenty days.)

(R: Reservationist, W: West)

R: Good afternoon. What can I do for you?

W: Good afternoon. I'm calling from Beijing Foreign Trade Company. Is it possible for me to have a suite?

R: Certainly, can you give me your name please, sir?

W: West, W-E-S-T.

R: Thank you, Mr. West. But by the way, how long will you stay here?

W: I'll stay here for quite a long time.

R: I'm glad you will be staying at our hotel for a long time.

W: How much is the suite, please?

R: Your suite is 860 yuan (RMB) per day.

W: Does that include attendance?

R: Eight hundred and sixty yuan a day, service included.

W: Meals included?

R: Meals are extra, not included.

W: What services come with that?

R: For eight hundred and sixty yuan a day, you will have one bedroom with air-conditioning, a sitting room, a bathroom, a colour TV set, Wireless WiFi, a telephone and a major international newspaper delivered to your room every day.

W: Do I have to pay in advance?

R: Yes, you may pay half of it. The account will be settled later.

W: On which floor is the suite?

R: We have reserved two suites for you to choose. One is on the first floor, the other on the thirteenth floor. Both of them have a bathroom and face to the south.

W: What's the difference between them?

R: The conditions and the prices are the same. No difference.

W: Which is quiet? I want a quiet one. I hate noise at night.

R: The one on the thirteenth floor is very quiet. The room number is 1316.

W: I think I'll take the one on the thirteenth floor.

R: OK. And your arrival and departure dates?

W: I don't know, but it could be seventeen to twenty days.

R: Then we can only confirm a room from the 10th to the 27th. I'm afraid we won't be able to guarantee you the room after the 27th.

W: What if there isn't any room then?

R: Don't worry, sir. We can either put you on a waiting list or find you a room in a nearby hotel.

W: Fine, thank you. Goodbye.

4. Reserving Rooms and a Conference Room

(Scene: John Berry on behalf of Mr. Smith of Oxford University is calling Zhang Li from Nelson Hotel to reserve four single rooms with bath for the nights of June 10th to 15th and a conference room for the afternoons of June 12th and 14th).

(J: John Berry, Z: Zhang Li)

Z: Hello. Nelson Hotel.

J: Hello, I'm calling on behalf of Mr. Smith of Oxford University. I'd like to reserve four single rooms with bath for the nights of June 10th to 15th.

Z: Hold on, please…Yes, we have rooms available for those dates. Can you repeat the name, please?

J: In the name of Mr. Smith of Oxford University. Mr. Smith will also require a conference room for the afternoons of June 12th and 14th.

Z: Yes, we can arrange that. For how many hours do you require the conference room and how many people?

J: It's for 8 people, from 3:30 p.m. to 6:30 p.m.

Z: Very good. For 8 people, from 3:30 p.m. to 6:30 p.m.

J: That's right. May I have the price for the single rooms and conference room, please?

Z: The single rooms will be US $80 per night. The charge for the conference room will be US $100 for two afternoons. Is that OK?

J: That's fine.

Z: Would you let us have your confirmation of the reservation and a deposit of US $40 as soon as possible?

J: Of course. I'll send them this afternoon.

Z: Thank you. Goodbye.

J: Goodbye.

Words and Expressions

departure	*n.*	离开，出发，起程	pick-up service			接车服务
escort	*n.*	护送	voucher	*n.*		凭单，收据，传单
vacancy	*n.*	空白，空地	suite	*n.*		套房

Learn by Heart

1. 订房的基本方式

柜台预订	talk	口头预订	verbal
信函预订	mail	合同预订	contract
电话预订	telephone	电脑预订	computer
传真预订	fax	电脑网络	computer network

2. 预订常用语

Do you have one single room for two nights?
我想订两晚的单人房一间，行吗？

(Room)Reservations. Can I help you?
客房预订部，可以为您效劳吗？

Which date would that be?
要订在什么时候？

What kind of room would you prefer?
您想要什么样的房间？

Could you hold the line please? I'll check our room availability.
请别挂断好吗？我来查一下是否有空房。

May I have your name /phone number /e-mail?

能告诉我您的姓名/电话/电子邮件吗？

We offer special rates for your company, sir. For a single room there is a 15% discount.

我们为贵公司提供特价，先生，单人可以打八五折。

May I have your airline and flight number, please?

请告诉我您搭乘的航空公司和班机号码，好吗？

We offer free transportation to and from the airport.

我们提供免费的机场接送服务。

Would you like to make a guaranteed reservation by credit card?

您愿意用信用卡来担保预订吗？

I'd like to confirm your reservation.

我想再确认一下您的预订。

Class Activity Role-Play

Scene One: A gentleman steps in, trying to find a room for the night.

Scene Two: John Smith from Peking University is calling to Shangri-La Hotel to reserve a conference room for an international academic conference.

Further Reading

Advance Reservation

Advance reservation service is provided by the Front Office. The reservationist works at the front desk by the lobby. What the reservationist should do involves answering questions concerning reservations, booking and assigning rooms for guests who request rooms in the hotel. The reservationist also takes reservations, cancellations and revisions, and types and sends out the hotel's letter of confirmation.

There are different ways of making reservations. You can send reservation e-mail to the hotel. You can go directly to the hotel and make reservations in person or call the hotel and make reservations over the telephone. You can also fax the hotel for reserving rooms. Nowadays fax reservation has become more and more popular, for with the fax, the communication is instantaneous.

When a reservationist receives a reservation request, he/she first checks the hotel's booking situation to see if the hotel has any vacancy during the specified period. If there are rooms available, the reservationist would fill out a reservation form and record the information in a reservation diary.

参考译文

预 订 房 间

　　客房预订服务由前厅部提供，预订员在大厅的前台工作。他的职责包括回答有关预订房间的询问，给有需要的客人订房间和具体安排房间。他还负责办理预订、取消预订、改变预订、打印并寄送确认预订书。

　　预订房间有多种方式。你可给酒店发邮件预订，可以亲自到酒店预订或给酒店打电话预订，还可以通过传真预订。如今，传真预订日益流行，因为使用传真沟通瞬时完成。

　　收到预订请求后，预订员首先要查看一下酒店的预订情况，看看在指定的日期内是否有空房。如果有空房，预订员就要填写一份预订单，并把有关情况记录在预订日志中。

【拓展习题】

Question

How to be a good reservationist?

Unit 2   Room Reservation (II)

Listening Practice

【听力音频】

1. Listen to the dialogue and fill in the blanks.

A: I would like_____.

B: Just a moment, please. Let me have a look. Yes, we still have a few vacant single rooms.

A: Do you have a single room with _____?

B: Yes, we do.

A: That's great! How much is the room, please?

B: Two hundred yuan per day. Would you like _____ in the room?

A: Yes. And I'd also like to know something about recreation in your hotel.

B: Yes, there's a recreation and fitness center in our hotel. We have a very well equipped bodybuilding gymnasium with all _____, such as pull weights and race apparatus etc.

A: Could you recommend some local exercise to me?

B: Have you heard about yoga? The movements are even and slow, very similar to Chinese Qigong exercise.

A: Thanks a lot for your information.

B: You're welcome.

2. Listen and fill in the missing information.

The single room's price: _____

The double room's price: _____

Discount: _____

The room type booked: _____

Situational Dialogues

【拓展音频】

1. Fully Booked

(Scene: A guest would like to reserve a single room for September 24th. But the rooms are fully booked on that day. The guest asks the clerk to recommend another hotel in the city center that are not full up.)

Clerk: Advance Reservations. Good morning. Can I help you?

Guest: Yes, I'd like to reserve a single room for September 24th.

Clerk: Just a moment, please. I'm sorry, miss. We are fully booked on that day.

Guest: Oh, that's too bad.

Clerk: Is it possible for you to change your reservation date?

Guest: I'm afraid not.

Clerk: Would you like us to put you on our waiting list and call you in case we have a cancellation?

Guest: Thank you. That's very kind of you. But could you recommend me another hotel which won't be full up?

Clerk: Yes, of course. Where would you rather like to be, in the city center or in the suburb?

Guest: I prefer a place close to the city center because most of our clients' offices are in the downtown business section.

Clerk: In that case, I would suggest that you try International Hotel.

Guest: Do you know the rate per night for a single there?

Clerk: Well, there is a minimum price for off-season stay and a maximun price for peak-season stay. A single with shower at the moment would run you between 380 yuan and 480 yuan.

Guest: I see. One last thing, do you know the telephone number?

Clerk: Yes. It's 500—4305. Shall I call the hotel for you now?

Guest: No, thank you very much. I really appreciate your help. Goodbye.

Clerk: Goodbye, and thank you for calling us.

2. Canceling a Reservation

(Scene: A guest would like to cancel a reservation which is under White's name. The reservation is from September 15th for 3 nights. The clerk helps the guest cancel the reservation.)

Clerk: Room Reservations. May I help you?

Guest: Yes. I'd like to cancel a reservation, because the travel schedule has been changed.

Clerk: That's OK. Could you tell me under whose name was the reservation made?

Guest: White. W—H—I—T—E.

Clerk: And what was the date of the reservation?

Guest: From September 15th for 3 nights.

Clerk: Excuse me, but is the reservation for yourself or for another party?

Guest: It's for my boss.

Clerk: Well, may I have your name and phone number, please?

Guest: Yes, it's Ellen Green, and my number is 245—3971.

Clerk: Thank you. ma'am. I will cancel Mr White's reservation for September 15th for 3 nights. My name is Wang Ying and we look forward to another chance to serve you.

Clerk: Thank you the same, Mr Wang.

Guest: It's my pleasure.

3. Adjusting a Reservation (R: Reservationist, G: Guest)

(Scene: Mr. Dunning calling from Los Angles has reserved a suite on Oct. 2nd. He would extend his stay in the hotel for two nights. The reservationist helps the guest reserve the suite for two nights from Oct. 2nd to 4th).

R: Advance Reservations. Good afternoon. This is Mary Wang speaking. What can I do for you?

G: This is Mr. Dunning speaking. I'm calling from Los Angles. I have reserved a suite on Oct. 2nd.

R: Just a minute, sir, I will look through the reservation records. Yes, we do have a reservation for you on that day. Are you calling to confirm it, Mr. Dunning?

G: Not really. I'd like to make an adjustment of my reservation. I know that my business negotiations will last more days than I have planned. I'll extend my stay in your hotel for two nights.

R: Would you please hold the line for a moment? I'll take a look at the hotel's booking record. Yes, sir. You can have the suite for two nights from Oct. 2nd to 4th.

G: That's great. Thank you very much.

R: You're welcome. We are expecting to see you soon.

Words and Expressions

fully booked	满额预订	cancellation	*n.*	取消
minimum price	最低价格	maximun price		最高价格
off-season	*n.* 淡季	make an adjustment		调整

Learn by Heart

1. 预订的基本步骤

Say hello to the guest.

Ask and record the reservation information of the guest.

Confirm the reservation.

Express your wishes.

Form the reservation record.

2. 预订常用语

But the rooms are fully booked on that day.

但是那天的房间已经订满了。

Would you like us to put you on our waiting list and call you in case we have a cancellation?

您需要我把您的名字列入等候名单吗？这样一旦有取消预订，我们就通知您。

Could you recommend me another hotel which won't be full up?

您能推荐另外一个没有预订满的酒店吗？

I'd like to cancel a reservation.

我想取消预订。

I'd like to make an adjustment of my reservation.

我想更改我的预订。

I'll extend my stay in your hotel for two nights.

我要把预订时间延长两个晚上。

I'll take a look at the hotel's booking record.

我来看一下酒店的预订记录。

What services come with that?

这个价格包括哪些服务项目呢？

By the way，I'd like a quiet room away from the street if it is possible.

顺便说一下，如有可能，我想要一个不临街的安静房间。

【情景演练】

Class Activity Role-Play

Scene One: A guest wants to extend his stay in the hotel for three nights.

Scene Two: A guest wants to book a cheaper room.

Further Reading

A Letter—Reserving a Room

Dear sir,

From the local tourist office I have learnt that Red Rose is a famous center for holiday. On a list of recommended hotels, I found the name of your hotel.

My family and that of my friend wish to spend about a fortnight at your resort. We require two double rooms, each with a private bath, and one twin-bedded room with a shower.

Would it be possible to let us have these rooms for the period from July 5th to July 19th? We would prefer half-board if possible. Kindly let us know your items.

I am looking forward to an early reply.

Yours faithfully,

(signature)

Oct.10th, 2015

参考译文

一封信——预订房间

尊敬的先生：

我从本地旅行社获悉，红玫瑰是著名的假日活动中心。在一份介绍饭店的目录上，我看到了贵店的名字。

我们和朋友两家人希望在贵店住大约两个星期的时间。因此，我们需要两间带洗澡间的双人房间和一间备有两张床铺的带淋浴的房间。

不知能否为我们提供上述房间，时间是从 7 月 5 日到 7 月 19 日。如果可能的话，我们要半膳(提供一日两餐)服务。请告知你们的价格。

盼早复函。

谨上

(签名)

2015 年 10 月 10 日

Question

【拓展习题】

How do you like letter-reserving?

Unit 3　Receptionist

Listening Practice

【听力音频】

1. Listen to the dialogue and fill in the blanks.

(R: Receptionist, G: Guest)

G: I want a double room with _____. How much a day do you charge?

R: It is a hundred yuan a day _____, but _____.

G: It's quite reasonable.

R: How long do you intend to stay in this hotel?

G: I shall leave in a fortnight (half a month).

R: Have you got through with the_____?

G: Oh, yes, I'm going to fill in the form of registration right now. Can I book a single room for my friend before hand as he will arrive in Shanghai tomorrow morning?

R: Sure. Here is the _____for reservations. Would you mind filling in this form and pay a hundred yuan _____for him.

G: All right. This is one hundred yuan to pay for my reservation.

R: Thank you. This is _____ in advance. Please keep it.

2. Listen and fill in the missing information.

Vacant room: _____　The Hotel recommended:_____

The plane ticket to book: _____

The train ticket to book: _____

Kinds of rooms: _____

Situational Dialogues

1. Receiving a Walk-in Guest

(Scene: Mr. Dudley who has not made a reservation tries to find a single room in Xin Zhong Hotel for tonight. The hotel will be able to arrange a room only after 6:00 this afternoon. The receptionist helps him to contact the Hilton Hotel.)

(R: Receptionist, D: Mr. Dudley)

R: Good morning, sir. May I help You?

D: Morning. Could I have a single room for tonight?

R: Have you made a reservation?

D: I'm afraid not.

R: Please wait a moment. Let me check.

...

Sorry to say that all the rooms are booked up. But don't worry. We'll be able to arrange a room after 6:00 this afternoon.

D: 6:00? Oh, I'm too tired to wait for that long.

R: Well, if you'd like to have a room right now, may I contact the Hilton Hotel for you? It's just minutes' walk to get there.

D: Why not? Do by all means.

R: (Making the call)Sorry to have kept you waiting, sir. There're some spare rooms in the Hilton Hotel.

D: Oh, good. I'll be going.

R: Let me get a bellman to help you with your baggage.

D: Thanks. You're really helpful.

2. Baggage Service

Scene: A car pulls up in front of Huatian Hotel. The doorman goes forward to meet the guest and opens the door of the car for the guest.

(D: Doorman, G: Guest)

D: Good evening, sir. Welcome to our hotel. Check in?

G: Yes. Good evening.

D: Do you have any baggage in the trunk?

G: Yes, four suitcases.

D: Is everything here?

G: Yes, that's all.

D: The Reception Desk is straight ahead. After you, please.

G: Thank you.

3. Recognizing a Tour Group

(Scene: Xu Zhen，the representative from International Hotel, welcomes Western America Industry and Commerce Union and Mr. Smith, the tour leader. There are 14 people. Another one has cancelled his trip for some reason. Liu, the bus driver, will take the union to the hotel.)

(R: Representative, S: Mr. Smith)

R: Good afternoon. Are you Mr. Smith, the tour leader of Western America Industry and Commerce Union?

S: Yes, I am.

R: I am Xu Zhen, the representative from International Hotel. On behalf of the hotel, I'm here to receive you.

S: Nice to meet you.

R: Welcome to China. And welcome to stay in International Hotel. Are there 15 members all together?

S: Oh, there are 14 people. Another one has cancelled his trip for some reason.

R: Are you tired after a long flight?

S: Yes, the plane had been flying 12 hours from the States to Shanghai, so they look a bit tired from the jet lag.

R: Well, let's get on the bus right now. Follow me, please. The bus is over there.

(Two minutes later.)

R: Please leave your big suitcases outside the bus. We'll help carry them on. Do check your baggage again.

S: So how long will it take to get to your hotel?

R: Around 2 hours. Remember to fasten your seat belt before starting. And this is Liu, the bus driver. He will take you to your destination. Have a nice trip. Goodbye.

4. Greeting a Guest on Arrival

(Scene: The bellman welcomes a guest to Wuxi International Hotel. The guest has two suitcases and two bags. The bellman shows the guest to the Front Desk.)

(B: Bellman, G: Guest)

B: Good evening, sir. Welcome to Wuxi International Hotel.

G: Thank you.

B: How many pieces of baggage do you have?

G: Just these four.

B: Two suit cases and two bags. Is that right?

G: Yes. That's all.

B: Let me take the baggage for you. I'll show you to the Front Desk. This way, please. I will put your bags by the post over there.

G: I see, thanks.

B: Did you have a good trip, sir?

G: Oh, it was very tiring.

B: I'm sorry to hear that. I will show you to your room when you finish checking in.

G: That's fine.

Words and Expressions

arrange	*v.*	安排	spare room		空房
baggage	*n.*	行李	suitcase	*n.*	手提箱
slippery	*adj.*	滑的	tour leader		旅游团领队

Learn by Heart

1. 接待的基本应对

未预订的顾客	walk-in guest	订满	book up
空房	spare rooms	行李服务	baggage service
检查，复核	have a check	领某人上楼	show sb. up
停下	pull up		

2. 接待常用语

Just a moment, please. I have to check if there's a room available.
请稍等，我要查一下有没有空房。

How many people do you have, please?
请问你们有多少人？

If you need any help, do let us know.
如果您需要任何帮助，请告知我们。

If you need a room right now, would you like me to get in touch with somewhere else for you?
如果您马上就需要一个房间，我帮您跟其他酒店联系，好吗？

Have you made a reservation?
您有预订吗？

Sorry to say that all the rooms are booked up. But don't worry.
很抱歉，所有的房间都订满了。但是不用担心。

Let me get a bellman to help you with your baggage.
让我找一个行李员帮你拿行李。

I will show you to your room when you finish checking in.
您办理入住登记后我带您去您的房间。

I'm the receptionist here，welcome to our hotel.
我是这儿的接待员，欢迎来到我们酒店。

Class Activity Role-Play

Scene One: The receptionist receives a walk-in guest.

Scene Two: Kane has made a reservation two days ago through a long distance call.

Now The receptionist receives her.

Further Reading

Receptionist Work

A receptionist must make sure that the guest's registration card correctly filled out. The following items are necessary in a registration record: the guest's full name, address, nationality, passport or visa number, purpose of his visit and his signature. Besides, information such as means of payment, arrival date, room type and rate must be also correctly recorded.

参考译文

接待员的工作

接待员必须确认顾客的登记卡填写正确。以下项目在一份登记记录中是有必要的：顾客的全名、地址、国籍、护照号或签证号、顾客访问意图及其签名。此外，诸如付款方式、抵达日期、房间类型和价格的信息也必须正确记录。

Question

【拓展习题】

What items are necessary in a registration record?

Unit 4   Check-in

Listening Practice

【听力音频】

1. Listen to the dialogue and fill in the blanks.

(R: Receptionist, G: Guest)

G: Hi, I'm here to _____.

R: You must be Mr. Larson.

G: Yes, that's right.

R: Welcome to _____. Would you please fill out this registration form?

(A moment later)

R: Thank you... Excuse me, sir. You forgot to fill in your_____.

G: Did I? Let me see that... Oh, sorry... Here you are.

R: And would you sign here, please? Thank you. May I see your _____, please... Thank you. Would you mind leaving your passport here for an hour or so? We must make a copy of your passport and visa for _____.

2. Listen and fill in the missing information.

Room type: _____   Guest's name: _____

The time to stay: _____   A private bath: _____

Beds: _____   Restaurant: _____

Situational Dialogues

1. Checking-in Guests with Reservations

【拓展音频】

(Scene: John Smith is at the Reception Desk of the Claude Hotel. The reception clerk handles the check-in.)

(R: Receptionist, S: John Smith)

R: Good afternoon, sir. Welcome to our hotel. May I help you?

S: Yes. I booked a room one week ago.

R: May I have your name please, sir?

S: John Smith.

R: Just a moment, sir. Yes, We do have a reservation for you, Mr. Smith. A city view single room with bath. You've paid RMB 2000 yuan as a deposit. Is that correct?

S: That's it.

R: Would you please fill in this registration card, sir?

S: Sure. Here you are. I think I've filled in everything correctly.

R: Let me see…Name, address, nationality, forwarding address, passport number, signature and date of departure. Oh, here, sir. You forget to fill in the date of departure. May I fill it in for you? You are leaving on…

S: October 24.

R: May I see your passport, please? Thank you, sir. Now everything is in order. Mr. Smith, your room number is 1107. It's on the 11th floor and your room rate is 500 RMB per night. Here is your key card with all the information on your booking, the hotel services and the hotel rules and regulations on it. Please make sure that you have it with you all the time. You need to show it when you sign for your meals and drinks in the restaurants and the bars.

S: Yes, I'll keep it with care. Thank you.

R: I hope you enjoy your stay with us.

2. Checking-in Walk-in Guests

(Scene: Mr. Findley and his friend come to the Reception Desk of the Claude Hotel to have a room for the night. The reception clerk receives them.)

(R: Reception Clerk, F: Mr. Findley)

R: Welcome to the Claude Hotel. May I help you?

F: I'd like a room, please.

R: And what type of room would you like? Single or double?

F: I'd like a double, please.

R: How many are in your party?

F: Just two.

R: How many nights would you like to stay?

F: Just tonight. How much is the room?

R: It's 980 yuan per night. How will you be paying?

F: Can I pay by credit card?

R: Certainly. We take Visa, Master Card and American Express.

F: Great. I have Visa Card.

R: That'll be fine. Let me help you fill in this registration form. May I have your name, please?

F: Timothy Findley.

R: Could you spell that please?

F: T—I—M—O—T—H—Y, F—I—N—D—L—E—Y.

R: OK. Would you like a wake-up call?

F: Yes, I'd like a wake-up call at 6:30a.m. Do you have a pool?

R: Yes, we do. On the 54th floor. Here's your key, Mr. Findley. That is Room 5604 on the 56th floor. The bellboy will show you up to your room.

3. Checking-in Guests with a Group Reservation

【拓展音频】

(Scene: A tour group arrives at the hotel, and the tour leader, Mr. Mills comes to the Reception Desk to check in. The reception clerk receives him.)

Staff: Good morning, sir. May I help you?

Guest: Yes, please. We'd like to check in.

Staff: Do you have reservations?

Guest: Yes. The Beijing CITS has booked 20 rooms for us.

Staff: Could you please tell me the name of your group?

Guest: The US Computer Association Delegation.

Staff: Just a moment, please.

(The staff checks on the computer.)

Staff: Yes, 20 twin rooms for three nights.

Guest: That's right. Here is the name-list with the group visa.

Staff: Thank you. Here are the keys to the rooms. Do you need morning call service?

Guest: Yes, please. 8:00 a.m. for tomorrow morning and 9:00 a.m. for the rest of the days.

Staff: And here are the vouchers for your breakfast buffet. The breakfast will be served at the Jing Tai Restaurant on the 4th floor.

Guest: Thank you.

Staff: We are always at your service. We hope you will enjoy your stay with us.

Words and Expressions

en suite bathroom	卫生间	conference	n.	会议
imprint	n.	印记	forwarding address	转寄地址
type of room	房间类型	delegation	n.	代表团

CITS(China International Travel Service) 中国国旅旅行社

Learn by Heart

1. 登记入住基本应对

in the names of...	在……的名下	take visa	接受签证
Master Card	万事达卡	American Express	美国运通卡
breakfast included	含早餐	key card	房卡

2. 登记入住常用语

Under what name is the reservation made?
这是以谁的名字预订的？

The porter will take your bag up to room.
行李员会帮你把行李放到房间里。

How long will you be staying?
您在这儿将会待多久？

May I see your passports, please?
我能看一下您的护照吗？

We hope you'll enjoy your stay with us.
我们希望您在我们酒店过得愉快。

Are you going to spend the whole week here?
您准备在这儿度过这个星期吗？

Would you fill in this form please?
请您填下这个表格，好吗？

You can order breakfast by the menu, too.
您也可以根据菜单来订早餐。

The bellboy will show you up to your room.
门童会带您到您的房间。

How will you be paying?
您想要怎么付费？

Let me help you fill in this registration form.
让我帮您填写这个登记表。

Could you please tell me the name of your group?
您能告诉我你们团队的名称吗？

Here are the keys to the rooms.
这是房间的钥匙。

Do you need morning call service?
您需要早上的叫醒服务吗？

Here are the vouchers for your breakfast buffet.
这是你们的早餐代金券。

Class Activity Role-Play

【情景演练】

Scene One: A guest named Tomlinson who has a reservation is checking in and the hotel staff would take a credit card for the deposit.

Scene Two: A guest made the reservation for tonight by fax is checking in, but the receptionist finds no record, and the room seems to be half-empty tonight.

Further Reading

【拓展知识】

Registration

A receptionist's job is to welcome and register the guest information. When a guest with a hotel reservation arrives at the front desk, the receptionist greets the guest and then gives out a registration form. When you arrive at a hotel, don't forget to fill out the form.

When you are filling out the form, make sure that such information items as your full name, address, nationality, forwarding address, the purpose of your visit and signature are entered correctly and legibly. When you are abroad, information about your passport number, place of issue and date also need to be recorded.

The receptionist will also check and make sure that such reservation details as room type and departure date are not changed. The receptionist is also responsible for answering any question from the telephones, taking messages for the guests and handling complaints form dissatisfied guests.

When you check in as a leader of large tour groups and conference guests, you should handle the registration forms and hand it over to the front desk yourself.

参考译文

住 宿 登 记

接待员的职责是欢迎客人，帮助他们办理登记入住手续。当已预订房间的客人来到前台时，接待员首先向客人问好，然后把入住登记表递给客人填写。当你入住酒店时，不要忘记填写登记表。

填完表格以后，你还要检查一下，要做到姓名(全名)、地址、国籍、转寄地址、来访缘由和签名等内容都填写得正确、字迹清晰。若是出国，还要填写护照号码、发照地点及日期等项目。

接待员还需检查并需确认房间类型及离店时间等项目没有更改。此外，接待员还负责回答客人的电话询问、替客人记录留言、处理客人因不满而提出的各种意见等。

　　如果你是旅游团领队或者某会议的客人，在登记入店时，要亲自填写登记表，并交给前台。

Question

Would you like to be a receptionist?

Unit 5 Foreign Currency Exchange

Listening Practice

【听力音频】

1. Listen to the dialogue and fill in the blanks.

C: Good afternoon, madam. Can I help you?

G: Good afternoon. May I exchange some money for _____?

C: What kind of _____ have you got?

G: _____.

C: Fine. How much have you got?

G: Two hundred dollars. Here you are.

C: Just a moment, please, madam.

…

Here's your money. _____ in all.

Please check it, madam.

C: It's quite correct. Thank you very much.

G: You are welcome, madam.

2. Listen and fill in the missing information.

Money to change: _____

Exchange rate: _____   Name: _____

Room number: _____

Situational Dialogues

1. Foreign Exchange

【拓展音频】

(Scene: An American tourist is approaching the foreign exchange counter.)

Cashier: Good morning, sir. May I help you?

Tourist: Good morning. Is this where I can change US dollars for RMB?

Cashier: Yes, sir. According to today's change rate, 100 US dollars in cash comes to
650 yuan. How much would you like to exchange, sir?

Tourist: 200, and here is the money.

Cashier: Thank you, sir.

(She holds the money under an ultraviolet light to check whether the notes are
forgeries or not.)

Well, sir. 200 US dollars, equal to 1,300 yuan. Please wait a moment.

...

Sorry to have kept you waiting, sir. Would you please write down your name, passport number, and room number or permanent address on the exchange memo?

Tourist: OK. I'll take care of it…Here you are.

Cashier: Thank you, Mr. Lawrance.

(She affixes her name seal on the memo and hands it to the guest.)

Please keep your memo, Mr. Lawrance. How would you like your money?

Tourist: In fifties, please.

Cashier: Here are twenty-six 50 yuan notes altogether 1,300 yuan RMB. Please check it. With the memo, you may have the leftover RMB changed back into US dollars at the Bank of China or the Airport Exchange Office.

Tourist: I see. Where is the Bank of China?

Cashier: It's just next to our hotel.

Tourist: Thank you for your help. Goodbye.

Cashier: You're most welcome, Mr. Lawrance. Goodbye.

2. Cashing Traveler's Checks

(Scene: A guest would like to cash some traveler's checks.)

Cashier: May I help you, sir?

Guest: Yes, I'd like to cash some traveler's checks.

Cashier: How much?

Guest: 100 pounds.

Cashier: That's all right. But please sign the checks on the back. May I see your passport?

Guest: Here you are. By the way, what is the exchange rate on pounds?

Cashier: 12.5 yuan to one pound. Would you sign here and fill in your room number, please? Thank you. That's 1,209 yuan and six jiao. Please count it to make sure it's correct.

3. Foreign Currency Exchange

(Scene: Mr. Bellow is making his way to the foreign exchange counter. He wants to change some US. dollars for RMB.)

(C: Cashier, B: Mr. Bellow)

C: Good afternoon, sir. Can I help you?

B: I'd like to change some US dollars and I'd like to know today's exchange rate.

C: According to today's exchange rate, 6.5 yuan, RMB. How much would you like to change, sir?

B: Well, I'll change one hundred and here's the money.

C: Would you please fill in this form?

B: All right.

C: Please write your name, passport number and room number on the slip.

B: Here you are.

C: Thank you. You'll have it right away. Will you sign your name here on this memo?

B: OK, Will you please give me some one-yuan notes? I need some small change.

C: All right.

   (Changing the money)

   Mr. Bellow, here it is. Please have a check and keep the exchange memo.

B: Oh, yes, thanks. By the way, can you tell me what I should do with the RMB left with me?

C: You'll have to go to the Bank of China or the Airport Exchange Office to changeIt backs into dollars.

B: I see. Thanks.

C: You are welcome.

4. Foreign Exchange

(Scene: A guest would like to change some pounds sterling into RMB.)

Guest: Excuse me, but is this where you exchange foreign money for RMB?

Clerk: Yes, sir. What can I do for you?

Guest: I want to have some pounds sterling changed into RMB.

Clerk: Very well. Please fill in this application form and sign your name, sir.

Guest: All right. Which address shall I give you, my home address or hotel address here?

Clerk: Your hotel address, please.

Guest: Right. Where am I supposed to sign my name?

Clerk: Here, on this dotted line, sir.

Guest: Here you are, is that all right?

Clerk: Let me see. Oh, would you mind telling me your passport number, sir?

Guest: Of course not. Let me see. It's E 56789.

Clerk: Thank you, sir.

Words and Expressions

exchange	v.	兑换	ultraviolet light		紫外灯
exchange memo		兑换备忘录	affix	v.	贴上
equivalent to		相当于	pounds sterling		英镑

Learn by Heart

1. 各国货币名称及货币的英文代码

Name of Currency 货币名称	Symbol or Abbreviation 标识或缩写	Country/Region 国家或地区
Baht 铢	B/THB	the Kindom of Thailand 泰国
Dollar (澳大利亚元)	$ A	The Commonwealth of Australia 澳大利亚
Dirham 迪拉姆	AED	The United Arab Emirates 阿拉伯联合酋长国
Won 韩元	₩Won	Republic of Korea 韩国
Euro 欧元	€	European Union 欧洲联盟
Dollar (美元)	US $	USA 美国
Dong (越南盾)	D	Vietnam 越南
Peso (菲律宾比索)	PHP ₱	Republic of the Philippines 菲律宾
Yen 日元	JPY ¥	Japan 日本
Rouble 卢布	R(或 rub, Rbl)	Russia 俄罗斯
Pound 英镑	£	UK 英国
Pound 埃及镑	LE	Egypt 埃及
Hong Kong Dollar 港元	HK$	Hong Kong 中国香港

2. 货币兑换常用语

Today's exchange rate of RMB to USD is 612 RMB yuan equal to 100 US dollars.
今天的汇率是 612 元人民币兑 100 美元。

What kind of foreign currency have you got? What's the exchange rate today?
您持有什么外币？今天的汇率是多少？

What kind of currency do you want to change?
您想换哪一种外币？

Sorry, you've filled a wrong account number. Please refill it.
对不起，您填错单子了。请重填一张。

What is the equivalent of five dollars in RMB yuan?
5 美元相当于人民币多少元？

We list the exchange rate issued by the People's Bank of China every morning.
我们是根据每天早上中国人民银行发布的汇率挂牌的。

What are you going to convert, bank notes or traveler's checks?
您要兑换什么，是现钞还是旅行支票？

How much would you like to exchange?
您要兑换多少钱？

Please write your name, passport number and room number on the form.

请在单子上写上您的姓名、护照号码和房号。

Class Activity Role-Play

Scene One: Mr. Bellow (B) is making his way to the foreign exchange counter. He wants to change some US dollars for RMB.

Scene Two: The guest want to break this 500 US dollars note into Japanese yen. And the buying rate is 120 yen to one US dollar. The guest need five 10,000 yen and the rest in small notes.

Further Reading

Banks in the West

In western countries, the banking industry is highly developed and advanced in terms of bank operational efficiency and scope of service. Customers generally follow the rule of "First come, first served". If you go to a bank, remember to stand in an orderly queue behind the yellow line, which is about a meter from the customer at the counter no matter how few the customers are. Do not go to the counter until the clerk says, "Next, please!"

The banking operations cover a wide range of services, including checking account, savings account, traveler's account, cashier's order, cashier's check, credit card, safety box, etc. Rather than a seal, customers generally use their signatures, which are, in fact, more reliable and hard to imitate.

参考译文

西方的银行

在西方国家中，无论从银行的服务效率还是服务范围来看，银行业都是十分先进，高度发达的。顾客们一般遵守"先到先接受服务"的原则。到了银行，无论顾客有多少，都要牢记应在黄线外排队等候。黄线一般距离站在柜台前的顾客一米左右。只有当银行职员喊"下一位"的时候，才可以走近柜台。

银行业服务内容十分广泛，包括活期存款账户、储蓄存款账户、旅行账户、现金汇票、现金支票、信用卡、贵重物品保险箱等。顾客常用签名，而不是用印章，因为签名难以模仿，更为可靠。

Question

Do you know the differences of banks in the west and in China?

【拓展习题】

Unit 6 Bell Service

【听力音频】

Listening Practice

1. Listen to the dialogue and fill in the blanks.

(B: Mr. Bellow, M: Mrs. Bellow)

Bm: Good evening, madam and sir. I'm the bellman.

B&M: Good evening.

Bm: Very glad to have you here. I'll get the _____ up to your room.

B&M: Thank you.

Bm: Let me carry your baggage. Are these all yours?

M: _____, Henry?

B: Yes.(Laughs)

Bm: Allow me, madam.

(Mr. Bellow tries carry one of the suitcases up to the_____.)

Bm: Oh, leave it to me. I'll do that for you.

B: Thanks.

Bm: It's my pleasure. This way, please.

       (They are going to the elevator entrance.)

       Here we are. Please take this elevator to the _____ floor. The floor attendant

       will meet you at your elevator entrance there and show you to Room _____.

       I'll take the baggage elevator and get your suitcases up to the room.

B: Very good. See you then.

Bm: See you.

2. Listen and fill in the missing information.

Room:_____   The corridor: _____

The hotel: _____

Other services:_____

Indoor swimming pool:_____

Brochure:_____

Situational Dialogues

【拓展音频】

1. Greeting the Guest at the Door

(Scene: The bellman is greeting a guest at the door.)

(B: Bellman, G: Guest)

B: Good afternoon, madam. Welcome to the Lake View Garden Hotel.

G: Thank you.

B: How many pieces of luggage do you have?

G: Just two pieces.

B: Two suitcases. Is that correct?

G: Yes. That's all.

B: I'll show you to the Front Desk. This way, please. I will put your suitcases by the Information Desk over there.

G: I see, thanks.

B: A bellman will show you to your room when you have finished checking in.

G: OK. Fine.

B: Please enjoy your stay.

2. Introducing Hotel Facilities

(Scene: The bellman carries the baggage for Mr. and Mrs. White and tell them about the hotel services.)

(B: Bellman, W: Mr. White, M: Mrs. White)

B: Good afternoon, madam and sir. I'm the bellman.

W&M: Good afternoon.

B: Very glad to have you here. Let me carry your baggage. This way, please.

(They are going to the elevator entrance.)

W: Could you tell us something about your hotel services?

B: Certainly, sir. Our hotel is a four-star hotel. There are over 400 international standard rooms which are very comfortable. If you want to have a walk, you can go to the garden of the hotel. It's very relaxing there.

W: That sounds good.

B: Also, there is a recreation center on the fourth floor. You can play billiards, table tennis and bowling.

W: Where can I listen to some music?

B: There is a music teahouse where you can enjoy both classical music and modern music. We also have saunas and after-sauna rooms. Guests can relax with soft drinks or snacks there.

W: How about other services?

B: Also available are a beauty salon，a barber shop，a souvenir shop...

W: Have you got an indoor swimming pool here?

B: Yes，it's on the top floor.

(Now they are at the elevator entrance.)

Here we are，please take this elevator to the eighth floor. I'll take the baggage elevator and get your baggage up to your room.

W: Thank you. See you then.

B: See you，Mr. and Mrs. White.

3. Bellman Service

【拓展音频】

(Scene: A guest has finished his check-in. The bellboy is accompanying the guest to his room.)

Staff: May I help you with your baggage，sir?

Guest: That'll be fine.

Staff: Let me take this suitcase for you.

Guest: Thank you.

Staff: Could you tell me your room number?

Guest: It's Room 1106.

Staff: This way, please. We shall take the lift on the right.

Guest: All right. The hotel looks like a maze.

Staff: Yes, the hotel has a lot of rooms and the corridors are twisting.

Guest: Very interesting.

Staff: Is it your first time here?

Guest: Yes，very first. By the way, do you have a bar?

Staff: Yes，we have a bar and a cafe on the third floor. Besides，we have a barber's shop，post service，a billiard room and a bowling alley.

Guest: Very good. Where can I send e-mail and fax?

Staff: You may do these in our Business Center. Oh，here we are，Room 1106.

Guest: Thank you for your help. Wait a moment. Eh，this is the tip for you.

Staff: We don't accept tips，I'm afraid，sir. Hope you will enjoy your stay with us. Goodbye.

4. On the Way to the Room

(Scene: The Bellman shows a guest to the room.)

(B: Bellman   G: Guest)

B: Good evening, sir. I'll show you to your room. You have two suitcases and one bag. Is that correct?

G: Yes, that's right.

B: Is there anything valuable or breakable in your bag?

G: Yes, there is a bottle of whiskey.

B: Could you carry this bag, sir? I'm afraid the contents might break.

G: Sure, no problem.

B: Thank you, sir. May I have your room key, please?

G: Yes, here you are.

B: Thank you, sir. Your room is on the 12th floor, please follow me, your elevator is this way.

G: I see.

B: Is this your first time to Hangzhou?

G: Yes, it is.

B: I hope you'll have time to see Hangzhou. There is a lot to see.

G: I'm sure there is.

B: This is the 12th floor. Your room is to the right. After you, sir. This way, please.

Words and Expressions

elevator entrance	电梯口	four-star hotel	四星级酒店
international standard	国际标准	relaxing *adj.*	舒适的
classical music	古典音乐	modern music	现代音乐
twisting *adj.*	曲折的	breakable *adj.*	易碎的

Learn by Heart

1. 行李员基本应对

贵重品	valuables	行李员	porter
行李	luggage/baggage	轻便行李	light luggage
行李电梯	baggage elevator	手推车	trolley
衣物袋	suit bag	旅行袋	travelling bag
背包	shoulder bag	大衣箱	trunk
手提箱	suitcase		

2. 行李员常用语

How many pieces of luggage do you have?
您有多少件行李？

I'll show you to the Front Desk.
我会带您到前台。

I will put your suitcases by the Information Desk over there.
我会把您的行李放到那边的问询处。

A bellman will show you to your room when you have finished checking in.
您登记完后，一个行李员会带您到您的房间。

Very glad to have you here.
很高兴你们来到这里。

Here we are, please take this elevator to the eighth floor.
我们到了，请乘这个电梯到 8 楼。

I'll take the baggage elevator and get your baggage up to your room.
我乘货运电梯，把您的行李送到您的房间。

Please take the elevator on the left.
请您搭乘左边的电梯。

May I help you with your baggage, sir?
先生，您需要帮忙拿行李吗？

Let me take this suitcase for you.
让我帮您拿这个行李箱吧。

Could you tell me your room number?
您能告诉我您的房号吗？

We don't accept tips, I'm afraid, sir.
先生，我们不收小费。

Is there anything valuable or breakable in it?
请问袋子里头有贵重或易碎物品吗？

Here is your tag. This cloakroom is open till 11:00 p.m., could you pick it up by then?
这是您的取物牌。本寄存处开放到晚上 11 点，您在那以前来领取好吗？

Class Activity Role-Play

Scene One: The Bellman carries the baggage for the guests and shows them up to the room.
Scene Two: The Bellman escorts a lady to her suite along the corridor and introduces the hotel services for her.

Further Reading

Telephone Service

Telephone service is very important in modern society. Information for phone calls can be found in the Phone Book, which is easily available near phones everywhere and provides local information, national dialing, international dialing and phone numbers for the area.

For international calls, you can find the code for the country you want in the Phone Book. The time of the day is particularly important for the call because in most countries there is a period when you can make calls at a cheaper rate. These periods are at a different time of the day in different countries. You can find information about international time difference in a post office or in some big hotels.

参考译文

电 话 服 务

电话在现代社会中起着非常重要的作用。关于电话方面的信息可以从电话本中获得。电话簿通常放在电话旁边，很容易就可找到。它提供很多方面的信息：当地拨号信息、国内和国际通话信息，以及当地的电话号码。

要挂国际长途，先从电话簿中找出该国的国家代码。打电话的时间也很重要，因为多数国家都规定在某一特定时间实行优惠价格。实行优惠价格的时间因国家而异。你可以从当地邮局或一些大酒店查询关于国际时差方面的信息。

Question

Have you made international calls?

【拓展习题】

Unit 7 Settling Guests Complaints

【听力音频】

Listening Practice

1. Listen to the dialogue and fill in the blanks.

(B: Mr. Bellow, A: assistant manager)

A: Good morning, sir. What can I do for you?

B: I'm Bellow. I'm in Room 908. Can you _____ for me? It's too noisy. My wife was woken up several times by the noise the baggage elevator made. She said it was too much for her.

A: I'm awfully sorry, sir. I do apologize. Room 908 is_____. It's possible that the noise is heard early in the morning when all is quiet.

B: Anyhow, I'd like to change our room.

A: No problem, sir. We'll _____ it, but we don't have _____today. Could you wait till tomorrow? The American People-to-People Education Delegation will be leaving tomorrow morning. There'll be some rooms for you to choose from.

B: All right. I hope we'll be able to enjoy our stay_____ tomorrow evening and have a sound sleep.

A: Be sure. I'll make a note of that. Everything will be taken care of. And if there is anything more you need, please let us know.

2. Listen and fill in the missing information.

Leaving time: _____ Regulations: _____

Porter: _____ Resting place: _____

Guest's request:_____

Situational Dialogues

1. Settling Guests Complaints about Room

(Scene: A guest telephones the Front Office clerk and complains that the room is smelly and there is someone's hair on her bed.)

Clerk: Good evening. Front Office. Can I help you?

Guest: This is Mrs. Stevenson, Room 1503. I've just checked in and I'm not happy with my room.

Clerk: May I know what is wrong?

Guest: The room is smelly and there is someone's hair on my bed! I didn't expect such things would happen in your hotel.

Clerk: I'm sorry to hear that, Mrs. Stevenson. I'll send a housemaid to your room at once. She will bring the air fresher and make up the bed again for you. We do apologize for the inconvenience.

Guest: That's fine. Thank you.

Clerk: You're welcome, Mrs. Stevenson. My name is Simon, and if there is anything else I can do for you, please don't hesitate to call me.

2. When the Room Is Not Ready

(Scene: A guest said to the receptionist that the room is not ready.)

(G: Guest, R: Receptionist)

G: Hello? ls that reception?

R: Yes, reception here. Carla Jones speaking. How can I help you?

G: I'm Mr. Arden in Room 346. I'm calling to complain about the state of the room.

R: I'm very sorry. What seems to be the problem?

G: Everything. The bed's not made, and the bathroom hasn't been cleaned.

R: I'm very sorry. The room should have been cleaned. I'll contact housekeeping straight away.

G: And that's not all. The television doesn't work either.

R: I do apologize. I'll send a new one up to your room.

G: Thank you.

3. When the Luggage Delivery Is Delayed

(Scene: A guest complains to the bell caption that the luggage delivery is delayed.)

(B: Bell caption, G: Guest)

B: Good evening! Bell captain. Georgia Smith speaking. Can I help you?

G: I'm Mr. Farmer. I have to make a complaint. I checked into my room 50 minutes ago and my luggage hasn't been delivered to my room yet.

B: I'm very sorry for the delay. Please let me ask you a few questions concerning your luggage. What kind of luggage is it?

G: It is a suitcase.

B: What color is it?

G: It is a brown leather suitcase.

B: Mr. Farmer, there's been an over-sight and your luggage is still here. I'll ask a bellboy to send it to your room at once. Sorry about the inconvenience.

4. Mis-calculation

(Scene: Mr. Bellow (B) goes back to the Cashier's Desk, thoughtfully and hurriedly.)

(B: Mr. Bellow, C: Cashier)

C: Good morning, sir. May I help you?

B: Just now I checked out here. But back in my room, I found that there might be something wrong with the bill.

C: Oh, yes?

B: I checked in on the 26th and will leave this morning. That's exactly three days, I think. But I paid for three days and a half.

C: Well, let me see. The 26th, the 27th, the 28th…Ah yes, you checked out in the morning, so you only stayed here for three days, no more. Sorry, sir. I do apologize for my mis-checking.

B: That's all right.

C: Now let me give you another receipt and please check it. Here is the money you overpaid.

B: Thank you.

C: I'm awfully sorry to have caused you so much trouble. I'll try to be more careful another time.

Words and Expressions

smelly	*adj.*	气味难闻的	housemaid	*n.*	客房服务员
air fresher		空气清新剂	make up the bed		整理床铺
straight away		直接	delivery	*v.*	送达

Learn by Heart

1. 处理客人投诉的步骤

倾听 listen

明白客人的需求 understand the guest needs

了解客人的动机 understand the guest motives by question

重复客人的需求并给予安抚 repeat the guest needs and comfort them

提供选择 offer alternatives

采取行动 take actions

跟踪客人满意度 follow up the guest satisfaction

2. 处理投诉常用语

I do apologize.

我向您道歉。

We'll manage it, but we don't have any spare room today.

我们会尽力办到，但是今天我们没有空余房间。

Could you wait till tomorrow?

等到明天好吗？

May I know what is wrong?

请问有什么问题吗？

I'm sorry to hear that.

很抱歉发生这种事情。

If there is anything else I can do for you, please don't hesitate to call me.

如果有什么我能效劳的，请尽管给我打电话。

The room should have been cleaned.

房间应该整理的。

I'll contact housekeeping straight away.

我会直接联系客房部。

I'm very sorry for the delay.

对不起，延迟送行李了。

Please let me ask you a few questions concerning your luggage.

请允许我问一些关于您行李的问题。

I'll ask a bellboy to send it to your room at once.

我会叫一个服务生马上送到您的房间。

Sorry about the inconvenience.

非常抱歉给您造成不便。

Class Activity Role-Play

Scene One: A guest wants to change a room. He goes to the assistant manager.

Scene Two: At the Reception Desk, a guest insists on staying longer without paying more.

Further Reading

【拓展知识】

Complaining of Bad Service

No one enjoys complaining, though some are in the habit of complaining, for it seldom brings positive feelings to oneself—especially when one is traveling abroad. But sometimes do make one unhappy. The most unbearable are:

(1) Inefficiency. Inefficiency results from inadequate training of the working staff.

(2) Aloofness. An aloof waiter wears an expression of studied indifference, serving the table with an air of injured dignity. His aloofness makes you feel unwelcome and lose interest in the food and drink.

(3) Over-attentiveness. Over-attentive waiters with effusive greeting, effusive talk about the specialties of the house and the distinguished spirits, eagerness to make recommendations, and frequent appearances are really annoying while you are enjoying the food.

There are several effective ways of complaining. Usually, politely informing the waiters or waitresses of your dissatisfaction could be very effective. When it is really necessary, you can go directly to the manager or other organizations concerned. In general, no business wants to spoil its image because it usually results in loss of profit.

参考译文

表达对劣质服务的不满

尽管少数人习惯发牢骚，却没有人真正喜欢发牢骚或抱怨，因为抱怨或不满极少能给人带来积极的影响。尤其是在外国旅行时，更是如此。但有时，有些事情的确使人不快。以下几种态度最令人不快，难以接受：

(1) 效率低。效率低主要是由工作人员受到的正规训练不足而致。

(2) 冷面孔。这类服务人员冷若冰霜，服务时一副受委屈的表情。他们的冷淡会使顾客觉得自己不受欢迎，从而失去进餐的胃口。

(3) 过分殷勤。这类服务员常常是过分殷勤，然后滔滔不绝地向你介绍店内的风味大菜和名酒，迫不及待地向顾客推荐饭菜。当你进餐时，他又在你面前频频出现，真是令人讨厌。

有几种有效的表达不满的方式。通常，礼貌地告知服务员，说明你的不满就很有效。如果真有必要，你可以向经理或有关部门反映。总的说来，任何商家都不愿损害自身形象，因为那样会带来经济损失。

Question

Can you endure bad services?

Unit 8　At the Information Desk

Listen Practice

1. Listen to the dialogue and fill in the blanks.

【听力音频】

A: Good afternoon. What can l do for you?

B: Good afternoon. I'm looking for _____Mr. Black. Could you tell me if he is in the hotel?

A: Mr. Black? Just a minute, please. I'll see if he is_____. Black, Mr. Black? There are _____here today... Mr. Charles Black, Mr. David Black…

B: Mr. Johnson Black from Chicago. Isn't he staying at this hotel?

A: Oh, yes, here's his name——Mr. and Mrs. Johnson Black and family. They are in _____. Please wait a moment, let phone him…Mr. Black said he's waiting for you in his room.

B: Thank you. Would you please show me where the _____ is?

A: OK. Step this way, please. Here it is.

B: Thank you.

A: It's my pleasure.

2. Listen and fill in the missing information.

Concierge's name: _____

Guest's name: _____　　Time: _____

Place to go: _____

Concierge's suggestion: _____

Situational Dialogues

1. Mail Service

【拓展音频】

(Scene: Mr. Bellow is going to the Information Desk with a letter in his hand.)

(R: Receptionist, B: Mr. Bellow)

R: Good afternoon, sir.

B: Good afternoon. Could you please mail a letter for me?

R: Yes. Have you stuck on the stamps yet?

B: No. I need to buy some.

R: (Looking at the letter.)

Is it to San Francisco?

B: Yes. And I'd like to send it by ordinary air mail.

R: (Weighing the letter on the scales.)

Two yuan and sixty fen.

B: Overweight?

R: Yes.

B: Thank you. Here it is.

(Giving the money.)

R: Here are your stamps. Please stick them on together with the air mail sticker on the front of the envelope.

B: All right. One more thing, I want to send a fax to New York. Can you arrange it for me?

R: Oh, yes, sir, We have fax service in our hotel. Would you please go to the business center? You can send your fax there.

B: Well, I'll be going there. Thank you for your information.

R: You are welcome.

2. Introducing Some Scenic Spots

(Scene: The Bellows plan to go around town. The Receptionist gives them some suggestions.)

(R: Receptionist, B: Mr. Bellow, M: Mrs. Bellow)

R: Good morning. Can I help you?

B: Good morning. Today we can afford a whole day for sightseeing. Could you tell us some places of historical interest in Shanghai?

R: Have you ever been Shanghai before?

B: No, this is our first trip here.

R: I'm very pleased to suggest that you go to visit the Yu Yuan Garden and the Jade Buddha Temple, the main attractions in Shanghai. They are often visited by foreign guests.

B: And why are those places so popular?

R: Because they are of typical Chinese national style. The Yu Yuan Garden is not only the pearl of Shanghai, but also called the "No.1 Vista in East China". You can see beautiful pavilions, terraces, rockeries, ponds, as well as buildings decorated with fine brick designs and wood carvings.

B: Good, I'll take some pictures. Then, how about the temple?

R: The Jade Buddha Temple is one of the most famous temples in China. There are two white jade statues of Sakyamuni brought from Burma more than a hundred years ago.

M: Oh, great! We'll have a good chance to feast our eyes.

R: What's more, the construction of the Grand Hall is magnificent. ˙

B: I think I'll enjoy the architecture of the temple, too.

M: Both places sound worth visiting. Henry, let's go.

3. Arranging a Tour Bus

(Scene: The receptionist suggests a guest traveling outside Nanjing by air-conditioned bus.)

(R: Receptionist, G: Guest.)

R: Is there anything I can do for you, Miss Watson?

G: Oh, yes. I'd like your advice on a weekend tour for my group of tourists.

R: I'll be delighted to help you. Let me write this down: A 2-day itinerary. What would you like to do most?

G: We want to see some of the famous scenic spots outside Nanjing. But there seems to be so many places to choose from. And we've got only two days.

R: Yes, two days is a bit tight. But you can cover a lot of places if you plan carefully. Are there any particular spots your tourists wish to see?

G: They are interested in some of the most famous scenic spots of Jiangsu province. And if you could arrange a visit to a folk arts and crafts factory, it would certainly be a great treat for them.

R: Let me make sure if I've got it right: you want to visit some scenic spots, for which Jiangsu province is well-known, and also to visit an arts and crafts factory.

G: That's right.

R: For the scenic spots, I would recommend Wuxi Yuantouzhu (or the Turtle-Head Park)and Ling-Shan Big Buddha. It's only 2-hour train ride from here. Then you can visit the famous Wuxi Hui-Shan Clay Figurines Factory. There you can see the artisans making the clay figurines.

G: Do we have to do a lot of walking to get to Yuantouzhu? I'm afraid I have to cut down on walking since my tourists are all a bit old!

R: Well, you don't have to do a lot of walking. Our bus can pick up your group at the gate. Do you want an air-conditioned bus?

G: Oh yes, that's most essential in this kind of heat. And we also need a tour guide.

R: All right. What about lunch? Do you want me to arrange a proper lunch or just packed lunches?

G: A good meal if you can.

R: Well, Lingshan Big Buddha is well known for vegetarian food. They can do you quite a variety of vegetarian dishes.

G: That's great! At least it'll be a new experience for most of us. You'd better tell me something about eating in a monastery so that I know what to tell them. I feel such a fool without knowing what food to expect, and I am the leader.

R: Don't worry. Here's all the information you need. Things like bean card, bamboo shoots, Chinese mushrooms, gingko nuts, cloud fungus, snow fungus, hair vegetable, etc.

G: Good, that's exactly the sort of information I need.

4. Asking the Way

(Scene: A guest asks the receptionist which is the simplest way to the Zhong-Shan Park.)

(R: Receptionist, G: Guest)

R: Good morning. Can I help you?

G: Yes, please. Will you please tell me the simplest way to the Zhong-Shan Park?

R: Yes. of course. The simplest way is by taxi. There is a taxi stand at the entrance here. If you can't find a taxi there，you can always hail one in the street. Shall I get one for you?

G: What are the rates, please?

R: It's 2.40 yuan for every kilometer. It's about 50 yuan to get to the Zhong-Shan Park.

G: Oh, I see. Would you please tell me how I can get there by bus?

R: Yes. You may take bus No.1. But l' m afraid the bus will be very crowded at this time of the day.

G: Oh, I like crowds. They make me warm.

R: Well, in that case, you can walk outside the hotel. Then turn right to Jingling Road，walk along the Jingling Road for about three minutes and the bus stop is right in front of you.

G: All right. Walk outside the hotel. Then turn right to Jin…Jin…What is the road，please?

R: Turn right to Jingling Road. Here, let me write it down for you.

G: No, thank you. I can't read the pinyin system anyway. Well, l think I'll have to resign myself to the taxi fare, then. Goodbye to the warm of the crowd.

Words and Expressions

ordinary air mail	普通航空信	fax service	传真服务
feast our eyes	让我们大饱眼福	a folk arts and crafts factory	民间工艺美术厂
packed lunches	打包的午餐	monastery　　*n.*	寺院
bean card	青瓜	gingko nuts	白果
cloud fungus	云耳	snow fungus	银耳
hair vegetable	发菜		

Learn by Heart

1. 北京主要景点

长城	Great Wall
紫禁城	Palace Museum (the Forbidden City)
北海公园	Beihai Park (Ancient Imperial Garden)
颐和园	Summer Palace (Ancient Imperial Garden)
天坛	Temple of Heaven

2. 问询处常用语

If you want to take a walk, you can go to the garden.
如果您想散步，可以去花园。

There is a recreation centre on the ground floor.
在一楼有个娱乐中心。

You can play billiards, table tennis, bridge, and go bowling.
您可以去打打台球、乒乓球、桥牌和保龄球。

There is a music teahouse where you can enjoy both classical music such as Beethoven, Mozart, Liszt, and modern music, while having some Chinese tea or other soft drinks.
有个音乐茶座，您可以一边欣赏古典音乐，如贝多芬、莫扎特、李斯特的乐曲，还有现代音乐，一边品尝中国茶和软饮料。

Don't worry. Here's all the information you need.
不用担心。这儿是所有您需要的信息。

Madam. What can I do for you?
夫人，我能为您做些什么？

Just a minute, please. I'll see if he is registered.
请稍等片刻，我看看他是否登记了。

There are two trains going to Hangzhou every morning，No.49 and No.79.
每天早晨有两列火车到杭州，49 次列车和 79 次列车。

They are in suite 705. Let me phone him.
他们住在 705 号套房，我来给他打电话。

Mr. Brown said he's waiting for you in his room.
布朗先生说他在房间里等您。

Class Activity Role-Play

Scene One: Mr. Brown needs some information about touring Hangzhou.

Scene Two: John Smith is looking for a man whose name is John in the hotel.

Further Reading

The Front Desk

A receptionist, belonging to the front office department, works side by side with the reservations at the front desk by the front hall. In small hotels a receptionist also serves as the bookkeeper, customer service and the advanced reservationist, while in bigger hotels they take over the work of the advance reservation department between 5:30 and 9:30 p.m.

If you come as a guest, a receptionist does your registration. After you are properly registered, the receptionist gives you your room key, tells you your room number, the floor it is on, and the daily room rate. You may get your key card that was prepared while you were completing the registration form. He explains the service to you or informs you of the place where you can find information about the service of the hotel by yourself.

参考译文

前　　台

接待员也属于前厅工作人员，他跟预订员一起在前大厅的前台工作。在小型酒店里，接待员还兼做记账员、解答员和预订员的工作。在大型酒店里，接待员在晚上 5:30～9:30 接管预订部的工作。

当你住店时，接待员将为你登记入住。当你登记好之后，接待员把钥匙交给你，告诉你房间号码、房间所在的楼层及每天的房费。接待员在你填写登记表时已为你准备好房卡。他会向你介绍酒店的各项服务，告诉你可以自己到哪里了解酒店的服务项目。

Question

Why does a receptionist belong to the front office department?

Unit 9 Check-out

Listening Practice

1. Listen to the dialogue and fill in the blanks.

【听力音频】

Staff: Good morning. sir. Can I help you?

Guest: I'd like to _____ now.

Staff: Your name and room number, please?

Guest: _____.

Staff: Yes, Mr. Bright. Have you used any hotel service this morning?

Guest: No, I haven't used any services.

Staff: Fine. This is your bill. Four nights at RMB_____ each, and here are the meals that you had at the hotel. That makes a total of RMB _____.

Guest: Exactly. Can I pay by _____?

Staff: Certainly. May I have your card，please?

Guest: Here you are.

Staff: Let me _____. Please sign your name here.

Guest: Oh, yes. Is it possible to leave my luggage here until I'm ready to leave this afternoon? I'd like to say goodbye to some of my friends.

Staff: Yes, we'll keep it for you. How many pieces of your luggage?

Guest: _____. I'll be back by 3:00 p.m.

Staff: That's fine. Have a nice day.

Guest: Thank you. See you later.

2. Listen and fill in the missing information.

Approximate figure of the account: _____

Check-out times: _____

Name: _____   Room number: _____

Way to pay: _____

Situational Dialogues

1. Checking-out

【拓展音频】

(Scene: A guest would like to check out right now and pay with traveler's checks.)

Guest: Good morning. Is this where I can pay my hotel bill?

Clerk: Yes. Please tell me your number and when you are checking out.

Guest: My room number is 1012 and I'd like to check out right now.

Clerk: Just a moment, please (checks files). Are you Mr. Steward from America?

Guest: Yes, Richard Steward.

Clerk: Mr. Steward, did you sign any bills in the last two hours in our hotel?

Guest: No.

Clerk: Have you used any hotel services this morning?

Guest: Ah, I used the mini-bar, drank a bottle of coca-cola and made a long distance call in my room.

Clerk: I'm afraid your final bill hasn't reached here yet. One moment, please. I'll call the department concerned. (He makes a call and then adds the amount to the bill.) Sorry to have kept you waiting, sir. Here is your hotel bill. Please check it.

Guest: I'm sorry. What's this for? (Pointing to figure.)

Clerk: That's for the drinks and phone calls you made from your room.

Guest: I see. Thank you. Can I pay with traveler's checks?

Clerk: Certainly, sir. (He fills out checks and hands them and his passport to the cashier.) Here are your bill and receipt, Mr. Steward. Hope you enjoyed your stay with us here and have a pleasant trip home.

Guest: Thank you.

2. Paying the Hotel Bill in Cash

(Scene: A guest wishes to pay his hotel bill, but finds he doesn't have enough Renminbi with him. He has his money exchanged and settles the accounts.)

Staff: Good morning, sir. Can I help you?

Guest: I'd like to know my account, so that I can have my money exchanged at the bank.

Staff: May I know your name and room number?

Guest: My name is Andrew Rich. Room 1246.

Staff: Let me see…Up to now, the total amount has been about 2,600 yuan.

Guest: OK. Thank you.

(Half an hour later.)

Guest: Excuse me. We're leaving today. Can we pay our bills now?

Staff: Certainly, sir. Oh, by the way, I'd like to tell you that the checkout time is 12:00 at noon. Your name and room number, please?

Guest: Andrew Rich in Room 1246.

Staff: Yes, Mr. Rich. How about the charge for the days you shared the room with your friend?

Guest: Please add it to my account.

Staff: Then we'll make out a bill for both of you.

Guest: OK.

Staff: Have you used any hotel services this morning or had breakfast at the hotel dining room, Mr. Rich?

Guest: We just had breakfast at the dining room, but we didn't use any services.

Staff: Fine. I'll need to find out what the charge is on the breakfast…Yes, the total for the six nights is 2,650yuan.

Guest: Oh, I didn't change enough money just now. Can I pay in US dollars?

Staff: Sorry, sir. But you can get your money changed at the Foreign Exchange Counter in our hotel, just over there.

(A few minutes later.)

Guest: Thank you. Here is the money I owe you.

Staff: Thank you, Mr. Rich. Here is your receipt. Have a nice trip.

3. Explaining the Bill

(Scene: A guest thinks the cost looks too high and wants the cashier to explain it.)

Guest: Good morning. Is this desk open?

Cashier: Yes, it is. Can I help you?

Guest: I'm leaving today. Can I see my bill, please?

Cashier: Just a moment, Mr. Baylor. I'll draw up your bill for you. Here is your bill. That's the total cost you owe the hotel.

Guest: This figure looks too high. Could you explain it a little bit?

Cashier: Sure. This is an itemized bill. So it is very easy to spot a mischarge if there exists one. A—P—T—S here stands for apartments your room charge. You stayed here for 5 nights, so the figure is repeated 5 times. Below the room charge are charges for the meals and drinks you put on your tab.

Guest: That's right. I had three drinks and three lunches at the lobby bar. But what is the next figure for?

Cashier: This is the charge for the drinks that you took from the mini-bar in your room.

Guest: Oh, I see. So that's accounted for. What is this figure under the item T—E—L—S—I —D—D?

Cashier: That means Telephone Subscriber International Direct Dialing. That's the charge for your international calls from your room.

Guest: But I only made a couple of calls to my wife and a couple of calls to our Hong Kong office.

Cashier: Mr. Baylor, international calls are rather expensive.

Guest: I know, but all of my calls were made during discount hours.

Cashier: Well, I'm sorry to tell you, sir, that there is no discount rate, or peak rate or any other rate for international calls here in the hotel. There is only one rate, the standard rate.

Guest: That's incredible. But it must be right of you say so. I just didn't expect it to be so expensive to make IDD calls from here. But now I don't have enough cash on me. Would credit card be all right?

Cashier: What kind are you holding, sir?

Guest: Bank of America Card.

Cashier: I'm sorry, sir. We only accept American express card, Master card and Visa.

Guest: Well, in that case, I want to pay the bill half in cash and half by traveler's cheques. Would that be all right?

Cashier: Yes, of course.

Guest: Here you are.

Cashier: Thank you. Have a pleasant journey home.

4. Postponing Checking out

(Scene: A guest wants to check out after 5:00 p.m.)

Cashier: Good morning. May I help you?

Guest: Yes, could you tell me what is the latest check out time?

Cashier: Our checking out time is from 11:00 to 12:30 o'clock.

Guest: Well, I planned to check out this morning, but my flight doesn't leave until 7:15 p.m. and I don't want to wait around at the airport all day. Could I check out after 5:00 p.m.

Cashier: Just a moment, please, sir. If we weren't so heavily booked, we could let you have a complimentary room. But now it is peak season and we've got a full house, so if you really want to keep your room this afternoon, we'll have to charge you 50% of the price.

Guest: Never mind, then, can I just leave my luggage somewhere until 5:00 p.m.?

Cashier: Certainly, sir. If you speak to the bellboy, he'll take care of it, but please take all valuables with you.

Guest: I'll do that.

Cashier: We are sorry for the inconvenience. Here is a complimentary coffee voucher. You can have a cup of coffee in our hotel bar on the second floor and spend your time there. We hope you have a nice time there.

Guest: Thank you very much.

Words and Expressions

add to my account	记在我的账里	make a total	总计
pay the bills	结账	receipt *n.*	收据
used any hotel services	使用酒店设施	an itemized bill	一个分项开列的账单

Learn by Heart

1. 几种支付方式

万事达信用卡	Master card	美国银行卡	Bank of America Card
美国运通卡	American express card	维萨卡	Visa
旅行支票	traveler's cheques	贷记卡(信用卡)	credit card
旅行娱乐信用卡(简称 T&E 卡)		travel and entertainment card	
储值卡	stored value card	附卡	supplementary card
银行卡	bank card		

2. 结账常用语

Please tell me your number and when you are checking out.
请您告诉我您的房号和结账时间。

Just a moment, please(checks files).
请稍等(查看记录)。

Have you used any hotel services this morning?
今天早上您是否使用过酒店内的服务设施？

I'm afraid your final bill hasn't reached here yet. One moment，please.
恐怕您最终的账单还没到。请稍等。

Here is your hotel bill. Please check it.
这是您的酒店账单，请结账。

"L" stands for laundry, and "T" means telephone call charge.
"L"代表洗衣费，"T"代表电话费。

Here are your bill and receipt.
这是您的账单和收据。

Oh, by the way, I'd like to tell you that the check-out time is 12:00 at noon.
顺便说一下，我们的结账时间是中午 12 点。

But you can get your money changed at the Foreign Exchange Counter in our hotel，just over there.
但是您可以在我们酒店的外币兑换处兑换货币，就在那里。

That's the total cost you owe the hotel.

这是您应付的所有费用。

This is an itemized bill. So it is very easy to spot a mischarge if there exists one.

这是一个分项开列的账单。如果有错误的话就很容易看出来。

What kind are you holding，sir?

先生，您有哪种卡？

Our checking out time is from 11:00 to 12:30 o'clock.

我们的结账时间是 11:00～12:30。

【情景演练】

Class Activity Role-Play

Scene One: A guest comes to the Front Desk to check out and he hasn't used any hotel services. He is ready to leave this afternoon and want to pay by bank card.

Scene Two: The guest would like to know the approximate figure of his account so that he can have his money exchanged at the bank. After checking his bill, the guest finds that he didn't change enough money just now. He want to pay in US dollars.

Further Reading

Checking-out

Hotel accounting has many distinctive features because a guest's bills must be entered, or posted, on his or her account as soon as possible. In addition to the charge for the guest's room, there may also be charges resulting from the use of the telephone, the laundry service, the restaurant, and room service. All the financial transactions not only must be posted, but also must be checked for accuracy. This is usually the job of a night auditor, who goes through this mass of figures on the night shift, where there is little activity in the hotel.

Cashiers provide financial services to the customers at the front desk including receiving payment for bills, making change, and exchanging foreign currency. When preparing a guest's bill, the cashier will pay special attention to the following things:

(1) Check if you have paid a reservation deposit. If you have, he/she will deduct the amount of your deposit from the bill.

(2) Check with you if you are entitled to any kind of discount or complimentary rate. If you are, he/she will make the necessary reduction.

(3) Remind you to return your room key to the reception desk before you leave the hotel.

(4) If you settle your account in traveler's checks, the cashier will make sure that you countersign the check in front of him/her. He/She won't accept checks that have already been countersigned.

参考译文

结 账 离 店

饭店会计业务有许多鲜明的特点，因为客人所有花费必须尽快入账。除了客人的房费外，还有电话费、洗衣费、餐饮费及客房服务费。所有账目不仅要登记入账，还要审核。审核工作一般由夜班审计员完成。他会在饭店业务较少的夜间将所有账目审核一遍。

出纳员的工作是在前台为客人提供财务服务，包括收款、找钱及兑换外币。在为客人结账时，出纳员会特别注意以下事项：

(1) 查看清楚你是否交过预订金。如果交过，就把预订金从账目中扣除。

(2) 查看你是否有条件享受折扣或优惠价格。如果有，就扣除应该去掉的数额。

(3) 提醒你在离店之前把房间钥匙交还给接待处。

(4) 如果你用旅行支票结账，他将要求你当面在支票上签字，不会接受事先签好了的支票。

Question

By which means do you like to check out?

Housekeeping

Unit 1 Showing Room

Listening Practice

1. Listen to the dialogue and fill in the blanks.

A: Mind your step, please. This way.

B: Thank you.

A: Here is your room, let me _____ for you, Mr. Lee.

B: Well, the air in the room was warm and _____. I like it!

A: That is our style. Shall I _____ for you?

B: OK, go ahead.

A: You will find a _____ with full information about the facilities and
services of our hotel in that drawer. The temperature control is here and there are
some light switches on the _____.

B: Good.

A: Please enjoy yourself, sir. And if there is anything we can do, please let us know.

2. Listen and fill in the missing information.

Room type: _____   Guest gender: _____

Room view: _____   Room number: _____

Festival: _____

Time of room service: _____

Situational Dialogues

1. Introducing the Room to the Guest

(Scene: Robin will meet some friends here and need to arrange some rooms for them.
But he wants to see the room first and then decide to choose the right hotel.)

(R: Robin, W: Wendy, T: Tony)

R: Excuse me, I need some rooms tomorrow. But could I check the room before
booking?

W: I'm sorry. Usually we do not have such a policy in the hotel. Why do you need to
check these rooms?

R: Well, the rooms are for my friends but they are very picky. Therefore, I'd like to
confirm that all rooms are nice for them and your service is quite satisfying.

W: I can understand what you are saying. Could you wait for a minute? I will check with my supervisor and arrange this for you.

R: How kind of you to help!

T: I am Tony, at your service, sir. Please follow me to see the room.

R: Thank you. Could you show me the single room first?

T: No problem, this way please.

R: Well, The room is about 20 or 30 square meters in the area. Am I right?

T: Exactly. It is about 25 square meters.

R: Spare blankets lay at the foot of each bed. That is a good idea.

T: Yes, we have many convenient facilities.

R: One of my friends has many requirements for the bathroom. He always spends hours in the bathroom or on the telephone.

T: Every room in the hotel has a private bathroom and they all have good decoration.

R: Good. By the way, will it be convenient to see the standard room now?

T: OK, this way please.

R: I am more concerned about the width of the bed in the standard room.

T: Don't worry about that. The bed is 1.5 meters wide and I think it is enough for one person.

R: Good. Do you have turn-down service in the hotel?

T: Yes, we start clearing up the mess, supplementing necessities from 5:30 p.m. or 6:00 p.m. in the evening.

R: Well, I think your hotel is perfect. I will book some rooms immediately.

2. Showing the Room

(Scene: A clerk named Bill is showing the room to a guest named Clark who visits the hotel for the first time．)

(B: Bill, C: Clark)

B: Here is your room, Mr. Clark. After you.

C: Thank you.

B: Shall I draw the curtain for you?

C: OK, thank you. By the way, do you know when room service is available?

B: It's available twenty-four hours a day. And in the first drawer of the dresser, you'll find a brochure with full information about the facilities and services of our hotel.

C: That's great. What kind of restaurant do you have?

B: There is a French café and a Korean barbeque restaurant on the 3rd Floor. And you can also enjoy yourself in the revolving cocktail lounge on the top floor.

C: OK. I think I can really enjoy my day here!

B: Of course. Here is the mini-bar. All the price tags have been already marked on the goods. And here is the water boiler ready for use.

C: That's great. Thanks for your kind introduction. Um…Here's something for you. (Giving tips)

B: That's very nice of you. Thank you. Is there anything else I can do for you?

C: No, thanks.

B: I'm always at your service, Mr. Clark. Have a nice day. Goodbye.

3. Taking the Guest to the Room

(Scene: A clerk named Peter is taking a guest to the room. The guest has many luggage.)

Peter: Good afternoon, Mr. Wang. Welcome to our hotel.

Guest: Oh, how do you know my name?

Peter: The labels on your luggage.

Guest: You are so clever. The label is from the airport.

Peter: Sir, I will show you to your room. Are there all your baggage?

Guest: Yes, could you give me a hand with the baggage?

Peter: Certainly, that is my responsibility.

Guest: Thank you.

Peter: Is there anything valuable or breakable in your bags?

Guest: Yes, there is a bottle of wine in this bag and that bag is full of books.

Peter: Sure, may I have a look at your room card, please?

Guest: Here you are.

Peter: Thank you. Your room is on the tenth floor, please follow me. We go up by the elevator.

Guest: OK.

Peter: This is your room. (Unlocking the door and switching on light.) After you, sir. Do you mind if I put your luggage by the wardrobe?

Guest: Not really.

Peter: If you need anything, just call the reception. The number is 9.

Guest: Thank you.

Peter: You are always welcome.

4. Introducing the Room and the Service in the Hotel

(Scene: Ellen has taken a guest into the room and the guest wants to know the services and the facilities in the room.)

Ellen: Please come in. This is the bathroom and the switch is here.

Guest: The room looks nice. It's comfortable.

Ellen: You are right. Our restaurant serves breakfast from 7 a.m. until 9 a.m. Here is a brochure explaining hotel services. The hot water is supplied round the clock. By the way, the extension number of the floor desk is 1001.

Guest: Thank you. Could you tell me something about the restaurant in your hotel?

Ellen: Sure, there is a French Café and a Korean barbeque restaurant on the third floor. Also we have a Chinese restaurant on the second floor.

Guest: Can I go shopping here?

Ellen: There are a lot of nice shops and boutiques nearby.

Guest: Thank you. That is very nice of you.

Ellen: You are welcome. We have both sauna and massage service in our hotel as well.

Guest: Good. Um…Here is something for you. (Giving tips.)

Ellen: Thank you, but I am afraid we don't accept tips. Is there anything else I can do for you?

Guest: No, thanks.

Ellen: Have a nice day!

Words and Expressions

confirm	*v.*	证实，批准，确定	arrange	*v.*	安排
convenient	*adj.*	便利的，方便的	necessities	*n.*	必需品
massage	*v.*	按摩	boutique	*n.*	精品店
lounge	*n.*	休息厅，酒廊			

Learn by Heart

1. 酒店的基本房型

标准间	standard room	高级间	superior room
豪华房	deluxe room	商务房	business room
行政房	executive room	套房	suite

2. 带客服务常用语

Please follow me, this way.
请跟我来，这边走。

Here is the wardrobe and there is the bathroom.
这是衣柜，那是浴室。

May I have your room key please?

能给我您的房卡吗？

Let me open the door for you.

请让我为您开门。

May I put your baggage here?

我可以把行李放在这里吗？

The switch is here.

开关在这里。

Here is a brochure explaining the hotel service.

这本手册介绍了饭店的一些服务。

Shall I draw the curtain for you?

我为您拉开窗帘好吗？

You can enjoy yourself in the revolving cocktail lounge on the top floor.

您可以在楼顶的旋转鸡尾酒吧里享受一下。

If there is anything else I can do for you, please call me.

如果需要我做什么，请给我打电话。

The room has a view of the West Lake.

从房间看出去是西湖。

There are a lot of nice shops and boutiques nearby.

附近有很多不错的商店和精品店。

There are several kinds of drinks in the mini-bar. Please help yourself to them. The cost of the drinks you've had will be added to your account.

迷你吧里有饮料，您可以随便用，用后统一结账。

If you don't want to be disturbed, you'd better press the "Don't Disturb" key on the bedside controls.

如果您不想被打扰，最好按床边的"请勿打扰"键。

Class Activity Role-Play

【情景演练】

Scene One: A floor attendant sees a guest coming out of a lift and comes up to greet him.

Scene Two: The floor attendant introduces the room facilities and services to a guest.

Further Reading

Welcoming and Guiding the Guest

Floor service is one important part of working organization in Housekeeping Department, where guests come and hope to be respected and concerned as well. Therefore, the floor attendant plays an important role in hotel service. The guests should be bowed in by the usher. Then the floor attendant needs to introduce the room service and explain the room facilities. Courteous and welcoming staff will leave guests with a good impression and cheerful temper, which speaks for the hotel at the same time.

Each hotel has different decoration or facilities in the room. Meanwhile, the buildings don't follow the same patterns as well. That means the attendant need to show guests the room and pick up their luggage thoughtfully. During the way to the room, the floor attendant should talk to the guest enthusiastically. Some information is useful for the guest such as festivals or promotions.

参考译文

来宾的迎接与引导

楼层服务是客房部工作组织中的重要部分，客人到达后也希望得到尊重与关心。因此，楼层服务员在此服务中起到了重要的作用。客人需要被指引到房间，然后服务员应该介绍房间服务与设施。员工的礼貌服务会给客人留下美好的印象，使之有一个好心情，同时也会给酒店加分。

每个酒店的房间都会有不同的装修或者设施。同时，每个酒店的建筑格局也是不一样的。这意味着服务员应该周到地带客并帮客人提取行李。在去房间的路上，楼层服务员可以与客人热情地交谈。有些信息对客人也是非常有用的，如酒店节日或促销等。

【拓展习题】

Question

How to be a good floor attendant?

Unit 2　Chamber Service

Listening Practice

【听力音频】

1. Listen to the dialogue and fill in the blanks.

(Knocking the door.)

A: Housekeeping. May I come in?

B: Come in, please.

A: Good evening, ma'am. Sorry to _____. May I do your room now?

B: Sure. Could you tidy up the _____ first? I've just taken a bath, and it's quite a mess.

A: Certainly, ma'am.

(Finish cleaning the room.)

A: Is there anything else I can do for you?

B: Oh yes. Where can I borrow a _____?

A: Don't worry. We provide the hair-dryer each room, you can find it _____.

B: Oh I see, thank you.

A: You're welcome. Good night, ma'am. _____.

2. Listen and fill in the missing information.

Time: _____　　Guest name: _____

Reason of cleaning late: _____

Weather tonight: _____

Situational Dialogues

1. Respond to the Request of Chamber Service

(Scene: A guest is leaving his room when coming across the housekeeper. He asks the housekeeper to do his room.)

(H: Housekeeper, G: Guest)

H: Good morning. May I come through, please?

G: Good morning. It's almost noon now, and our room has not been made up yet. I wonder when you are going to do it.

H: Truly sorry. I'm now on my way to your room as soon as I just finished this one.

G: Really? But I think you could do our room first, since we want to have a nap after lunch.

H: Well. We always do the check-out rooms first, unless there is a request.

G: What do you mean check-out rooms?

H: A check-out room means guests are leaving the hotel at the end of their stay. We have to get the rooms ready for sale by the front desk.

G: OK. In that case, I can understand. I suppose it's a lot of work for you since it's now the peak season for tourism in this area.

H: Thanks. Our hotel is full nearly everyday. Your room will be ready in half an hour.

G: That's fine.

H: Is your room number 3008?

G: Yes. Well, we are going to have lunch. Thank you.

H: My pleasure. Hope you are having nice stay here.

G: Sure we are. Goodbye.

2. The Turn-down Service

【拓展音频】

(Scene: The Whites are sitting in the room when a chamber maid knocks at the door.)

(C: Chamber maid, M: Mrs. White, W: Mr. White)

C: Housekeeping. May I come in?

W: Yes, please.

C: Good evening, Mr. and Mrs. White. May I do the turn-down service for you now?

M: Oh, thank you. But you see, we are having some friends to celebrate my birthday here. Could you come back later?

C: Certainly, Mr. White, What time would it be convenient for you?

M: Could you come again in there hours?

C: I'm afraid I'll be off then. But I will let the overnight staff know. They will come then.

M: That's fine. Well, our friends seem to be a little late. Would you tidy up a bit in the bathroom? I've just taken a bath and it is quite a mess now. Besides, please bring us a bottle of just boiled water. We'd treat our guests with typical Chinese tea.

C: Yes, Mr. White. I'll bring in some fresh towels together with the drinking water.

M: That's fine.

C: (Having done all on the request.)

It's growing dark. Would you like me to draw the curtains for you?

M: Why not? That would be so cozy.

C: May I turn on the lights for you?

W: No, thanks. I like this atmosphere.

C: Yes, sir. Is there anything else I can do for you?

M: No more. You're a smart girl indeed. Thank you very much.

C: I'm always at your service. Goodbye, Mr. and Mrs. White, and do have a very pleasant evening.

3. Borrowing Things

(Scene: A guest wants to borrow something in the room.)

(H: Housekeeper, G: Guest)

H: Housekeeping. May I help you?

G: Yes. I need to borrow a trouser press.

H: Your name and room number, please?

G: I'm Alice Wilson in 317.

H: There is absolutely no problem, Mrs. Wilson. For how long will you need to borrow the trouser press?

G: For about three hours.

H: The charge will be 10 yuan per hour.

Gt: That's fine. By the way, could you also send your seamstress right up? I'll need her to do some sewing.

H: Right, I'll ask the seamstress to bring a trouser press up to 317 right away.

G: Thanks a lot.

H: You are welcome. Will there be anything else?

G: No, thank you. Goodbye.

4. Repairing Service

(Scene: A guest had a problem with the TV set. Besides, he also has some other requirements for the room.)

(G: Guest, F: Floor Clerk)

G: Excuse me, but could you do something about the TV set in my room?

F: Yes, sir. What's wrong with it?

G: The picture is wobbling. The sound is not clear and there is a lot of static.

F: I see. Maybe it needs to adjust the channels. I will send for a repairman from the Maintenance Department to your room at once to look at it. We apologize for the inconvenience. Anything else, sir?

G: Yes. Do you have large slippers than the ones I have in my room? They are too small for me.

F: I'm not really sure, sir. But I'll try and see if I can get you a pair of larger ones.

G: One more thing, I also need a couple more of hangers.

F: I'll fetch you some more right away. Is four enough?

G: Yes, that's more than enough. Thank you.

Words and Expressions

nap	*n.*	小睡，打盹	check-out		退房
courier	*n.*	快递，快递员	vacuum	*v.*	用吸尘器打扫

turn-down service		开夜床服务	towel	n.	毛巾
atmosphere	n.	气氛	trouser press	n.	裤子熨斗
seamstress	n.	女裁缝	static	n.	静电
fetch	v.	拿来，取得			

Learn by Heart

1. 客房服务员了解客人姓名的途径

行李标签	luggage tag	来客单	arrival list
入住登记表	registration form	餐厅预订	restaurant reservation
会议姓名牌	convention name tag	询问客人	asking the guest

2. 客房服务常用语

Housekeeping. May I come in?
客房服务，我可以进来吗？

When would you like me to do your room，sir?
您需要我什么时间来给您打扫房间呢，先生？

I'm sorry that your flask is empty.
很抱歉您的水壶空了。

May I do the turn-down service for you now?
现在可以为您开夜床服务了吗？

I hope I'm not disturbing you.
我希望我没有打扰到您。

Certainly, madam. I'll let the overnight staff know.
当然可以，女士。我会转告夜班服务员。

It's growing dark. Would you like me to draw the curtains for you?
天黑下来了，要不要我拉上窗帘？

Shall I come back later, sir?
先生，要我等一会再来吗？

What time would you like me to come back?
您希望我什么时候再来？

You can call the front desk when you want your room done.

当您需要清理房间时，可以给前台打电话。

Just leave the things as they are, please.

就把它们放在那儿吧。

Where can I borrow a hair-dryer?

我从哪儿能借到吹风机？

I will send one up right away.

我马上送一个上来。

Is there anything I can do for you?

您还有什么事要我做吗？

I'm always at your service.

乐意效劳。

Class Activity Role-Play

Scene One: A housekeeper comes into a room and identifies the guest, and finds out if he
would like to have the room cleaned.

Scene Two: A guest wants to recharge his electric shaver and he needs a converter as well. But
another guest has borrowed it, so you promise to lend it to him in 30 minutes.

Further Reading

About Housekeeping

Housekeeping department, together with front office, food and beverage department, auditing
department and the engineering department, make up the five basic departments of a hotel. It is
responsible for cleaning the guestrooms and making them look clean, tidy, well-appointed and
comfortable. The housekeeping department also does such work as to set up and to take apart
banquets, exhibitions, conventions and conferences.

The housekeeping department is headed by the executive housekeeper and its staff includes
housemaids, housemen (room boys), floor clerks, porters, room attendants, and seamstresses, and
in some hotels the painters, plumbers, general maintenance men and window washers. Such
housekeeping staff as porters, floor clerks, housemaids and room boys all have direct contact with
the guest and contribute to the guest's overall experience with the hotel. The job of a housemaid or
houseman is especially important, for a comfortable, clean, quiet and well-appointed room with a
large soft bed is what every traveler looks for at the end of his/her journey or a day's sightseeing.
Even such trivial carelessness as an impaired ashtray or waste basket, an improperly cleaned bath
tub can upset a frazzled guest and thus affect his/her impression of the hotel.

参考译文

关于客房部

客房部与前厅部、餐饮部、审计部和工程部一起，构成了酒店的 5 个基本部门。客房部的职责是打扫客房，使它们看上去干净、整洁、设备齐全、舒适。客房部还参与举办宴会、展览、会议，并负责收场的工作。

客房部以行政管家为首，工作人员包括女服务员、男服务员(客房部服务生)、楼层文员、行李员、客房服务员和裁缝，有些酒店还有画家、水暖工、一般维修人员和窗户清洁工。行李员、楼层文员、女服务员和客房部服务生这样的家政人员都会与客人直接接触，这有助于客人的酒店整体体验。一个女服务员或客房服务生的工作显得尤为重要，因为一个舒适、整洁、安静和设备齐全的客房加上一张大软床，是每位旅客在他/她的旅程或一天的观光结束后所寻找的目标。一些微不足道的疏忽，如损坏的烟灰缸或废纸篓、清洗不当的浴缸都会使一个疲惫的旅客心烦，从而影响他/她对酒店的印象。

Question

How to make sure that there is no trivial carelessness in the room?

Unit 3   Laundry

Listening Practice

【听力音频】

1. Listen to the dialogue and fill in the blanks.

A: Excuse me. Have you any laundry? The laundry man is here to _____.

B: No, not now. Thank you.

A: If you have any, please just leave it in the _____ behind the
bathroom door. The laundry man comes over to collect it every morning.

B: Thank you.

A: Please _____ in the list whether you need your clothes
ironed, washed, dry-cleaned or mended and also what time you want to get them
back.

B: I see. What if there is any laundry damage? I wonder if your hotel has a policy on
dealing with it.

A: In such a case, the hotel should certainly pay for it. The indemnity shall not exceed
_____ the laundry.

B: That sounds quite reasonable. I hope there's no damage at all.

A: Don't worry, sir. The Laundry Department has _____ in their
work.

B: All right. Thank you for your information.

A: Not at all.

2. Listen and fill in the missing information.

Room number: _____ Guest name: _____

How to wash a silk dress: _____

Duration of laundry: _____ Price of express service: _____

Situational Dialogues

1. Providing the Laundry Service to the Guest

【拓展音频】

(Scene: A guest called the laundry service center before and put forward her needs. A
room maid then came to her room and is offering laundry service to the guest now.)

(M: Room maid, G: Guest)

M: Good evening. Housekeeping. May I pick up your laundry?

G: Yes, it is in the laundry bag.

M: Thank you, ma'am. Is the laundry form in the bag?

G: Yes. I'd like to know how long your laundry service usually takes.

M: For clothes received before 11:00 a.m., we'll deliver them to your room by 9:00 p.m. the same day; and for those received before 3:00 p.m., you may get them back by noon the next day.

G: Got it. By the way, I may need dry-cleaning for my sweater. How long does it usually take?

M: It usually takes two days.

G: Oh, it might be a little bit long. We're leaving tomorrow.

M: If you are in a hurry, we have a two-hour quick service with an extra charge of 50%.

G: Well, if that's the case, I'd like this sweater dry-cleaned by hand in cold water.

M: Sure, the laundry will be done as you asked before. But, let me see, there should be three T-shirts in your form, but there are only two in the bag.

G: Oh, sorry. I can't find another T-shirt now, just send the laundry as it is.

M: OK. Could you sign for the change please?

G: No problem.

M: Anything else, ma'am?

G: No, that's all.

M: Thanks for your cooperation. Goodbye.

2. Laundry Service

(Scene: A guest is calling for laundry service in the room.)

Staff: Good morning. Housekeeping. May I help you?

Guest: Yes. Please send someone to pick up my laundry.

Staff: Your room number, please?

Guest: 1102.

Staff: A valet will be up in a few minutes.

Valet: Housekeeping. May I come in?

Guest: Yes. I'd like to have this laundry done.

Valet: Certainly, sir. Would you please fill out a laundry form?

Guest: Yes. Here you are.

Valet: Would you like regular service or express service?

Guest: What's the difference?

Valet: For regular service, laundry is collected before 9:30 a.m. and returned at 6:00 p.m. the same day. For express service，the laundry is returned within four hours. The charge for express service is double.

Guest: I see. Regular will be all right.

Valet: I guess your skirt need steamed and pressed, am I right?

Guest: Yes, of course. And there is a spot on the right side, see if you can remove it.

Valet: Could you tell me what the stain is made of then we can use the best way to deal with it.

Guest: I think it is an oil stain but I am not sure.

Valet: OK. We will do our best. May I do anything else for you?

Guest: No, that is all.

Valet: Could you please sign your name here?

Guest: Sure.

3. Complaints about Laundry Service

(Scene: A guest is complaining that the laundry service is not very good. Some clothes have shrunk to half size and some are even missing.)

(L: Laundress, G: Guest)

L: Laundry service. May I help you?

G: Yes. I have a lot of complaints about the laundry.

L: What is the problem exactly, madam?

G: First of all, I sent a pair of tights to the laundry and now they are full of runs. I also sent a T-shirt and a nightgown which have shrunk to half size.

L: I am terribly sorry, madam. However, according to the hotel rules we are allowed to pay up to ten times the price for laundering the items for the damage. I hope this will help.

G: That's very kind of you, but this isn't the only problem. We are also missing a singlet and a panties girdle. They were never returned.

L: I see that you have some serious problems, madam. I am going to contact the laundry manager right this moment and ask her to attend to your problems personally.

G: That's very kind of you.

L: Please let me apologize on the part of the management of our hotel for all the inconvenience. We will pay as much as is allowed by hotel rules for the damaged articles and we will do our utmost to find the missing things.

G: I hope so. I'm checking out in two hours.

L: We will take immediate action, madam. Thank you for calling.

G: You have been very helpful. Thank you very much. Goodbye.

L: Goodbye, madam.

4. The Error of the Laundry Service

(Scene: A guest is going to check out, however, the laundry was not returned by the hotel. There must have something wrong about the laundry service.)

(L: Launderss, G: Guest)

L: Good afternoon. The laundry. May I help you?

G: Yes. You took my laundry two days ago and I'd like to know where it is.

L: I am terribly sorry for the inconvenience, sir. Could you tell me your name and room number?

G: I'm George Ellington in 311.

L: Please hold on a moment, Mr. Ellington. I will try to locate your laundry.

(After one minute…)

L: Are you still there, Mr. Ellington?

G: Yes, I am.

L: We have found your laundry，Mr. Ellington. It went to 312 by mistake. I am terribly sorry about this error.

G: That's all right, but please bring my laundry right up because I will check out right away.

L: Your laundry is on its way up right now, Mr. Ellington.

G: Thank you very much.

L: You are welcome, sir. Please let me apologize again for the mistake.

G: Thank you for finding my laundry. Goodbye.

L: Goodbye, sir.

(After five minutes…)

L: Mr. Ellington, your clothes are ready. Here they are.

G: Well, let me check. The stain on my skirt has all been removed and the skirt looks like a new one. How nice!

L: Thank you, but we still feel sorry for our mistake.

G: To err is human. Forget it.

L: That is very kind of you.

Words and Expressions

dry-cleaning		干洗		quick service		加急服务
starch	v.	给……上浆		shrink	v.	缩水，起皱
valet	n.	服务员，侍者		steam	n.	蒸汽
tights	n.	紧身衣		nightgown	n.	睡衣
singlet	n.	汗衫		panties girdle	n.	裤带，腰带
To err is human		人非圣贤，孰能无过				

Learn by Heart

1. 洗衣服务的种类

干洗　dry clean　　　　湿洗　wet clean

手洗　hand wash　　　　熨烫　ironing

2. 洗衣服务常用语

Excuse me. Do you have any laundry?

请问您有没有要洗的衣服？

The laundry man is here to collect it.

洗衣房服务员来这里收要洗的衣服了。

If you have any, please just leave it in the laundry bag behind the bathroom door.

如果您有衣服要洗，请放在浴室门后的洗衣袋里。

I'm afraid it is too late for today's laundry.

恐怕已经过了今天的洗衣时间。

I'm sorry, but we don't have the special equipment necessary to clean leather.

很抱歉，我们没有清洗皮料所需要的特别设备。

Please tell us or notify in the list whether you need your clothes ironed, washed, dry-cleaned or mended and also what time you want to get them back.

请告诉我们或在洗衣单上写明您的衣服是否需要熨烫、水洗、干洗或缝补，还要写明何时需要取衣服。

In such a case, the hotel should certainly pay for it.

如果是这样，饭店当然应该赔偿。

A valet will be up in a few minutes.

洗熨工马上就到。

We'll dry-clean the dress.

我们要干洗这条裙子。

We'll stitch it before washing.

我们会在洗之前把衬里缝好。

But would you like express service or same-day service?

不过，您是要快洗服务还是当日取？

Could you fill out the laundry form, please?

请您填一下洗衣单，好吗？

We will deliver them around 5 tomorrow evening.

我们会在明晚 5 点左右给您送回。

Please refer to your laundry list for further information.

详细情况，您可以参考洗衣表。

Class Activity Role-Play

Scene One: You are the guest in the hotel and ask your floor attendant for laundry service. You want your clothes to be washed by hand in cold water, no starch and no bleach.

Scene Two: You are the floor attendant. You return a guest's laundry and tell the guest that one button has missed. Try to explain for this and find a way to deal with this problem.

Further Reading

The Laundry Service

In a hotel, the laundry service, the prime duty of which is to see to the cleanliness of the hotel linens, the staff's uniforms and the guest's personal laundry, belongs to the Housekeeping Department. The laundry service can be divided into washing, dry-clean and pressing. According to the length of time needed, it also falls into two categories: ordinary and express. Good laundry service is a very important aspect of a hotel, and it makes the guest feel at home. Furthermore, the guest is more likely to complain about the service if it is not performed well. Consequently, the hotel attaches importance to laundry service, too. In fact, the laundry service can be outsourced to dry clean company in some hotels. However, the quality is the major point in hotel's service.

参考译文

洗 衣 服 务

在酒店，洗衣服务的首要任务是清洗酒店的床上用品、工作人员的制服和客人的个人衣物，它属于客房部的工作范畴。洗衣服务可分为洗涤、干洗和熨烫。根据所需的时间长度，也可以分为两类：普通和特快。良好的洗衣服务是酒店的一个非常重要的方面，它使客人有宾至如归的感觉。此外，如果服务欠佳，宾客更容易对服务产生抱怨。因此，酒店也非常重视洗衣服务。事实上，有些酒店采取的是将洗衣服务外包给干洗公司，但不管怎样，质量仍然是酒店追求的首要目标。

Question

How to make sure to keep guest's laundry in good condition?

Unit 4　Dealing with Emergencies

Listening Practice

【听力音频】

1. Listen to the dialogue and fill in the blanks.

A: Hello, could you ask someone to come to my room?

B: Sure, do you need any help?

A: I have a _____. Maybe I had too much seafood. Besides, one
can get stomachache from eating hot food rinsed with _____.

B: Shall I call a doctor for you?

A: Yes, please do and make it quick. Or I will squirm with stomachache on bed.

B: Right away，sir. _____, please?

A: Room 809.

B: I see, sir. Before the doctor's arrival，is there anything else I can do for you?

A: Yes. I want to know if there is any medicine in your hotel.

B: Of course, sir. The doctor will give you explicit instructions on _____
to take the medicine.

A: Wonderful. Thank you very much.

B: _____.

2. Listen and fill in the missing information.

Room number:_____　　Guest name: _____

Reason for complaint: _____

Location of the room: _____

Available time of changing room: _____

Situational Dialogues

1. A Drunken Guest

(Scene: A guest is smoking in the room, which makes the detector flash. The floor
attendant has to check the room.)

Staff:　Excuse me. May I come in?

Guest:　Yes, the door is open.

Staff:　I am sorry, some guests complained about the noise in your room. They said
someone were shouting and singing loudly in the room. However, there is
something more terrible that the smoke detector is flashing and warning.

Guest: I can't tell you how sorry I am. You see, my husband had drunk so much that he found it hard to remain perpendicular.

Staff: I think the gentleman may need a cup of tea. It's very stuffy here. Would you mind taking your husband out for some fresh air?

Guest: I hope so. But I guess he is so tired that he feels as if he could sleep the clock around.

Staff: Well, do you mind that I need to check the smoke detector?

Guest: No problem, go ahead.

Staff: Smoke sensors warned us of the fire for the smoke triggered off the alarm.

Guest: We are truly sorry for the inconvenience. It was thoughtless of him to forget your hotel's policy after drinking.

Staff: I can make sense. Please take care of him and avoid disturbing others. By the way, if you need any help, just let us know.

Guest: Yes, thank you.

2. Repairing the Room

(Scene: A guest is calling the housekeeping center to complain the bad facilities in the bathroom.)

(H: Housekeeper, G: Guest, R: Repairman)

H: Good evening. Housekeeping. May I help you?

G: Yes. There is something wrong with some of the facilities in the bathroom. I usually take a bath shower before I go to bed. But could you deal with this immediately?

H: I'm sorry to hear that. What exactly is the matter?

G: The toilet doesn't flush, the shower head and washbasin faucet keep dripping, and the bathtub drain is clogged as well.

H: First, I do apologize for the inconvenience. I will have the Maintenance Department fix these right now. Would you please tell me your room number?

G: 1205.

H: Room 1205. Thank you for bringing the problems to our attention. And I apologize for the inconvenience again. The repairman will come to your room soon.

G: Yes, I see.

(5 minutes later.)

R: Housekeeping. May I come in?

G: Come in, please.

R: Good evening, sir. I have come to repair the bathroom facilities and I will take a look at them as well.

G: Good. Go ahead. How long will I have to wait?

R: Fifteen minutes or so.

G: OK.

R: Everything is all right, sir. You can use the bathroom now.

G: Thank you. And another thing, the people next door are very noisy.

R: I'm very sorry about the noise. We will check into it.

G: Fine, don't forget.

R: I'll take care of it. Have a good night.

3. Asking for First Aid

(Scene: A guest just slipped in the bathroom and got injured. Her husband is asking for help in the room.)

(A: Floor Attendant, G: Guest)

A: Good afternoon. Sarah speaking. What can I do for you?

G: My wife has slipped in the bathroom. She can't stand up. I'm afraid she sprained her ankle.

A: Shall I call a doctor for you?

G: Yes, please do and make it quick.

A: Right away, sir. May I have your room number, please?

G: Room 1008. Oh, no! Her left leg is also bleeding now.

A: Sir, I'll call the ambulance and get help immediately. Please don't move her.

G: Hurry up.

A: Help is on the way, sir. Everything will be alright. We will bring some bandages and absorbent cotton to your room to give her first aid before the doctor comes.

G: OK. Thank you!

A: We are on the way. Bye.

4. Saving the Guest

(Scene: The hotel will hold a fire drill this morning. But a guest did not get the information and went to the wrong place with panic.)

(Broadcasting: May I have your attention, please? This is an emergency. The place is on fire now. Please leave your room immediately and follow the emergency exit door. Withdraw this building immediately. Thank you for your cooperation, this is a fire drill.)

(E: Ellen, G: Guest, H: Housekeeper)

E: Housekeeping, Ellen speaking. May I help you?

G: I'm outside on the fire escape and can't get in. What shall I do?

E: Which floor are you on, madam?

G: The 15th floor.

E: Could you stay where you are, madam? We will send someone immediately.

G: OK, please be quick!

H: Hello, is anyone there?

G: Yes, I am here.

H: Could you step to the left as the door opens outwards, madam?

G: Sure.

H: I am opening the door now.

G: Thank goodness you came! I was beginning to give up hope.

H: I'm very sorry, madam. But for security reasons the fire doors cannot be opened from the outside.

G: I can understand. I just don't know this is a fire drill.

H: Did you get the message on your table in the room?

G: No. I slept early last night.

H: I am sorry. But happily, you are safe and sound.

Words and Expressions

sprain	v.	扭伤	bandages and absorbent cotton		绷带和脱脂棉
drunken	adj.	喝醉的	perpendicular	adj.	站直的
stuffy	adj.	不通气的，闷	faucet	n.	水龙头
tablet	n.	药丸	fire drill		消防演习
safe and sound		平安无事			

Learn by Heart

1. 酒店常见突发事件

火灾	fire	受伤	suffer injuries
失窃事故	theft incidents	醉酒的客人	drunken guest
食物中毒	food poisoning	停电	power cut

2. 处理突发事件常用语

We'll send someone to repair it immediately.
我们会马上派人来修。
What's the trouble?
哪儿坏了？

Some part needs to be replaced. I will be back soon.

某些零件要换。我马上就到。

I'm sorry. May I have a look at it?

很遗憾，我可以看看吗？

I'll send for an electrician from the maintenance department.

我去请维修部的电工来。

We can have it repaired.

我们可以修理。

Please wait just a few minutes.

请稍等几分钟。

Let me pinch your nose to stop the bleeding.

让我捏住您的鼻子来止血。

Everything will be all right, I will send for the doctor, just relax!

一切都会好的，我叫个医生过来，请放松！

I hope you will feel better soon.

我希望您会马上好起来。

Are you feeling better now?

您现在感觉好些了吗？

Would you please give her one more pillow so that she can lie better?

请再给她一个枕头好吗，这样她躺着可以舒服点。

But all you have to do now is to take a good rest in your room.

您现在最好在房间里好好休息。

Class Activity Role-Play

Scene One: A guest is hurt when he was shaving and he can't stop bleeding on his face.

Scene Two: You have caught a cold because of the low temperature. So you ask the floor attendant to give you some help.

Further Reading

Rescue Teams in Hotel Emergencies

Shanghai has established teams in its 18 districts and Chongming County to help with emergencies involving hotels.

The teams, which will have about 10 members each, will be made up of hotel and tourism agency employees, said the Shanghai Tourism Administrative Commission. Team members will be responsible for evacuations, first aid and raising the alarm when fire or other emergencies strike. They'll also teach disaster prevention and first-aid to other employees and tourists, said the commission. The commission's districts and county branches have held lectures and practical drills for team members to educate them about what to do in an emergency.

Yesterday, a fire drill was successfully carried out at the Sofitel, Jin Jiang, Oriental, Pudong Hotel in Pudong New Area. "The team members are still relatively inexperienced, but we expect them to play important roles in the future in ensuring tourists' safety," said Su Guangjian, director of the commission's market management section.

参考译文

酒店突发事件救援小组

上海在 18 个区和崇明县成立了救援小组，专门帮助处理发生在酒店中的突发事件。

这些小组每组大概有 10 个队员。据上海旅游事务管理委员会透露，组员大多来自酒店和旅行社员工。组员负责协助人员撤离、急救和紧急报警或其他突发事件。他们也会传授灾难预防、急救等知识给其他员工。委员会所在地和县市分公司已经举办了讲座和实际演练来教导组员学会正确处理突发事件。

昨天，位于浦东新区的索菲特酒店、锦江大酒店、东方大酒店和浦东酒店成功举行了一次消防演习。委员会市场管理科主任苏广建说："这些组员仍然相对缺乏经验，但我们希望在未来，他们在确保游客的安全方面发挥的重要作用。"

Question

In your opinion, what skills are useful in hotel emergencies?

Unit 5 Lost and Found

Listening Practice

【听力音频】

1. Listen to the dialogue and fill in the blanks.

A: Housekeeping. May I help you?

B: Yes. I'm Mrs. Parker_____. I just do not know what to do!

A: What is the problem, Mrs. Parker?

B: It's Oliver and Elizabeth! _____. I've looked everywhere. I thought that the room attendant might have seen where they went.

A: You mean that you _____?

B: No! Oliver and Elizabeth are pets! Oliver is my little dog. He is very cute with black spots. And Elizabeth is a cat.

A: We will do everything we can to help you find your pets，Mrs. Parker. I will immediately _____. They have closed circuit television so they should be able to spot Olive and Elizabeth.

B: Please catch them if you see them.

A: I will telephone you_____, Mrs. Parker. If your pets are still in the hotel, we will find them.

B: Thank you so much. I will be waiting by the telephone.

2. Listen and fill in the missing information.

Room number:_____   Guest name: _____

Dog's name: _____   Cat's name: _____

The place of dog be caught: _____

The place of cat be caught: _____

Situational Dialogues

1. The Missing Coat

(Scene: A guest has just checked out but he found that he must have left something in the room.)

Staff: Housekeeping. May I help you?

Guest: Yes, I have just checked out but I think I must have left my coat in my room.

Staff: May I have your name and room number, please?

Guest: Yes, I'm Wilson and I was in room 1508.

Staff:　Are you still in hotel?

Guest: Yes, I am in the lobby.

Staff:　Could you come to Room 1508 now? We will wait for you there.

Guest: OK. I will be there right away.

(5 minutes later.)

Staff:　Excuse me, but are you Mr. Wilson?

Guest: Yes, that's right.

Staff:　Could you fill out this request slip, please?

Guest: Sure. Here you are.

Staff:　I'm sorry, sir. May I see some identification, please?

Guest: Of course, here is my passport.

Staff:　Thank you. Please come in.

Guest: I think I must have left it in the closet. Eh…where is my coat?

Staff:　Don't worry. Maybe our attendant had just collected it. I will call the housekeeping center to confirm it.

Guest: OK, please do it.

Staff:　Mr. Wilson, my colleague told me your coat is in the Lost and Found Office now.

Guest: Wonderful, thank you.

2. The Missing Suitcase

(Scene: A guest came to the information desk in the lobby and asked the clerk about his missing suitcase.)

(S: Staff, G: Guest)

S: Good morning, ma'am.

G: Good morning, Miss. I'm worried because I have lost my suitcase this morning.

S: Where did you lose it?

G: I still had it when I got off the taxi. And I just couldn't remember where I misplaced it.

S: Can you describe your suitcase please?

G: Sure, it is a black, medium size suitcase with four wheels.

S: En, I'm afraid we've got nothing like that, sorry.

G: Oh, I made a mistake. I carried the brown one today. It must be very like because there is nothing but a Xiao in it.

S: A Xiao?

G: Well, Xiao is a kind of Chinese vertical bamboo flute. I will play at night at the annual party of our company.

S: Let me see. Yeah, we do have a brown suitcase. Do you have the key?

(The customer hands over the key, and the clerk opens the suitcase.)

S: You are right, sir. This is your Xiao(The clerk takes out a notebook).

Please sign your name here, miss.

G: OK, thank you for your help.

S: With pleasure. Enjoy yourself tonight.

3. The Missing Cell-phone

(Scene: A guest has just lost his cell-phone and he is asking for help.)

Clerk:　Good afternoon, sir. May I help you?

Guest:　It is a pity that I have just lost my cell-phone. All my contacts are in it. It's really important to me.

Clerk:　I can understand how you feel, sir. Don't worry. We will try our best to help you. Do you remember the last time you used it or saw it, and where was it?

Guest:　This morning. I got a call from my daughter, and then I left the room with the phone on me.

Clerk:　Where did you go after that?

Guest:　A lot of places. The restaurant, the lobby and then I had my hair cut at the barber's. I think the phone is still in the building.

Clerk:　What's your phone number? Has the phone been connected yet?

Guest:　No, the phone was shut down.

Clerk:　Could you tell me your name and room number, please?

Guest:　Yes, Mr. Jackson in Room 1058.

Clerk:　What is the model of your phone? And what's the color?

Guest:　It's a white iphone 4S. By the way, do guest ever steal anything?

Clerk:　I am not sure. We will arrange a search for it as soon as possible. If we find it, we will let you know immediately.

Guest:　I hope you can. Thank you for your help.

Clerk:　You are welcome.

4. Claiming the Battery Charger

(Scene: A guest has just lost his charger and he is calling for help.)

Clerk: Good afternoon, sir. Lost and found office, can I help you?

Guest: Hello, this is Robert Brown.

Clerk: Mr. Brown, what can I do for you?

Guest: I just checked out one hour ago, but I am afraid that I left my battery charger in the bathroom.

Clerk: May I have your room number, please?

Guest: It is Room 1305.

Clerk: Mr. Brown, what is the model of the charger?

Guest: It is a mobile phone charger for my Nokia N5800.

Clerk: All right, we will send the room attendant for it now. We will see you at the Lost and Found Office.

Guest: Thank you very much.

(5 minutes later.)

Clerk: Excuse me, are you Mr. Brown?

Guest: Yes, I am here to claim my charger. Sorry about that.

Clerk: Don't mention it. Can I see your ID?

Guest: Yes, here you are.

Clerk: Could you fill in this request slip?

Guest: Sure.

Clerk: Here is your charger, sir.

Guest: Thank you very much.

Clerk: You are welcome. Have a nice day!

Words and Expressions

slip	n.	纸片	identification	n.	身份证
closet	n.	壁橱	a set of		一串
FuWa ornament		福娃装饰物	barber	n.	理发师
charger	n.	充电器			

Learn by Heart

1. 酒店常见遗失物品

充电器	charger	剃须刀	shaver
内衣	underwear	毛巾	towel
笔记本	note book	钢笔	pen
化妆包	cosmetic case	房卡	room key

2. 失物招领服务常用语

We'll see to it immediately.
我们将立刻为您查询。

I am really sorry to hear this, but we will try our best to help you with it.

很遗憾，但是我们将尽力帮助您。

I am sorry, it has not been found yet.

对不起，还没找到。

What is the make of your (item)?

您的物品是什么牌子的？

Do you remember the last time you had it?

您记得最后看见它是什么时候吗？

Could you show me your ID card?

能给我看下您的身份证吗？

Could you fill in the lost report?

您能填写失物招领单吗？

Where had you been this morning?

今天早上您去过哪里？

My bag was stolen, and my passport was in it.

我的包被偷了，护照还在里面呢。

Would you tell us when and where you last saw it?

您最后一次见到它是在什么时候，什么地方呢？

I'm afraid we had warned you to mind your valuables, sir. And if you'll excuse me, I'll find our duty manager for you.

很抱歉，我们已经告知过您要小心贵重物品了，先生。如果您允许的话，我去叫值班经理来。

Class Activity Role-Play

Scene One: On receiving a report of lost items, use the polite language and show your sympathy to the guest.

Scene Two: Mr. Bentley calls the lost and found office to see if they found his CD of Whitney Houston. The clerk is answering the phone and checking the lost and found log.

Further Reading

Standard Lost Property Letter

Dear Mr. Smith:

Thank you for your letter of May 8th, 2011. We hope that you enjoyed your stay with us.

Regarding the pair of trousers and the belt which you think you might have left in your room, we regret that despite a diligent search by our housekeeping staff, we have been unable to locate them.

All items which have been lost or left behind at the hotel are immediately deposited with our Housekeeping Department, the owner on request. We have checked the lists for May 27th—May 30th, but unfortunately neither your trousers nor your belt were among the many articles received at that time. We sincerely regret, therefore, that we are unable to assist you.

We hope that this will not have marred your memories of your stay with us and we look forward to welcoming you on any future visits you might take to our city.

Sincerely yours!

参考译文

关于丢失物品的标准信件

尊敬的史密斯先生：

感谢您在 2011 年 5 月 8 号的来信，但愿您在此与我们共度了快乐的时光。

有关您认为可能遗失在房里的长裤与皮带，很遗憾，尽管客房部员工仔细检查过，仍旧无法找到。

遗失或遗忘在酒店的物品，向来都是立刻存放到我们的客房管理部，填入登记表，并交还前来询问的失主。我们已查过 5 月 27 日至 30 日的记录，很遗憾，您的长裤和皮带并不在该时间收到的众多遗失物品中。因此，非常抱歉，我们无能为力。

我们希望这件事不会破坏您在本店的美好回忆，并期待您下次来本市会再度光临本饭店。

谨上

Question

How to explain to a guest if you could not find the guest's lost items?

Unit 6　Wake-up Service

Listening Practice

1. Listen to the dialogue and fill in the blanks.

A: Operator. I wonder if your hotel has the _____ service.

B: Yes. Anyone who stays in our hotel can ask for the service. Would you like a wake-up call?

A: Yes. I'd like to be woken up at 6:30 _____.

B: What kind of wake-up call would you like, by _____?

A: But I don't know the differences between the computer and the phone.

B: If you want to use computer wake-up call service, just dial 9 first and then 0630 for the time. There must be five digits in the final number and it's only available _____.

A: _____, I see.

B: That is all right, sir. Our computer will record the time and your room number.

A: Thank you.

B: You are welcome. Have a good night.

2. Listen and fill in the missing information.

Room number.: _____　　Guest name: _____

Wake-up time of tomorrow morning: _____

Wake-up time of this afternoon: _____

Schedule of tomorrow morning: _____

Situational Dialogues

1. Providing Wake-up Service

(Scene: A guest is consulting some wake-up call service in the hotel.)

(G: Guest, R: Receptionist)

G: Good evening. This is Mr. Johnson in Room 303.

R: Good evening，Mr. Johnson. What can I do for you?

G: I'm going to Wuhan early tomorrow morning. So I wonder if your hotel has the morning call service.

R: Yes, sir. Anyone who stays in our hotel can ask for the service. At what time would you like us to call you tomorrow morning?

G: Well，actually I'm not really sure. But I have to be at the conference room of the Eastern Garden Hotel in Wuhan by 10 o'clock. You wouldn't know how long it takes to drive to Wuhan from the hotel，would you?

R: I would give it three to three and a half hours.

G: That means that I'll have to be on the road by 7 o'clock at the latest.

R: That's right.

G: Well，in that case，I would like you to call me at 5:45?

R: OK. So we will wake you up at 5:45 tomorrow morning. What kind of call would you like，by phone or by knocking at the door?

G: By phone. I don't want to disturb my neighbors.

R: Yes, sir. I'll tell the operator to call you up at 5:45 tomorrow morning. Anything else I can do for you?

G: No. Thanks. Good night.

R: Good night, Mr. Johnson. Have a good sleep.

2. Wake-up Call for Traveling

(Scene: A guest is calling the reception to book a wake-up call service.)

(R: Receptionist, G: Guest)

R: Reception. Good evening. I'm Marry Lee.

G: Good evening. This is John Anderson from Room 1208.

R: What can I do for you, Mr. Anderson?

G: I'd like to request a morning call.

R: At what time would you like us to call you tomorrow morning?

G: I'm not sure. But I have to be at Tianhe Airport before 9 o'clock. I'm not an early riser because of the time difference, perhaps you understand.

R: I know. It usually takes one hour to drive to the airport from our hotel.

G: Well, in that case, how about 7:30?

R: I'm afraid that period of time is during rush hour. I advise you to be on the road by 7:30 at the latest.

G: OK. I'd like you to call me at 7:00 a.m.

R: All right. Mr. Anderson, Room 1208, the calling time is 7:00.

G: Yes, thank you.

R: Good night. Have a nice sleep.

3. A Wake-up Call for a Meeting

(Scene: A guest is asking for a wake-up call service for a meeting.)

(S: Staff, G: Guest)

G: Good evening．This is Mr. Green in Room 303．

S: Good evening, Mr. Green. What call I do for you?

G: I'm going to Los Angeles early tomorrow morning. I would like a morning call, but it seems something wrong with your computer wake-up call system. There's always busy tone.

S: Sorry, Mr. Green. The system has a breakdown recently and our repairman is trying to figure it out. We can call you in the morning if you need, sir.

G: Oh, I see. That's fine.

S: Yes, Mr. Green. At what time would you like us to call you tomorrow morning?

G: Well, I'm not really sure. But I have to be at the banquet hall of the Four Seasons Hotel in Los Angeles by 12 o'clock. You wouldn't know how long it takes to drive to Los Angeles from the hotel, would you?

S: I would give it two and a half hours.

G: That means that I'll have to be on the road by 9 o'clock at the latest.

S: That's right.

G: Well, in that case, I would like you to call me at 7 a.m.?

S: OK. So we will wake you up at 7 tomorrow morning. Good night, Mr. Green. Have a good sleep.

G: Good night.

4. Wake-up Call for Early Exercise

(Scene: A guest wants to find some places to do some exercises and she hates to be a late sleeper.)

Ellen: Operator, Ellen speaking, may I help you?

Guest: Yes, would you do me a favor?

Ellen: Certainly, madam. What can I do for you?

Guest: I wonder if you can help me. We have just come from London and we are not at all used to the time difference here. But I hate to be a late sleeper as I'm fond of fresh air in the morning and I will see if I can find some places like public gardens or somewhere to do some exercises.

Ellen: I see. It's three o'clock in the afternoon now. I suggest you have a good rest in the room. It usually takes a while to recover after a long flight. Some guests may have jet lag for a few days.

Guest: That's very nice of you for your consideration. Would you recommend some places for me?

Ellen: Yes, I think the Zhong Shan Park is the closest park from our hotel. The park borders on the shores of the lake as well. Besides, there is a gymnasium nearby.

Guest: Wonderful. Would you please wake me up tomorrow morning?

Ellen: That's for sure. At what time do you want us to call you up?

Guest: At 7 sharp tomorrow morning, please.

Ellen: OK. We will wake you up at 7:00 a.m. Anything else I can do for you?

Guest: Yes, could you bring me some English newspaper? I'm used to reading something before sleeping.

Ellen: Yes, what about *Times*?

Guest: That's good.

Ellen: OK, see you soon.

Guest: See you.

Words and Expressions

complicated	*adj.*	复杂的		rush hour		(交通)高峰时间
jet lag		时差反应		recommend	*v.*	推荐
gymnasium	*n.*	体育馆		sharp	*adv.*	准时地
breakdown	*n.*	崩溃，故障				

Learn by Heart

1. 叫醒服务的方法

总机人工叫醒　　　　wake-up service by operator

计算机自动叫醒　　　wake-up service by computer

服务员敲门叫醒　　　wake-up service by knocking at the door

2. 叫醒服务常用语

At what time would you like us to call you tomorrow morning?
您想让我们明天早上什么时候叫醒您？

OK. So we will wake you up at 5:45 tomorrow morning.
好，那么我们明早 5:45 叫醒您。

Would you like a morning call?

您需要叫醒服务吗？

At what time do you want me to call you up, sir?

您需要我什么时候叫醒您，先生？

What kind of call do you like, by phone or by knocking at the door?

您需要哪种叫醒服务，电话还是敲门叫醒？

By phone. I don't want to disturb my neighbors.

电话叫醒，我不想吵醒邻居。

We have a computer wake-up service.

我们有电脑叫醒服务。

May I repeat your room number and the time, sir?

先生，我重复一遍您的房号和叫醒时间好吗？

Sure, we will call you by phone at that time.

当然，我们到时候会电话叫醒您的。

Class Activity Role-Play

Scene One: You are the guest in a hotel. You will have a meeting and require a morning call at 7:00 a.m. tomorrow morning.

Scene Two: Suppose you are an operator. A guest asks if he could be waken-up at 7:30 a.m. and how to use the computer wake-up call service.

Further Reading

Wake-up Call Service

Wake-up call service is a daily service which receptionists or room attendants are responsible for in a hotel. The evening and night shift employees will make a note of guests' request and the time for wake-up call service. Next morning, the guests will receive a wake-up call by telephone or a hotel staff on time.

Actually, different hotels may have different details on wake-up call service. Wake-up by operator is normal in most hotels. Besides, wake-up service by computer is common in 4 or 5 stars hotels. Sometimes you can hear a piece of music from the telephone or a women's voice on the phone. In case of emergency, the attendant would knock at the door to wake you up every 5 minutes.

参考译文

叫 醒 服 务

叫醒服务是酒店提供的一项日常服务项目，由前台服务人员或客房部服务员负责。通常晚班和夜班员工负责记录客人的叫醒服务要求及时间。第二天早晨，客人将按时被电话叫醒或人工叫醒。

事实上，在叫醒服务的细节上每个酒店都不太一样。由总机人工叫醒是最常见的。此外，在一些四星级、五星级酒店，电脑叫醒服务是常见的。有时，你可以从电话中听到一段音乐或者一段女声播报。在紧急情况下，服务员会通过每 5 分钟一次的敲门来叫醒你。

【拓展习题】

Question

How to make sure to wake the guest up on time?

Unit 7　Miscellaneous Service

Listening Practice

【听力音频】

1. Listen to the dialogue and fill in the blanks.

A: Could you bring me an English newspaper, please?

B: Certainly, sir. We will bring one_____. Would you like an _____ tonight, too?

A: No, that's all right. How much will it be?

B: It's free, sir.

A: Fine. I'm sorry to bother you but I will need some_____ as well.

B: That's no trouble at all, sir. Which brand would you prefer?

A: Marlboro.

B: _____ will you need, sir?

A: Two, please. Here are five dollars.

B: Thank you. We will bring your _____ immediately.

2. Listen and fill in the missing information.

New room number.:_____　　Guest name: _____

Time of return: _____

Reason of changing room: _____

Situational Dialogues

1. Booking a Tour

(Scene: A guest decides to start their tour immediately. But they have some questions and need some suggestions as well.)

Guest:　Good morning.

Staff:　　Good morning. What can I do for you?

Guest:　I'm looking for some places to spend the weekend. What do you have that's good and not too expensive?

Staff:　　Do you want to go alone, or with a group?

Guest:　I think group is cheaper. Do you have any special offers?

Staff:　　Yes, for a group tour, we have the Emperor Tomb package. It includes transportation, tour guides, hotels, meals and the entrance fee for Dong Ling. It is an all-expenses-paid tour: the price includes all meals and insurance.

Guest: How much is that?

Staff:　1,000 yuan per person.

Guest: How about their service?

Staff:　I guess they are very good for we haven't received any complaints about them so far. They take care of their guests very well.

Guest: Well, I'll have to see about that…OK, deal.

Staff:　That's fine. I can book that for you. Could you tell me your name, room number and cell phone number, please?

Guest: Sure. Grace Smith in Room 1025 and my cell phone number is 1397—147—3683.

Staff:　Here are the details of the trip and the contract. Could you read and sign your name at the bottom?

Guest: OK.

Staff:　By the way. Most tour companies insist on advance payment when a booking is made.

Guest: Sure. I will pay by credit card.

Staff:　Thank you. The travel agency will pick you up at the hotel at 7 o'clock this Saturday morning.

Guest: Good, see you.

Staff:　See you. Have a nice trip!

2.　A Babysitter

【拓展音频】

(Scene: A guest is not in the room this evening so she needs a babysitter to take care of her children.)

(H: Housekeeper, G: Guest)

H: Housekeeping. Good morning. May I help you?

G: I'm Kathy Jenkins in two-one-two. I need a babysitter for tonight.

H: (The housekeeper begins taking notes.)At what time will you need a babysitter?

G: From eight until eleven.

H: And how old are the children?

G: My little girl is two years old and the boy is three.

H: At what time would you like the babysitter to come to your room?

G: Just before eight.

H: I will arrange everything for you.

G: Thank you very much.

H: Is there anything special that you would like the babysitter to do, Mrs. Jenkins?

G: The babysitter should just give them some milk and put them in bed.

H: Very well.

G: The little girl still wears Pampers. I'll leave some on the bed.

H: Is there anything else we should know, Mrs. Jenkins?

G: No. I think that's about everything.

H: I'll arrange for the babysitter right now.

G: Thank you very much.

3. Renting a Car

(Scene: A guest wants to rent a car to go for an excursion. So he asks for some information when Lily is doing the room.)

(L: Lily, G: Guest)

L: Good morning Mr. Stevens. I am now ready to do your room. Glad to serve you.

G: Thanks. By the way, Miss, is there car rental service in your hotel?

L: Yes, sir. We have many kinds of cars for you to rent. As far as I know, we have compact or sports car, jeep, coach, SUV and so on. What kind of car do you have in mind?

G: Well, it's my son's first time to come to Wuhan. We want to go for an excursion in the East Lake Scenic Area. I suppose a five-seat SUV would be fine.

L: Aha, since the road condition is quite acceptable around the area, a mid-sized car should also be available for you guys.

G: Um…I'll think over and the price should also be taken into account. How much does it cost to rent a mid-size car?

L: That would be US $45 a day excluding fuel.

G: The price is reasonable. But is there any discount if we rent for relatively long time?

L: Of course. It's US $280 per week plus taxes. All cars come with unlimited mileage.

G: Oh, I see. Are the cars filled before I take them?

L: We fill all the cars before they leave. But be sure you bring it back filled, because we charge you two dollars a gallon to fill it here.

G: OK. I'm going to make decision after discussing with my son. Thanks.

L: My pleasure. You can just contact the concierge desk for further information.

4. Introduction for Miscellaneous Service

(Scene: A guest may be new in the hotel and have many questions about the hotel's services.)

(G: Guest, H: Housekeeper)

G: Would you please tell me the daily service hours of the dining room?

H: Certainly. From 7:00 a.m. till 10:00 p.m. nearly serving all day long.

G: When will the bar and cafe open?

H: From 3:00 p.m. till midnight.

G: Does the guest house offer any other service?

H: Oh, we have a barber shop, a laundry, a store, post and telegram services, a newspaper stand, a billiard, table tennis, video games.

G: It's jolly good.

H: You may have your shopping and amusements there.

G: Thank you for your concern. Can I get a tourist map in the hotel?

H: Yes, you may go to the lobby and buy it from the newspaper stand there. With the map, you can find your way around.

G: Good. And where can I have my laundry done?

H: There's a plastic bag in the bathroom. Just put your laundry in it. It will be picked up after I make the bed every morning. Here is the room key.

G: Do I keep the key?

H: At the Service Counter, there are attendants on duty all day. Please leave the key with Service Counter when you go out.

G: Yes, I know. Thanks.

H: And then, you might keep your valuables: diamonds, necklace, ear-rings, etc. in the vault of the guest house.

G: You give very good service in this guest house. Thank you a lot.

H: My pleasure. I hope you will enjoy staying here. In the mean time, the hot water supply in this guest house is from 6:00 a.m. up to 12:00 p.m.

G: Oh, that sounds good. I feel like taking a bath right now. I'm used to having a bath at 9 o'clock every morning.

H: In the bathroom, everything has already been prepared, such as toilet soaps, towels, bathing towels, bathrobes slippers, toilet paper, shampoo combs, brushes, shavers, an ashtray and bathing caps.

G: Thank you for your information.

Words and Expressions

babysitter	*n.*	保姆	mineral	*adj.*	矿物质的
Pampers	*n.*	帮宝适(纸尿裤品牌)	nappy	*n.*	尿布
billiard	*n.*	台球	jolly	*adj.*	愉快的
amusement	*n.*	娱乐，消遣	bathrobe	*n.*	浴衣
all-expenses-paid tour		(费用)全包团			
compact or sports car		紧凑型车，跑车	coach	*n.*	大客车
SUV(sport-utility vehicle)		运动型多功能车			

Learn by Heart

1. 酒店常见杂项服务

车辆预订服务	car reservation service	外币兑换服务	foreign currency exchange
留言	leaving the message	维修服务	maintenance service
文秘服务	secretarial service	订票服务	ticket booking
委托代办服务	entrusted service	托婴服务	babysitting service

2. 杂项服务常用语

Would you like me to book a ticket for you?
需要我帮您订张票吗？

The travel agency in the hotel takes all kinds of booking.
饭店的旅行社代办各种预订票。

I'm sorry, there aren't any tickets left for the tour.
对不起，旅游团的票已经没有了。

Will there be anything else?
还有什么可以帮助您吗？

There is no fee for registered guests.
对于入住酒店的客人是免费的。

Will you come to pick up your ticket or should we send it to your room?
您是自己来取票还是我们给您送到房间？

Do you have any special requirement in the service?
您有什么特别的要求吗？

You'll have to use credit card or leave a US $100 deposit.
您可以使用信用卡，也可以支付 100 美元的押金。

What's your high-end card?
你们最好的车是什么车？

Can I have a look car first?
我可以先看看车子吗？

Can I drop it off at another branch?
我可以在其他分店还车吗？

Class Activity Role-Play

Scene One: Mr. Smith wants to book a train ticket. Please try to help him.

Scene Two: Please ask the guest to fill in the babysitting service application form to ensure all the important information about the baby is included.

Further Reading

Babysitting Service

The hotel can provide many kinds of services, some belong to miscellaneous service that means they are uncommon or trivial. However, babysitting service is one of the most important services for its unpredictable process.

Babysitting is the practice of temporarily caring for a baby on behalf of his/her parents. The sitter is normally contracted one night at a time. The term probably originated from the action of the caretaker "sitting on" the baby in one room, while the parents were entertaining or busy.

In providing the babysitting service, the clerk needs to equip himself with career morals and the awareness of quality service. Keep a clear record of the baby's situation, the parent's requirement and the accurate starting time of the service so as to coordinate the qualified babysitters to carry out the service.

参考译文

托 婴 服 务

酒店能提供各种服务，有一些属于杂项服务的范畴，这意味着这些服务比较不常见或者琐碎。但是，托婴服务是其中最重要的服务之一，因为，总会有一些不可预知的事发生。

托婴服务是暂时代替家长照看婴儿的一项临时服务。保姆通常是照看一个晚上。"Babysitting"这个术语可能是来源于照顾者让婴儿"坐好"的一个行为，而他们的父母可能出去娱乐或者忙其他事去了。

提供婴儿照看服务的时候，员工需要有一定的职业道德和优质的服务意识。要清楚地记录宝宝的情况、父母的需求和准确的服务时间，这样可以协助保姆良好地开展服务。

Question

【拓展习题】

Why does babysitting service have unpredictable process?

Food & Beverage

使用方法：
USAGE

1、靠近门锁
KEEP THE CARD CLOSE TO
THE LOCK

2、绿灯亮
GREEN LIGHT ON

3、转动把手，门即开
TURN HANDLE, THE DOOR
OPENED

如遗失卡请向总台挂失，离店退房请将卡交回总台
IF LOSING THE CARD,PLEASE TELL THE FRONT
DESK IMMEDIATELY; PLEASE RETURN THE
CARD TO THE FRONT DESK WHEN CHECK-OUT.

地址(ADD）：中国山西省太原市建设北大街146号
电话(TEL）：86-0351-8827777
传真(FAX）：86-0351-4042531
邮编(CODE）：030001

Unit 1　Reservation

【听力音频】

Listening Practice

1. Listen to the dialogue and fill in the blanks.

A: Good morning. Rose restaurant.

B: Hello. I'd like to _____.

A: For when, sir?

B: Tomorrow evening, say, around _____.

A: How many in your party?

B: There will be_____.

A: Smoking or non-smoking?

B: Oh, I didn't think about that. _____, I guess.

A: May I have your _____?

B: Oh, it's Smith. And my mobile phone number is 1397—147—3683.

A: OK, Mr. Smith. That's party of six for tomorrow evening at 6:00. Is that correct?

B: That's right. Thank you.

2. Listen and fill in the missing information.

Guest name: _____　Estimated arrival time: _____

Number of guest: _____　Preferred table: _____

Any information is missing in the dialogue: _____

Situational Dialogues

1. Reserving a Table on Valentine's Day

(Scene: Tomorrow is the Valentine's Day and the Stevens want to have a dinner in the Swan Restaurant.)

Clerk: Good afternoon, Swan Restaurant. May I help you?

Guest: I'd like to reserve a table for dinner for tomorrow night.

Clerk: Certainly, sir. Tomorrow is the Valentine's Day. So you have only two people in the party?

Guest: Yes, my wife and me.

Clerk: At what time can we expect you, sir?

Guest: Around 7:00 p.m.

Clerk: I see. Would you like a table in the main restaurant or in a private room, sir?

Guest: A private room, please.

Clerk: Certainly, sir. We will have Rose Hall reserved for you, will that be all right? May I have your name and telephone number, please?

Guest: Sure, it's Stevens and my cell-phone number is 13971473683.

Clerk: Thank you. By the way, we can only keep your room till 8:00 p.m. since it's the peak season now.

Guest: I understand.

Clerk: I'd like to confirm your reservation: Rose Hall for Mr. Stevens on Valentine's Day; arrival time is around 7:00 p.m. and your phone number is 13971473683. Is that correct?

Guest: Exactly, thank you.

Clerk: We look forward to serving you. Thanks for calling.

2. Banquet Reservations

(Scene: There will be a banquet following the conference. Therefore, a guest is booking a banquet in a private room.)

Clerk: Good afternoon. Banquet Reservations. May I help you?

Guest: Yes. I'd like to book a banquet in a private room at 6:30 p.m. tomorrow.

Clerk: Would you like Chinese，Western，Japanese or Korean cuisine?

Guest: Chinese food, please.

Clerk: For how many people?

Guest: Let me see, 9 persons.

Clerk: Yes, sir, 9 persons. The minimum charge for a private room is 100 yuan per person.

Guest: How much for food per person?

Clerk: 120 yuan per person. And what drinks are you going to have?

Guest: Just get ready Hennessy XO. We're going to order other drinks at the dinner time. All the drinks are on consumption basis.

Clerk: Yes，sir. May I know your name，please?

Guest: Galley Spencer.

Clerk: How do you spell it?

Guest: G—A—LL—E—Y，S—P—E—N—C—E—R.

Clerk: G—A—LL—E—Y，S—P—E—N—C—E—R. Yes，Mr. Spencer. And what is your telephone number?

Guest: 660—782—19.

Clerk: 660—782—19. You are not calling from Wuxi，are you?

Guest: No, I'm calling form Shanghai. How do you know?

Clerk: The phone numbers in Wuxi are all 7 digit ones.

Guest: I see. By the way，could you fax us the menu with the name of the banquet room? My fax number is 660—782—18.

Clerk: Yes, 660—782—18. We'll be sure to fax you the menu with the name of banquet room, Mr. Spencer. Is there anything else I can do for you?

Guest: No, thanks.

Clerk: So, the reservation is made by Mr. Spencer，a Chinese banquet for 9 people at 6:30 p.m. tomorrow evening. The price is 120 yuan per person excluding drinks. We'll prepare Hennessy XO.

Guest: That's fine. Thank you.

Clerk: My pleasure. We look forward to seeing you tomorrow evening，Mr. Spencer.

3. Providing Specific Reservation Information

(Scene: A headwaiter is receiving a telephone call from a local customer to book a table for dinner. The guest has a lot of requests and she may ask for more information.)

(C: Clerk, G: Guest)

C: Good morning. Ascot Cafe at your service. May I help you?

G: Yes. I'd like to make a dinner reservation for this Friday, the 8th.

C: Alright, just a moment please and I'll check our reservation book. OK, how many people are there in your party?

G: There'll be six, four adults and two children. We prefer table by the window.

C: Sure, we can arrange that. When would you like to take the table?

G: 6 p.m., please.

C: Alright. And what is your name and phone number, please?

G: It's Sherry Jackson, and my phone number is 588-776-01.

C: OK, Ms. Sherry. So, that's a party reservation for Friday the 8th, at 6 p.m. Your number is 588-776-01.

G: Yes, that's right. Thank you very much. When do I need to arrive at the latest?

C: Ms. Sherry, as that is the peak hour, please be aware that the reservation will be kept for 30 minutes after the reserved time. That means you ordered a table for 6, and we will hold the table for you till 6:30 p.m.

G: Fine. By the way, shall I bring drinks by myself?

C: Well, according to our policy, all liquors brought in will be subject to a 20% service charge based on the market price of the liquor. But we can give you 10% off if your consumption reaches US $288.

G: Um…that's reasonable. Shall I bring my Corgi when dinning there?

C: Sorry, Ms. Sherry, dogs are not allowed in our restaurant.

G: OK. I see.

C: Thanks for calling, Mrs. Sherry. We look forward to having you with us.

4. A Failed Reservation

(Scene: A man wants to book a table tonight, but there are not enough tables for the guest.

Finally, the man has to make a reservation some other time.)

Guest: Hello, is that the Happy Hour Restaurant?

Clerk: Yes. May I help you?

Guest: Yes. I'd like a table for eight at 7:00 this evening. Can you arrange it for us?

Clerk: Just a minute. I'll check if there is any available.

(After a while.)

I'm sorry, sir. There aren't any tables left for 7:00, but we can give you one at 8:30. Would you like to make a reservation at that time?

Guest: Well, let me see. It seems a little late.

Clerk: Usually, the restaurant will be quieter at that time, sir.

Guest: That's the truth, and we need a quiet place in fact.

Clerk: Then I will recommend the West Lake Room. It is quiet and spacious. And we offer free fruit juice after 8:30.

Guest: Fine. I will change the time to 8:30.

Clerk: Very good, sir. A table for eight at 8:30 this evening in West Lake Room. May I have your name, please?

Guest: It's Smith.

Clerk: Thank you very much, Mr. Smith, see you soon.

Words and Expressions

swan	*n.*	天鹅	Valentine's Day		情人节
private	*adj.*	私人的	banquet	*n.*	宴会
cuisine	*n.*	烹饪，佳肴	consumption	*n.*	消费
code	*n.*	密码，规则			

Learn by Heart

1. 餐厅常见订餐方式

面对面预订	face-to-face reservation	电话预订	telephone reservation
传真预订	fax reservation	网上预订	Internet reservation

2. 订餐服务常用语

Just a moment, please. I will check the availability for you.
请稍等，我为您查看下有无空位。

I'm afraid we are fully booked for that time.
恐怕那个时间餐位全部订满了。

At what time can we expect you?
您几点光临呢？

Would you like a table in the hall or in a private room?
您喜欢大厅的座位还是包间呢？

We can only keep your table till 8:00 p.m.
我们只能为您把餐位保留到晚上 8 点钟。

What kinds of fruit/dessert/drinks would you like?
您想要什么样的水果/甜品/酒水？

We will get everything ready in advance.
我们会提前准备好一切的。

I'm sorry, all these tables are reserved until 7:00.
非常抱歉，7 点以前的桌位全部订完了。

Would you like to make a reservation some other time?
您能否换个时间订餐呢？

Would you like to make a guaranteed reservation by credit card?
您愿意用信用卡来担保预订吗？

Is there any minimum charge for my table?
请问我们订的位子有没有最低消费？

Since we have a long waiting list, we would appreciate receiving your call if you are unable to come.
因为还有很多客人需要订座，如果不能来，请电话通知。

【情景演练】

Class Activity Role-Play

Scene One: Mr. Green is calling to reserve a table for 10 persons at 7:00 tonight, but there are no tables available.

Scene Two: One guest is calling to book a table to celebrate their tenth wedding anniversary with his wife. He wants a table by the window at the non-smoking section.

Further Reading

Position Knowledge for Reservation

If the restaurant has extra requirements, such as the room charge or minimum charge, you should make it clear in advance to the guest who makes the reservation of a private room or a banquet. There are four different ways of reserving table: face-to-face reservation, telephone reservation, fax reservation and Internet reservation. No matter in which kind of way the reservation is made by the guest, you should make clear the following information: the name of the guest who makes the reservation, his phone number, the time of arrival and the number of the guests. Be sure to confirm the information at the end.

参考译文

位置预订知识

如果餐厅有像包间费和最低消费这样的额外要求，要事先给预订包间或宴会的客人解释清楚。通常有 4 种不同的预订方式：面对面预订、电话预订、传真预订和网上预订。无论客人使用哪一种预订方式，都要弄清楚下列信息：预订人姓名、电话号码、客人抵达餐厅的时间和用餐人数。最后一定要再次确认这些信息。

Question

How to be a good reservationist in a restaurant?

Unit 2 Seating Guests

Listening Practice

【听力音频】

1. Listen to the dialogue and fill in the blanks.

A: Good evening, madam. Welcome to _____.

B: Thanks.

A: May I ask if anyone is _____?

B: _____. I have come alone.

A: Do you have a _____?

B: I'm afraid not.

A: OK, where would you prefer to sit? What about a seat _____?

B: I prefer to sit close to the air-conditioner.

A: Sure, _____, please.

2. Listen and fill in the missing information.

Guest name: _____   Frequent guest or unfamiliar guest: _____

Number of guest: _____

Position of the seat: _____

Situational Dialogues

1. I Need a Baby Chair

(Scene: Mr. Lauren had a reservation before. He came to the restaurant with his wife and little baby. He asked for an extra baby chair.)

(H: Hostess, L: Lauren)

H: Good afternoon. Welcome to Peach Queen Restaurant. Do you have a reservation?

L: Yes, I have.

H: OK. May I have your name please?

L: My name is Lauren.

H: Let me see… here is your information. You have reserved a table for two. We have been holding it for you. Could you follow me, please?

L: Fine. Thank you.

H: The floor is a little bit wet, please mind your steps. (A moment later) This is your table. Please be seated.

L: Oh, by the way, we may need a baby chair.

H: That's exactly what I'm going to say, Mr. Lauren. I'll bring a baby chair for your baby, a moment please. (A moment later) Here it is. You can put your baby in the baby chair. Remember to tie the belts for safety.

L: Thank you. That's very kind of you.

H: My pleasure. Here's the menu. The waiter will be with you in a moment.

2. A Table Too Close to the Toilet

(Scene: The waitress is seating the guests and the guest doesn't like the position of the seat.)

(W: Waitress, G: Guest)

W: Good evening. Do you have a reservation?

G: Yes. The name is Billings.

W: Please follow me, Mr. Billings. Your table is here.

G: This table is too close to the toilet. Could we have another one?

W: Would you prefer a table in the corner?

G: Yes, a table in the corner would be fine.

W: Please come this way. Here is your menu. Can I get you something to drink while you are waiting?

G: Can you bring us 3 cold beers right away?

W: We have Heineken, Tuborg and Guinness.

G: Do you have Beck's?

W: No. I'm sorry, sir.

G: Three Tuborg will be fine.

3. Arranging One Table for the Non-reserved Guests

(Scene: Four people entered the restaurant without reservation.)

(H: Hostess, G: Guest)

H: Good evening, sir and madam. Welcome to our restaurant. Do you have a reservation?

G: I don't think I have.

H: How many are there in your party?

G: 4.

H: This way, please. How about the centre table? It sits up to 6 seats.

G: That's fine.

H: Here's the menu. Please take your time. The waiter will be at your service soon.

G: Thank you.

4. Arranging One Table for the Non-reserved Guests

(Scene: 8 people entered the restaurant without reservation.)

(H: Hostess, G: Guest)

H: Good evening. Welcome here. Do you have a reservation?

【拓展音频】

G: No, I'm afraid we don't.

H: How many are there in your party?

G: 8.

H: I'm sorry, we don't have a table for 8 people now, but there will be one after about 20 minutes. Do you mind waiting in the lounge? You can have a drink there or reading newspaper.

G: That's a good idea.

H: May I have your name?

G: Robert.

H: We'll seat you when we have a table.

(20 minutes later)

H: Excuse me, sir. We can seat your party now.

G: Good.

H: Please step this way.

Words and Expressions

menu	*n.*	菜单	lounge	*n.*	休息室
Heineken	*n.*	喜力啤酒	Guinness	*n.*	英国产吉尼斯黑啤酒
Beck's	*n.*	贝克啤酒	Tuborg	*n.*	乐堡啤酒
Hostess	*n.*	女领台员			

Learn by Heart

1. 领台服务员常见动作

问好	greeting	指路	give directions
拉椅	pull the chair out	打开餐巾	unfold napkins
上茶	serve tea		

2. 领台服务常用语

I'm sorry，that table is already reserved. You can sit where you like.

对不起，这张桌子已经被预订了，其他的位置您可以随便坐。

Would you like a cover for your coat？

需要罩子盖住您的外衣吗？

Just a moment, please. I will check the availability for you.

请稍等，我为您查看下有无空位。

Welcome to our restaurant.

欢迎光临本餐厅。

Do you have a reservation?

您有预订吗？

How many persons, please?

请问您几位？

Where do you prefer to sit?

您想坐在哪里？

Would you please come with me?

请跟我来好吗？

A waiter will come to take your order.

服务员会来为您点菜的。

Another guest wishes to sit at the counter. Could you move down one seat, please?

另一位客人想坐在柜台边，您可以挪过去一点吗？

We can seat you very soon.

我们马上安排您入座。

Would you mind waiting until one is free?

您介意等到有空位吗？

Class Activity Role-Play

Scene One: Mr. Green comes to your restaurant with his 5 friends without reservation.

Scene Two: Mr. Johnson comes to the Chengdu Snacks Restaurant in the evening. He has reserved a table by the window, but there is no vacancy at that time. Mr. Johnson is very angry and he asks when he will get one table.

Further Reading

Position Knowledge for Seating Guest

When directing the guest, the receptionist should ask the guest whether there is a reservation and the number of persons firstly. This is very important for the restaurant may not provide the service properly. When there is no vacancy, we should ask the guest, "Would you mind sharing a table with others?" In fact, most people do not like sharing a table with unfamiliar people unless in fast food restaurant. When we have to keep the guest waiting, we can say, "I'm afraid all our tables are taken." or "Would you mind waiting?"

There is the special requirement about the guest's dress in some top restaurants. We should explain it to the guest politely and give him some solutions. For example, we can say, "I'm afraid we require our guests to wear a jacket and tie. We can lend you one." When the guest comes into the restaurant, the waiter should greet the guest, pull the chair out for the guest, unfold napkins and put them on the guest's laps.

参考译文

为客人引座的知识

为客人引座时，迎宾员应该先询问客人是否有预订及客人的数量。这非常重要，否则可能导致餐厅不能提供合适的服务。若餐厅客满，我们应该问客人："您是否介意与他人共用餐桌？"事实上，大多数人不愿意与不熟悉的人共用餐桌，除非是在快餐店。当我们不得不让客人等待的时候，我们可以说："恐怕我们已经客满了。"或者"您介意等一会吗？"

有的高档餐厅对客人的着装有特殊要求，这时，要礼貌地向客人解释说明并提供解决办法。例如，我们可以说："抱歉，我们要求客人穿外衣打领带，我们可以借给您。"当客人到餐厅的时候，服务生应问候客人，为客人拉椅、让座，打开餐巾放在客人膝盖上。

Question

How to pacify the guest when your restaurant was full?

Unit 3 Taking Orders for the Western Food

Listening Practice

【听力音频】

1. Listen to the dialogue and fill in the blanks.

A: Good evening，sir. _____.

B: Thank you. What is the "Supreme" like?

A: It is a pizza with pepperoni, beef, pork, onion, _____.

B: That sounds good，I'll take one. _____?

A: Chef's salad, Waldorf salad and shrimp salad.

B: What is the shrimp salad? _____?

A: It is a salad with fresh shrimps, cucumber slices, eggs, and diced potato. It doesn't contain any carrot.

B: That'll be fine. _____.

2. Listen and fill in the missing information.

Today's special: _____

Guest's selection of salad: _____

Guest's selection of drinks: _____

Guest's selection of time for cooking steak: _____

Situational Dialogues

1. Taking an Order for Western-style Food

(Scene: After drinks being served, a waiter asks the dining guests about their orders for some dishes.)

(S: Staff, C1: Customer 1, C2: Customer 2)

S: Excuse me, may I take your order now? A la carte or table d'hote?

C1: I'd like a la carte, a steak with egg, a side salad.

S: How would you like your steak, sir?

C1: Medium rare.

S: And your egg, poached, fried or scrambled?

C1: Poached, please.

S: How about your salad? Today we have garden salad, Caesar salad，Greek salad and Asian salad. Which do you prefer?

C1: I think I might go for the garden salad.

S: Great. And ma'am, what will you be having today?

C2: I'd like to have the beef stewed with potato with a side serving of vegetables.

S: OK. How would you like your potato done, smashed or baked?

C2: Baked, please.

S: And your vegetables, would you like them boiled or stir-fried?

C2: Stir-fried.

S: Would you like to order dessert now or wait until after your main course?

C2: We might wait until later.

S: OK. You have ordered steak, medium rare with poached egg accompanied by a garden salad and beef stewed with baked potato accompanied by stir-fried vegetables. We'll have your meals out to you shortly. Thank you.

2. Western Food for Dinner

【拓展音频】

(Scene: A waiter is taking orders for the guest.)

(W: Waiter, G: Guest)

W: Good evening. Would you like to order now?

G: Yes, I'd like to start with shrimp cocktail, then the veal cutlet, I'll have a vanilla ice-cream for dessert, and some coffee with cream.

W: I'm sorry, the veal cutlet is not being served today, but we have sirloin steak, it's very delicious. Would you like to try it, sir?

G: That sounds like a good idea. I'll have a sirloin steak.

W: How do you like your steak done, sir?

G: Rare, please.

W: OK.

G: Please bring me two slices of bread and butter with the soup.

W: Yes, sir. Can I get you something to drink with your meal?

G: I'll have a gin and tonics with lemon and ice, please.

W: Anything else, sir?

G: No, thanks. I think that's enough.

W: Yes. So one shrimp cocktail, a cup of coffee with cream, a gin and tonic with lemon and ice and two slices of bread and butter. And the main course is a rare sirloin steak.

G: Thank you.

W: Thank you, sir. Just a moment please, I'll go to place your order and get it for you right away.

3. Western Food for Dinner

(Scene: The guests met with the waiter to talk about plans for the dinner.)

(W: Waiter, C1: Customer 1, C1: Customer 2)

W:　Good evening，ladies. Here's your menus. What can I get you to drink?

C1:　I'd like a martini，please.

C2:　A glass of white wine for me.

W:　OK. We have two specials, charbroiled steak and leg of lamb. Which one do you prefer?

C2:　What are you having, Susan?

C1:　The leg of lamb sounds good to me.

C2:　I think I'll get the charbroiled steak.

W:　OK. What about vegetables? Peas and carrots, broccoli, corn, or string beans?

C1:　Peas and carrots.

C2:　Baked.

W:　OK. What kind of dressing? French, Italian, or Russian?

C1:　Italian.

W:　OK.

C2:　And I'd like it medium-rare. And with the broccoli. And baked potato.

W:　OK, fine.

C2:　Oh, and French dressing on the salad, please.

W:　OK, fine. I'll take your menus.

4. Ordering Western-style Breakfast

【拓展音频】

(Scene: A waiter is taking orders for the guest who's trying to choose Western-style dishes for breakfast)

(W: Waitress, G: Guest)

W: Good morning, madam. Are you ready to order? Would you like to have breakfast buffet or A la carte?

G: A la carte, please. I'll choose something from the menu.

W: May I take your order now, madam?

G: Please give me a few minutes. I'm not yet ready.

W: Please take your time, ma'am.

G: Yes. Um…Your menu for continental breakfast seems tasty.

W: Indeed, ma'am. We offer a quite wide variety of dishes. Would you like toast, breakfast rolls, croissants or Danish pastries?

G: Croissants, please.

W: OK. What kind of fruit juice would you like?

G: Pineapple juice would be fine.

W: Coffee or tea, ma'am?

G: Black coffee. Please.

W: So that's croissants, pineapple juice and black coffee. Would you like something else?

G: Let me see. I would like two more eggs.

W: OK. How would you like your eggs? Sunny-side up or fried over?

G: Fried over, please.

W: Certainly, ma'am. We'll cook your breakfast about 10 minutes.

G: That's fine. Thanks.

W: You are welcome. It's our pleasure to serve you.

Words and Expressions

a la carte		零点，照菜单点		table d'hote		套餐
poach	v.	水煮		fry	v.	油炸
scramble	v.	炒		stew	v.	炖汤
smash	v.	弄碎		stir-fried		用旺火炒
veal cutlet		小牛肉排		sirloin	n.	牛里脊肉
gin	n.	杜松子酒		martini	n.	马提尼酒
charbroil	v.	用炭烧烤		broccoli	n.	西兰花
dressing	n.	调料，打扮		continental breakfast		欧式早餐
croissant	n.	牛角包		Danish pastries		丹麦包
Sunny-side up		单面煎		fried over		双面煎

Learn by Heart

1. 西餐常见菜点

清汤	light soup; clear soup; consomme			
浓汤	thick soup; potage		肉汤	broth
茶点	refreshment		开胃菜	appetizer
沙拉	salad		什锦肉	mixed meat
鱼虾	fish and prawn		家禽	poultry
素菜	vegetable dish		通心粉	macaroni
粥	porridge		炒饭	fried rice

面包	bread	馅饼	pie
肉饼	cutlet	卷饼	pancake roll
布丁	pudding		

2. 西餐的上菜顺序

开胃菜(appetizer)—汤类(soup)—沙拉(salad)—主菜(main course)—甜点(dessert)

3. 西餐点菜服务常用语

May I have a menu, please?
请给我菜单，好吗？

May I order, please?
我可以点餐了吗？

Do you have a menu in English?
是否有英文菜单？

Can I order set lunch?
我可以点中午套餐吗？

What is the specialty of the house?
餐厅特色菜是什么？

Would you like something to drink before dinner?
在用晚餐前想喝些什么吗？

Do you have today's special?
餐厅有今日特餐吗？

What kind of drinks do you have for an aperitif?
餐厅有些什么餐前酒？

Can I have the same dish as that?
我可以点与那份相同的餐吗？

May I see the wine list?
可否让我看看酒单？

I'd like appetizers and meat(fish) dish.
我想要一份开胃菜和肉类(鱼)。

May I order a glass of wine?
我可以点杯酒吗？

We offer special menus for different diets.
我们有特殊食谱，可以满足不同的饮食需求。

What kind of wine do you have?
餐厅有哪几类酒？

If you are in a hurry, I would recommend…
如果您赶时间，我可以推荐……

I'd like to have some local wine.
我想点当地出产的酒。

Do you have vegetarian dishes?
餐厅是否供应素食？

I'm afraid … is not on our menu.
恐怕我们的菜单上没有这道菜。

How do you like your steak?
你的牛排要如何烹调？

How would you like your sirloin steak done?
请问您的西冷牛扒要几成熟？

Could you recommend some good wine?
是否可推荐一些不错的酒？

Do you have a special diet?
您对饮食有什么特别的要求吗？

Class Activity Role-Play

Scene One: Mr. Green and his girl friend are sitting in a western restaurant, but they don't know how to take order.

Scene Two: Mr. Johnson and his wife come to the restaurant. Mr. Johnson orders a beef steak and his wife orders some vegetables.

Further Reading

Ten Meals for Briton

The average Briton can make 10 meals from scratch without having to look at a recipe, a survey suggests. Spaghetti Bolognese is the most popular dish, with 65% of people saying they know the recipe by heart. The traditional roast dinner comes in second place with 54% of people able to prepare it unaided. The survey, commissioned by the UKTV Food channel to mark the return of its Market Kitchen show, involved questioning 3,000 people. The survey suggests the average cook is more comfortable preparing foreign dishes than British classics at home. Chilli con carne is the third most popular dish for cooks to attempt, with 42% saying they can manage it without looking at a cookbook or recipe online. Some 41% of cooks feel confident they can prepare the classic Italian dish lasagna. The research defined a recipe as a main course dish containing four or more ingredients. Matthew Fort, presenter of Market Kitchen, said, "The results provide a good snapshot of what Brits are eating week in, week out, because if you cook something regularly enough you will remember the recipe." The study revealed British cooks own an average of five recipe books each but are increasingly turning to the Internet and television cooking shows for inspiration.

参考译文

英国人的 10 道菜

调查显示，多数英国人不看菜谱就能直接烹制的佳肴共有 10 道。最受追捧的当属意大利肉酱面，65%的英国人表示这个菜谱已经烂熟于心了。排在第二位的是英式传统烤菜，54%的人可以轻松烹制这道美味。这项由 UKTV 食品频道委托进行的调查共走访问了 3000 多人，调查结果在该频道的"市场厨房"节目播出。调查发现，英国人居家做的多半是外国美食，而非本国佳肴。香辣肉酱排在最受欢迎榜单的第三位，42%的英国人表示无需菜谱或上网查询就会做这道菜。还有 41%的人表示，自己能够信心十足地烹制意大利千层面。该项调查中的主菜指的是含有 4 种或 4 种以上配料的菜式。"市场厨房"的节目主持人马修·福特说："这项调查让我们了解到英国人平时常吃哪些菜。因为一道菜只有常做常吃，你才能记住菜谱。"调查发现，英国人人均拥有 5 本菜谱，不过，如今越来越多的人通过互联网或是电视上的烹饪节目去获得美食的灵感。

Dishes made without recipe 不看菜谱就能做的 10 道佳肴：

Spaghetti Bolognese 意大利肉酱面 (65%)

Roasted dinner 传统英式烤肉/菜 (54%)

Chili con carne 香辣肉酱 (42%)

Lasagna 意大利千层面 (41%)

Cottage or shepherd's pie 农家馅饼/牧羊人馅饼 (38%)

Meat or fish stir fry 爆炒肉片/鱼片 (38%)

Beef casserole 炖牛肉 (34%)

Macaroni cheese 奶酪烤通心粉 (32%)

Toad in the hole 约克郡烤饼卷香肠 (30%)

Meat, fish or vegetable curry 咖喱肉/鱼/蔬菜 (26%)

Question

Do you have any ideas about western food?

【拓展习题】

Unit 4 Taking Orders for the Chinese Food

【听力音频】

Listening Practice

1. Listen to the dialogue and fill in the blanks.

A: Are you ready to order now, sir?

B: No, I'm still _____. You see, this is my first trip to China. I don't know much about Chinese food.

A: Chinese food is divided into _____, and Chinese cuisine is very different from European. Our restaurant is noted for_____.

B: I have heard Sichuan food is spicy and hot.

A: Yes. Cantonese food is lighter.

B: But I really like hot food. Could you recommend something?

A: What about the boiled fish with pickled cabbage and chili sauce, and the spicy Sichuan beancurd? _____.

B: OK. I will have them.

A: Would you like some vegetables for your lunch? How about spicy cabbage of Sichuan style? It's our chef's dish.

B: That' fine. _____.

2. Listen and fill in the missing information.

Guest's name: _____   Number of guest: _____

Guest's selection of Chinese food: _____

Guest's selection of drinks: _____

Situational Dialogues

1. Ordering From the Sichuan Restaurant Menu

(Scene: The waitress is bringing a menu to a guest and the guest has many questions about Chinese food.)

(W: Waitress, G: Guest)

W: Good evening, sir. May I get you something to drink while you read the menu?

G: Yes, please. We'd like to try some Chinese beer. What brand do you recommend?

W: Beijing Beer is very popular.

G: We'll take five Beijing Beers ...eh...very cold, please.

(The waitress comes back after 5 minutes...)

W: Are you ready to order, sir?

G: We are interested in the sautéed chicken gizzards with pepper. Is it hot?

W: Yes, sir. It's quite hot.

G: What is the Sichuan drunken chicken?

W: It is chicken cooked in rice wine.

G: Is it hot?

W: No, it's not hot.

G: That's all right. We'll take the diced chicken with dried red pepper.

W: Very well.

G: We'd like a pork dish, too. What do you suggest?

W: Most guests like the sweet and sour pork.

G: Hum...No, I think we'll take the deep fried suckling pig.

(The guest stops ordering.)

W: Would you care for soup?

G: Where are the soups listed?

W: On the next page, sir.

(The waitress shows the guest where the soups are listed.)

G: We'll take the Sichuan hot and sour soup. By the way, have we ordered enough for five people?

W: You might want to order two more dishes. Perhaps beef, seafood or a vegetable...

G: Let me take another look at the menu. Yes, the sliced beef with celery and chili should be nice.

W: Yes, sir.

G: Also, we'd like the deep fried king prawns.

W: For how many persons?

G: For five, please.

W: Would you like to see the wine list?

G: No, thank you. We'll just have tea.

2. Recommendations for Chinese Food

(Scene: Mr. Greg and his family are having dinner at Xinyue Chinese Restaurant. The waitress helps him make his order.)

【拓展音频】

(W: Waiter, G: Greg)

W: Good evening. Welcome to Xinyue Chinese Restaurant. May I take your order now?

G: Yes, we are. But there are so many things on the menu and they all look good. Actually, it's our first time in China, we know a little about Chinese food. Could you recommend something special in your restaurant?

W: With pleasure. We offer a wide variety of typical Chinese food. I think Kongbao chicken is quite stir-fried together, with our special sauce.

G: Sounds great. We'll try it then.

W: Oh, well. Broccoli with Crabmeat Sauce is also our specialty. The broccoli is a local vegetable, very delicious, actually also quite different from yours. It's also worth a try.

G: All right. We do like broccoli. Let's see the difference.

W: OK, sir. Those pictures on the menu could be helpful. Which else would you like to try?

G: What is this dish then? It looks red and a little… greasy.

W: Aha, that's fried fish slices with sweet and sour sauce, it tastes sweet.

G: Fish could be cooked like this. That's interesting. We'll take it.

W: Very well.

G: We also want to try Chinese rice. What do you suggest?

W: Yes, sir. You could try boiled seafood and rice with abalone sauce. Many guests like it.

G: OK. We take it. I think that's enough for us. Um…Where is the Chinese tea listed? We also want to have a try.

W: It's on the last page. What kind of tea would you like? We have Longjing, puer tea, Jasmine tea Tieguanyin and so on.

G: Longjing please. We heard a lot about it.

W: OK. So you have ordered Kongbao chicken, broccoli with crabmeat sauce, fried fish slices with sweet and sour sauce, boiled seafood and rice with abalone sauce, and Longjing tea. Is that right?

G: That's right. Thank you.

W: My pleasure. Your dishes will be sent to you in 15 minutes.

3. Eating Chinese Food in Chinatown

(Scene: Mr. Brown and Mr. Zhang had some business in the Chinatown. After that, they might end their day dining in a restaurant that serves Chinese cuisine.)

(B: Mr. Brown, Z: Mr. Zhang)

B: Well, Mr. Zhang, Chinese cuisine is famous throughout the world. I've been looking forward to having my first real Chinese meal while I'm in Chinatown.

Z: We're here in a restaurant famous for its Chinese food.

B: Ah, here comes the first course. Tell me please what it is.

Z: It is chicken soup. At a restaurant that serves Cantonese dishes, we usually start off with soup.

B: Oh, this soup is delicious. What's this second course?

Z: It's "sweet and sour pork ribs". It's very popular with our foreign friends.

B: I also like it. It tastes good.

Z: Don't you like sea-food, Mr. Brown?

B: I can manage shrimps all right, but I'm afraid crabs don't agree with me.

Z: Here comes the "steamed fish". According to the menu, there are "stir-fried rice", "rolls" and "dumplings". Which do you prefer?

B: I think I'll try the dumplings.

Z: Now we'll end up with some fruit. Please help yourself to it.

B: Thank you, I've done very well. I feel so full. You've treated me to a very nice Chinese meal.

4. Chinese Restaurant Service

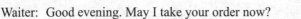

【拓展音频】

(Scene: A guest is having dinner at a Wuxi restaurant. The waiter helps him make his order.)

Waiter: Good evening. May I take your order now?

Guest: Yes.

Waiter: "Liangxi Crispy Eel" is a Wuxi specialty. It's crisp and savory. It's tasty and worth a try.

Guest: OK. We'll take one.

Waiter: How about the "Quick-boiled White Shrimps"? The white shrimp is a specialty from the Taihu Lake. Would you try one?

Guest: Yes, please. Any other local specialties you could recommend?

Waiter: Yes, what about a" Wuxi Pork Spare Ribs", "Steamed White Fish", "Whitebait Fish Soup with Egg Flakes", "Wuxi Pork Ravioli" and "Stir-fried Greens with Gluten"?

Guest: We'll take them all.

Waiter: Yes, sir. So that's one "Liangxi Crispy Eel"，one "Quick-boiled White Shrimps", One "Wuxi Pork Spare Ribs", one "Whitebait Fish Soup with Egg Flakes".

Guest: Yes, that's enough.

Waiter: How about a fruit combination?

Guest: No, thanks.

Waiter: While you are waiting. May I suggest a drink for you?

Guest: No, thanks.

Waiter: One moment, please. Excuse me, here is the "Quick-boiled White Shrimps".

Guest: All the dishes are tasty. But we are full now. Can you cancel the Pork Ravioli please?

Waiter: One moment, please. I'll check with the chef right now. Excuse me, sir. The Pork Ravioli is being steamed now and will be ready in a minute.

Guest: All right, but can you pack them for me so that I may take them back?

Waiter: No problem. Here is the Pork Ravioli.

Guest: Thank you.

Words and Expressions

cucumber	*n.*	黄瓜	broccoli	*n.*	花椰菜
boiled seafood and rice with abalone sauce					鲍汁海鲜烩饭
fried fish slices with sweet and sour sauce					糖醋鱼片
greasy	*adj.*	油腻的	jasmine tea		茉莉花茶
sautéed chicken gizzards		炒鸡杂	dice	*v.*	切成丁状
suckling pig		乳猪	celery	*n.*	芹菜
prawns	*n.*	对虾	oyster sauce		耗油
tender	*adj.*	温柔的，嫩的	mince	*v.*	切碎
rib	*n.*	排骨	roll	*n.*	花卷
crispy	*adj.*	卷曲的，香脆的	eel	*n.*	鳗鱼，鳝鱼
savory	*adj.*	可口的，香辣的	whitebait	*n.*	银鱼
ravioli	*n.*	馄饨	gluten	*n.*	面筋

Learn by Heart

1. 中餐菜名的翻译方法

"烹调法+主料"，如：白切鸡 blanched chicken

"主料+with+辅料" 或 "烹调法+主料+with+辅料"，如：洋葱煮鱼 fried fish with onion

"主料+with+酱汁" 或 "烹调法+主料+with+酱汁"，如：红烧牛肉 braised beef with brown sauce

"口感+主料(+with+辅料/酱汁)"，如：香酥排骨 crisp fried spareribs

"人名/地名+主料"，如：北京烤鸭 Beijing roast duck

2. 中餐点菜服务常用语

Are you ready to order now, sir?
先生，您准备点菜了吗？

Have you decided on anything?
决定点什么了么？

Do you have a menu in Chinese?
是否有中文菜单？

What would you like to have today?

您今天要吃点什么？

Would you like something to drink before dinner?

在用晚餐前想喝些什么吗？

I'm sorry. There are no chops left.

抱歉，没有排骨了。

I'm afraid that this vegetable is not in season. Would you like to try something else?

恐怕这种蔬菜不是时令蔬菜，您来点别的可以吗？

We offer special menus for different diets.

我们有特殊食谱，可以满足不同的饮食需求。

I'm afraid … is not on our menu.

恐怕我们的菜单上没有这道菜。

Do you have a special diet?

您对饮食有什么特别的要求吗？

Would you like to try some Chinese alcohol?

您想不想尝试下中国酒？

Would you like your beer draught or bottled?

您喜欢扎啤还是瓶装啤酒？

I'm afraid it will take some time for this dish, about 25 minutes. Do you mind waiting a little bit longer?

恐怕这道菜要等 25 分钟，您介意吗？

Could you like some more red wine?

给您再添点红酒好吗？

May I suggest the Roast Crispy Chicken? It's our chef recommendation.

我能推荐烤脆皮鸡吗？那是我们大厨的拿手菜。

Class Activity Role-Play

Scene One: It's the first time that a guest has been to China, and he wants to have some authentic Chinese food.

Scene Two: Mr. Robin likes spicy food and he comes into a Sichuan restaurant. The waiter recommends some Sichuan dishes to him warm-heartedly.

Further Reading

Chinese Cuisine

The art of cooking in China dates back several thousand years and it is an integral part of Chinese civilization. Today, Chinese cuisine is ranked among the world's best and Chinese restaurants can be found nearly in every corner of the world.

Chinese cooking pays great attention to color, fragrance, taste, form and nutrition of the food. It requires the technique of cutting and temperature control. By rough estimate, there are about 5,000 different local cooking styles in China. The most popular cuisines are those of Sichuan, Guangdong, Shandong and Jiangsu. They may be subdivided into eight: Shandong, Hunan, Sichuan, Fujian, Guangdong, Jiangsu, Zhejiang and Anhui cuisine. In addition to the major regional cuisines, there are about twenty local cuisines, including Muslim, Henan and Hubei cuisine.

参考译文

中 国 菜

中国烹调艺术的历史可以追溯到几千年，它是中国文明的组成部分。今天，中国菜是世界上的顶级菜肴，在世界的任何角落都几乎可以看见中餐馆。

中国烹饪注重食物的色、香、味、形态和营养。它需要切割和温度控制技术。粗略估计，有大约 5000 种不同的中国本土的烹饪风格。最流行的美食来自四川、广东、山东和江苏。它们又可以细分为八大菜系：山东菜、湖南菜、四川菜、福建菜、广东菜、江苏菜、浙江菜和安徽菜。除了主要的区域美食，还有大约 20 个当地美食，包括穆斯林、河南、湖北美食。

Question

How to introduce Chinese food to western guests?

Unit 5   Room Service

Listening Practice

【听力音频】

1. Listen to the dialogue and fill in the blanks.

A: Good morning. Reception. May I help you?

B: Good morning. _____. Can I have breakfast in my room tomorrow morning?

A: Certainly, Mr. White. Breakfast can be served in your room from_____. Our hotel has very good room service.

B: When shall I order that?

A: You can use our doorknob menu if you'd like. Please check the items you would like to have for breakfast. Just _____ before you go to bed.

B: Is there any other way to have room service?

A: Yes, Mr. White. You may have breakfast arranged _____. The extension number for room service is 9.

B: Thank you for your information. By the way, what shall I do with the plates when we finish eating?

A: You may just _____. We will take care of it.

B: Thank you very much.

A: You are welcome. Have a pleasant stay with us.

2. Listen and fill in the missing information.

Guest name: _____   Room number: _____
Number of guest: _____
Preferred food: _____

Situational Dialogues

1. Taking Telephone Order for Breakfast

(Scene: Mr. White wants to have breakfast in his room tomorrow, so he telephones the Reception and talks to the clerk about it. Wang Qiang is answering the phone.)

(W: Wang Qiang, G: Guest)

W: Good afternoon, Reception. May I help you?

G: Hello, room service. This is Room 508. We'd like to order breakfast for tomorrow.

W: Yes, sir. What would you like?

G: We'd like to start with fruit juice, orange for me and grapefruit for my wife. Fresh juice, please. Not canned or frozen.

W: Right, sir. One fresh orange and one fresh grapefruit.

G: Good. And then bacon, egg and tomato for me, two soft-boiled eggs for my wife. And toast, butter, and marmalades. Do you have different marmalade?

W: Yes, sir. We will put a selection of preserves on your tray. And is it tea or coffee?

G: One coffee, with milk and one hot chocolate, unsweetened, please.

W: Certainly, sir. And when is it for, please?

G: Oh, about 8:30 a.m. Would it be fine?

W: Fine, and could I have your name and room number again, please?

G: It's Mr. White, Room 508.

W: Thank you, Mr. White.

【拓展音频】

2. Providing Room Service

(Scene: Mr. Black calls room service. The clerk is taking the order on the phone.)

(C: Clerk, B: Mr. Black)

C: Good morning, Room Service. May I help you?

B: I'd like to have a meal in my room.

C: Certainly, sir. We offer two types of breakfast. American and continental. Which one would you prefer?

B: I'd like continental breakfast. Do you have cheese omelet?

C: I'm sorry. We're currently out of cheese omelet. We now offer chilled orange juice, toast with butter, coffee or tea.

B: In that case, I'll take two slices of buttered toast and a bottle of orange juice.

C: I see. May I have your name and room number, please?

B: Sure. It's Jefferson Black in Room 1608.

C: Let me confirm your order. Mr. Jefferson Black in Room 1608, two slices of buttered toast and a bottle of orange juice. Is that right?

B: Exactly.

C: OK, sir. There is an extra charge of 15% for room service. Room service will be charged to your amenities account. Is that alright?

B: That's fine.

C: Your order will be ready soon. Thank you for calling.

3. Ordering Room Service

(Scene: Mr. Smith calls the Room Service. The clerk is taking the order on the phone.)

Clerk: Good evening. Room Service. May I help you?

Guest: Yes. Please send one "Fried Rice，Yangzhou Style" and one "Fruit Combination" to our room.

Clerk: Anything to drink, sir?

Guest: Yes, two bottles of beer.

Clerk: Is there any particular brand you like, sir?

Guest: Heineken or Carlsberg.

Clerk: Yes, sir. Is there anything else you want, sir?

Guest: No, thanks.

Clerk: May I know how many people of you so that I can prepare the right set of tableware?

Guest: Well, two of us.

Clerk: Excuse me, sir. May I know your name and room number?

Guest: Yes, Ted Smith, in Room 1107.

Clerk: OK. Mr. Smith, Room 1107. So, that's one "Fried Rice, Yangzhou Style", one "Fruit Combination" and two bottles of Heineken beer. We'll bring them to your room in twenty minutes.

Guest: Thank you.

4. Sending the Room Service Order

(Scene: There is a DND sign on the door knob. The room service staff goes to make a phone call before sending the meal.)

(S: Staff, G: Guest)

S: Room Service. There's a Do-Not-Disturb sign on your door knob. Could I bring the food to your room now?

G: Yes, please.

S: Wait a minute, please.

(One minute later.)

S: Good evening, gentlemen. May I put them here?

G: OK.

S: This is your meal: mushroom omelette, French fries and a steak sandwich. Please enjoy the food.

G: Thanks.

S: Excuse me, who's going to sign the bill, please?

G: Please give it to me.

S: Here you are. Thank you. For more orders, please dial "7" for room service.

G: OK.

S: When could I come back to take away the plates and glasses?

G: I think 8:30 tomorrow morning would be fine.

S: Yes, sir. Also you can just put them outside your door. We will take care of it. Good night.

G: The same to you.

Words and Expressions

grapefruit	*n.*	西柚		marmalade	*n.*	柠檬等制成的果酱
continental	*adj.*	大陆的，欧洲大陆的		tableware	*n.*	餐具
mushroom	*n.*	蘑菇		omelette	*n.*	煎蛋，煎蛋饼
steak	*n.*	牛排		cheese omelet		奶酪蛋卷
toast with butter		黄油吐司				

Learn by Heart

1. 客房送餐服务常见器具

餐具	tableware		酒杯	goblet
餐车	serving trolley		账单	bill
托盘	serving tray		花瓶	vase

2. 客房送餐服务常用语

What would you like to have?
您想要点些什么？

Is there anything else to have?
您还要点别的吗？

Would you please sign the bill?
您可以签下账单吗？

May I come in?
我可以进来吗？

Enjoy your meal.
祝您用餐愉快。

Would you prefer rolls or toast?
您想要早餐包还是吐司呢？

There is an extra service charge of 15% for room service.
客房送餐服务要加收 15%的服务费。

Room service is available 24 hours a day.
客房送餐服务一天 24 小时都提供。

It will take ten minutes to prepare.
大约需要 10 分钟来准备。

We will deliver your food in about 20 minutes.
大概 20 分钟后我们会把食物送到您的房间。

Where shall I put your breakfast, sir?
先生，我把早餐放在哪里？

When you finish your meal. Please dial "2" to call us to remove the tray /trolley.

当您用完餐后，请拨电话"2"。我们将会为您提供收拾餐具服务。

Class Activity Role-Play

Scene One: Mr. White is calling to Room Service. He would like to have supper in the room.

Scene Two: Mr. Robin likes American breakfast with coffee. He is calling in the room.

Further Reading

Room Service

The business time of the restaurant service is usually limited in the hotel. But if you are back too late and the restaurant is closed, please do not worry. Because most star-rated hotels provide 24-hours room service for you, except some hotels in the scenic spots. Besides, guests can choose to have breakfast or others in the room. Room service is usually provided by the food and beverage department and the waiter of the housekeeping department may also provide this service. Room service is usually a sign of high star-rated hotel. The service cost is a little higher than the cost of the restaurant, but it's just the smaller profit item in the hotel catering industry.

参考译文

客房送餐服务

酒店的餐厅服务通常都有营业时间的限制。但是如果回来太晚，无法在餐厅用餐，请不要担心，因为，大多数星级酒店，除了一些景区的酒店外，都提供 24 小时房内送餐服务。此外，顾客可以选择在房内用早餐或其他餐饮。此项服务通常由餐饮部提供，客房部的服务员也可以配合提供此项服务。送餐服务通常是一个高星级酒店的标志。这项服务的费用虽然相对餐厅用餐的费用较高一些，但这只是酒店餐饮业中盈利较小的项目。

Question

Shall we encourage guests to have dinner in the room? Why?

Unit 6　Paying the Bill

【听力音频】

Listening Practice

1. Listen to the dialogue and fill in the blanks.

A: Waiter, please!

B: Yes, sir. _____?

A: No, thank you. Can I _____?

B: Yes, sir. Here it is.

A: Would you please explain_____?

B: That's your soup.

A: Oh, I see. And what about the service? _____?

B: Yes, here it is. Five percent for service charge.

A: So it totals US $52.8. Here is the money. _____. Thank
you for your nice service.

B: Thank you. Goodbye.

2. Listen and fill in the missing information.

Total bill: _____　　　Room number: _____

How to pay the bill in the plan: _____

How to pay the bill actually: _____

Situational Dialogues

1. Checking the Bill

(Scene: A guest is going to pay the bill but he finds it a little expensive when checking
it out. The cashier is trying to explain and offer necessary information.)

(G: Guest, C: Cashier)

G: Excuse me. I'm checking out now. Can I have my bill, please?

C: Yes, sir. Just a moment, please. I'll draw up your bill for you. (After a while) Sorry
to have kept you waiting. Here's your bill. The total is RMB 499 yuan, including
15 percent surcharge. Here is your bill.

G: What? 499 yuan! That's much more than I expected. Is there a mistake? Please
examine the bill carefully and see if there's any mistake.

C: Of course. I'll check it.

G: 160 yuan for a pot of Herbal Tea. That's really too expensive!

C: Well, sir. Herbal Tea is our specialty and the price is on the menu. I think you've already had a taste for its fragrance and special flavor.

G: Fine, I see. I haven't noticed the price before. It seems that I'll have to pay what you ask. I hope I'm not being ripped off.

C: Ripped off? That's out of the question in our restaurant. How would you settle the bill?

G: With credit cards. What card do you honor?

C: American Express, Master, International Diner's Club, Visa, International Great Wall are all available. What kind of card have you got?

G: Master card, please.

C: Find, Let me take a print of your card. Wait a moment, please... Sorry to have kept you waiting, please sign on the print.

G: Sure.

C: Thank you, sir. Take your credit card and the invoice. Hope you have a nice stay in our city.

2. Some Mistakes in the Bill

(Scene: A guest is going to pay the bill but there seems to be many problems with the bill.)

(C: Customer, W: Waiter)

C: Excuse me, but I have some questions with the bill.

W: Oh, what seems to be the problem?

C: Well, first of all, we only had one soda, not three.

W: OK. Anything else?

C: Secondly, the waitress told us that the pizza was going to be on the house.

W: I see. She must have forgotten to change your bill. Was there anything else?

C: Actually, there were two more things.

W: Oh. What things might those be?

C: Well, we want to split the bill and that wasn't done.

W: I can do that for you now. Would you still like me to do this?

C: Yes, please.

W: And the final problem?

C: Do you accept American credit cards?

W: Yes, sir. What kind of card will you use?

C: VISA card.

W: That'll be fine. May I take an imprint of your card, please?

C: OK. That's it.

W: Thank you, sir. I must apologize for any inconvenience. Have a nice evening.

3. Payment in Foreign Currency

(Scene: A guest is going to pay the bill in US dollars and the barman has to explain some polices of the restaurant.)

Barman: How about another drink, sir?

Guest: No, thanks. I'm just leaving. My bill, please.

Barman: Your bill, sir. The total is RMB 88 yuan.

Guest: What? 88 yuan for a drink?

Barman: I'm sorry, sir. That's our minimum charge: two drinks at 40 yuan each, plus 10% service charge.

Guest: Why didn't you tell me? Had I known it, I wouldn't have come.

Barman: I'm awfully sorry, sir. There's a sign at the door as well as this tent card on the counter. Since you are going to pay for it, you might stay and enjoy the other half, sir. The orchestra is giving a wonderful performance.

Guest: OK. I'll stay a bit longer. But I haven't got any RMB. May I pay in foreign currency?

Barman: What kind of currency have you got?

Guest: US dollars.

Barman: Yes, you can. Let me see what the exchange rate for today is. Today's exchange rate is 6.50 yuan RMB for one US dollar. So it comes to 13.5 dollars.

Guest: Here's 14 dollars. Please keep the changes.

Barman: Thank you, sir. But we are not allowed to accept tips. It's our hotel policy. Enjoy your drink.

4. Explaining the Credit Limit

(Scene: Credit cards sometimes are inconvenient in that they cannot be used in most small restaurant or hotels. Besides, there are still some limits in using credit card.)

Guest A: Hello, miss.

Waiter: Yes, sir. Can I help you?

Guest A: The bill, please.

Waiter: One bill or separate bills?

Guest A: Two separate bills, each for three tables.

Waiter: Yes, sir. How would you like to settle the bill?

Guest A: I'll sign my bill.

Guest B: Can I pay by credit card?

Waiter: Yes, of course. (The waiter gets the two separate bills and presents them to the guests. Guest A signs the bill and returns it to the waiter. Guest B gives him the Million Card.) Sorry, sir. But we don't accept Million. (The waiter gives the card back to the guest in a professional way.)

Guest B: Do you accept Visa Card then?

Waiter: Yes, sir.

Guest B: Here you are.

Waiter: Do you have another card?

Guest B: Yes, but it's not with me. Why?

Waiter: The credit limit set by the Visa Card office is 1,000 US dollars. We need their permission to extend credit over that amount. Would you kindly settle the difference in cash?

Guest B: Well, if that's the case, I think I might make all my payment in cash.

Waiter: Thank you, but we don't accept US dollars in this restaurant. I'll change it for you at the front cashier if you don't mind.

Guest B: I'll appreciate that.

Waiter: According to today's exchange rate, one hundred US dollars is equivalent to 620 RMB.

Guest B: All right.

Waiter: Excuse me, sir. Here're the change and the receipt.

Guest B: Keep the change.

Waiter: No, thank you, sir. But we don't accept tips.

Words and Expressions

Gordon's Dry Gin		哥顿金酒	on the house			免费
split	v.	分离，分开	orchestra	n.		管弦乐队
settle	v.	解决，处理	equivalent	adj.		相等的
exchange rate		汇率				

Learn by Heart

1. 餐厅结账常见方式

现金	cash	信用卡	credit card
支票	check	签单	sign the bill

| 免单 | on the house | 优惠券 | coupon |

2. 餐厅结账服务常用语

Your check, madam.

您的账单，女士。

Please wait a moment while I correct the bill.

请稍等，我去把账单改过来。

I'm sorry but we are not allowed to accept personal checks.

很抱歉，我们不能接受个人支票。

I'll need your signature and room number.

我需要您的签名和您的房号。

Shall I explain some items for you?

需要解释收费款项吗？

I am afraid it is not enough to cover the amount/ can't cover the amount.

恐怕那不够付账。

I neglected that detail when I drew up your bill.

我在开账单时忽略了那个细节。

The exchange rate today is ×× for ××× RMB.

今天的兑换率是××兑换×××人民币。

Here's your change and receipt.

这是您的找零和发票。

There are several ways of paying for the drinks.

饮料费的收付方法有几种。

Please feel free to contact us if you have any questions or requests.

如果有什么事情或要求，请与我们联系，不必客气。

Hope to see you again soon.

欢迎下次光临。

Could you pay at the Cashier's Desk at the entrance, please?

请到门口收银处付款，好吗？

Class Activity Role-Play

Scene One: Jerry and Lily are having dinner at restaurant. They almost finish the meal but they don't know how to pay the bill by US dollars.

Scene Two: Mr. Black is going to pay the bill at Greenery Café, but his credit card is expired, so he has to pay in cash.

Further Reading

Go Dutch

I was at a restaurant the other day with a couple of friends and one of them suggested we went Dutch. As none of us had much money we all agreed but it got me to thinking about why we use this expression. Of course what it means is that each person pays his share of the bill and nobody tries to foot the whole bill. We also say it is a "Dutch treat" when we "go Dutch".

The origins go back to a time when the people of Holland and the people of the UK weren't such good friends as they are today. In fact they were at war. During the 17th century the Dutch and the British were enemies fighting to control the spice trade and they fought 3 wars between 1652 and 1674. During wars the propaganda machines did their best to demonize the enemy and to make them seem as nasty as possible so everyone would hate them. The Dutch were depicted as mean and bad tempered and therefore unlikely to ever invite anyone to a meal.

There is a delicate etiquette surrounding going Dutch. It is widely accepted in some situations, such as between non-intimate friends or less affluent people, but can be considered stingy in other circumstances, such as on a romantic date or at a business lunch.

参考译文

AA 制

有一天，我在一个餐厅与几个朋友吃饭，其中一个朋友建议我们都各自付账。我们每个人都没带很多钱，于是所有人都同意，但它使我思考我们为什么用这个表达。当然，这意味着每个人只付他的那份账单，没有人需要请客。当我们"各自付账"的时候，我们也会说"AA 制"。

这个起源要追溯到荷兰人和英国人没有如今这么好的关系的时候。事实上，他们在打仗。在 17 世纪，荷兰人和英国人处于敌对状态，他们通过战争来控制香料贸易。1652 年到 1674 年间，他们打过 3 次仗。一般，战争期间的宣传机器会尽它们最大的努力来妖魔化敌人，使人们尽可能地认为敌人很卑鄙以至于憎恨他们。荷兰人被描述为小气的、坏脾气的，绝不乐意请人吃饭。

AA 制是一种得体的礼仪，现在被人们普遍接受，普通朋友或者经济条件不好的人之间常遵循这一礼仪。但是，在其他一些场合，比如，浪漫的约会或者商务聚餐中，遵循 AA 制的人常常被视为小气或吝啬的人。

Question

How to make out the bill when guests going Dutch?

Unit 7 Beverage Service during the Service

【听力音频】

Listening Practice

1. Listen to the dialogue and fill in the blanks.

A: Excuse me, _____?

B: Sure, go ahead.

A: May I show you the _____?

B: OK.

A: Here you are.

B: Can you tell me what the mead is?

A: Oh, I see. It's a beverage typically made of fermented _____.

B: But I never drink alcoholic beverage. So I'd like to _____.

A: Certainly, sir. Here is your coffee. _____?

B: Fine, thank you.

2. Listen and fill in the missing information.

Some hard drinks in the list: _____

Some soft drinks in the list: _____

Man's choice: _____   Women's choice: _____

Situational Dialogues

1. Ordering Drinks

(Scene: Three guests are ordering drinks. They ask for recommendations from the waiter.)

Guest 1: Waiter, the menu, please.

Waiter: Here is the menu. May I take your order now?

Guest 1: I don't know what I want. I'm not really a drinker.

Waiter: Tea or coffee?

Guest 1: What do you suggest for tea?

Waiter: We have black tea, green tea, pu'er tea, jasmine tea and oolong tea. What kind of teas would you like?

Guest 1: I will take a cup of pu'er tea. How about you, Sara?

Guest 2: I don't drink tea at all. Do you serve coffee?

Waiter: Of course, madam. What kind of coffee do you like? Plain or blended?

Guest 2: Blended?

Waiter: Yes, coffee with cream and sugar, cappuccino is a good choice.

Guest 2: It sounds interesting. I will take one cappuccino.

Waiter: What would you like to drink, sir?

Guest 3: Well, I suppose I will have the usual tea. I'm very thirsty.

Waiter: Any snack for drink, sir?

Guest 3: What about cakes made by your own shop? I heard they are good.

Waiter: Yes. They are really delicious. How about three Black Forest Cakes?

Guest 3: All right.

Waiter: Fine. One pu'er tea, one cappuccino and one usual tea, three Black Forest Cakes.

Guest 2: Could we have some fruits?

Waiter: Certainly, I will get you a fresh supply.

2. Recommending a New Brand of Coffee

(Scene: Mr. Robin is a frequenter of the restaurant. Now he is asking the waiter to order some beverage. The waiter recommends a new brand of coffee to him and teaches him how to taste it.)

(W: Waiter, R: Mr. Robin)

W: Excuse me, Mr. Robin. Do you need any beverage during your dinner?

R: En, what would you recommend for today? I have tasted more kinds of coffee in your shop. Is there anything fresh?

W: Yes, we have purchased a kind of new cold brew coffee toddy from America. What about a cup of it? You know, many guests give it high praise.

R: Cold coffee? I don't like to drink cold coffee.

W: The cold brewed coffee doesn't mean it has to be consumed cold. Well, this coffee is 67% less acidic and smoother than many other brew methods. Add boiling water, which dilutes it a smidgen.

R: Sounds good. OK, give me a cup of it.

W: Thank you. Would you like any refreshment?

R: No, thanks.

W: Wait a moment, please.

(5 minutes later)

W: This is your cup of toddy cold brewed coffee. Could I tell you something about it?

R: Yes, please.

W: The cold brewed coffee comes out very strong. But the lack of acidity and bitterness makes it much easier to drink than espresso. When drinking, you can pour it over ice, or in a blender. It is perfect for an iced coffee or any kind of blended coffee drink. Would you like to taste it?

R: Excellent! Thanks for your recommendation.

W: You are welcome and enjoy your coffee please.

3. Trying Traditional Chinese Wine

(Scene: Mr. White and his friend are having dinner at Orchid Restaurant in Chinatown. They are ordering some traditional Chinese beverage.)

(G1: Guest 1, G2: Guest 2, W: Waiter)

W: Your Light Rum, sir. May I serve you now?

G1: Sure, go ahead.

W: How is it, sir?

G1: Very good.

G2: Maybe we need something more. I don't like soft drinks. What would you recommend?

W: Here is the wine list, sir. We have a very extensive cellar. Would you like to try some Chinese alcohol?

G1: Oh, we heard a lot about it. It seems quite strong.

G2: I know Mao Tai. Do you have it?

W: Yes, sir. Mao Tai is the best Chinese spirit. It's rather strong, but never goes to the head. I think it's worth to try.

G1: OK. We'll take some. The small bottle is enough for us.

W: Indeed. That's 125ml for small bottle. Chilled or at room temperature?

G2: At room temperature.

W: Very well. Would you like to have some snacks with your wine?

G1: Let me see…Four Hong Kong egg tarts and two Margaret cakes, please.

W: OK, sir. An extra small bottle of Mao Tai, Four Hong Kong egg tarts and two Margaret cakes. Is that right?

G1: Exactly.

W: OK. Just a moment please.

Words and Expressions

jasmine	*n.* 茉莉花	plain	*adj.* 纯的
blended	*adj.* 混合的	toddy	*n.* 棕榈汁，棕榈酒
brew	*v.* 酿，泡	acidic	*adj.* 酸的
dilute	*v.* 稀释	smidgen	*n.* 少量，一点点
refreshment	*n.* 小吃，茶点	bitterness	*n.* 苦
espresso	*n.* 浓咖啡	full-bodied	*adj.* 醇厚的

Learn by Heart

1. 餐厅的常见饮料

矿泉水	mineral water	橙汁	orange juice
柠檬水	lemonade	苹果酒	cider
红茶	black tea	牛奶咖啡	white coffee
豆浆	soya-bean milk	酸梅汤	syrup of plum

2. 酒水饮料服务常用语

Would you care for another drink, madam?
您介意再来点其他饮料吗，女士？

Would you care for anything else, sir?
您是否还需要其他饮料呢，先生？

How about one for the road?
上路前再来一杯怎么样？

Would you like to try some Chinese alcohol?
您要不要尝点中国酒？

Have you decided what you would like to drink?
您决定好喝什么了吗？

I would recommend…
我推荐……

What kind of drinks do you like?
您喜欢什么样的饮料？

What would you like for a drink?
您想喝什么？

How would you like it, straight up or on the rock?
您想怎么喝，直接饮用还是加冰？

I think that a Chablis would go very well with your oysters.
我想夏布利白葡萄酒会和您点的生蚝很相配。

If we add ice, the taste will be spoiled.
如果我们加冰，会破坏它的味道。

How is the taste/color/bouquet/temperature/... of the wine?

酒的味道/颜色/香味/温度/……如何？

Class Activity Role-Play

Scene One: You are a waitress in a restaurant and is ordering some drinks of foreign brands.

Scene Two: A guest asks the waiter to order two cups of coffee, one cup with sugar and others without.

Further Reading

Coffee and Coffee Shop

The word "coffee" entered English in 1598 via Italian caffé, via Turkish *kahve*. Its ultimate origin is uncertain, there being several legendary accounts of the origin of the drink. One possible explanation is the Kaffa region in Ethiopia, where the plant originated.

A coffee shop or café shares some of the characteristics of a bar, and some of the characteristics of a restaurant. As the name suggests, coffeehouses focus on providing coffee and tea as well as light snacks. In some countries, cafés may more closely resemble restaurants, offering a range of hot meals, and possibly being licensed to serve alcohol.

After several centuries of development, a coffeehouse is not only a place to have a cup of coffee, but a symbol of lifestyle, a landmark for certain social group. No matter you like it or not, let's just enjoy a cup of coffee!

参考译文

咖啡和咖啡店

"咖啡"这个词进入英语领域是在 1598 年，它是由意大利语 caffé 和土耳其语 *kahve* 演变而来的。它的最终来源不太确定，关于这个饮料的起源有多种传说版本。一种比较可信的解释是其来自埃塞俄比亚的卡法地区，也就是这种植物的来源地。

咖啡店或者咖啡厅共享了一些酒吧和餐厅的特点。顾名思义，咖啡馆主要提供咖啡、茶和一些小吃。在一些国家，咖啡馆更接近于餐馆，能提供热腾腾的饭菜，还可以持执照卖酒。

经过几百年的发展，咖啡馆已经不仅是喝咖啡的地方了，它也是一种生活方式的象征，一个特定社会群体的标签。不管你喜欢与否，让我们来喝杯咖啡吧！

Question

How to introduce the history of coffee to the guests?

Unit 8　Bar Service

Listening Practice

【听力音频】

1. Listen to the dialogue and fill in the blanks.

A: Your Muscatel, sir. _____?

B: Sure, go ahead.

A: How is it, sir?

B: _____.

A: May I decant it now to _____?

B: Certainly.

A: (Pouring the wine.) _____.

B: OK, that's enough.

A: Thanks, _____.

2. Listen and fill in the missing information.

Name of the bar: _____　　　Number of its famous liqueurs: _____

Waiter's first recommendation: _____

Waiter's second recommendation: _____

Situational Dialogues

1. Serving Cocktails for Reserved Guests

(Scene: The bartender is serving drinks for two guests in the bar. The guests have a reservation.)

(B: Bartender, G1: Guest 1, G2: Guest 2)

B:　Welcome to our bar. Do you have a reservation?

G1:　Yes, we do.

B:　May I have your name please?

G1:　Jordan Baermann.

B:　OK. Let me check our reservation book. Would you prefer smoking area or non-smoking area?

G2:　Non-smoking area please.

B:　This way, please. Mind your step. (after seating the guests) Here is the wine list, please take your time.

G1:　We would like some cocktails. But there are so many things on the list. Could you recommend something?

B: Well, Tequila Sunrise is our newly-developed and our barmaid recommended. Many guests like it.

G1: OK, I'll try it then. What about you, Miss Young?

G2: Um… I've tried Pink Lady before. It tastes different everywhere.

B: Indeed. But the ingredients should be similar. It's slightly pink or red, very aromatic. It's said that Pink Lady has got an implied meaning of love and kindness. You can have a try, Miss.

G2: Aha, what you said is quite interesting. OK, then.

B: Well. Do you like the cocktails on the rocks or straight up?

G1: With ice please.

B: OK. And you, Miss?

G2: Straight up, please.

B: So, that's one Tequila Sunrise on the rocks, Pink Lady straight up. Just a moment, please.

2. Chinese Liquors and Wines

(Scene: The bartender is serving drinks for two guests in a bar. They are talking about Chinese liquors.)

(B: Bartender, G1: Guest 1, G2: Guest 2)

B: Anything to drink, gentlemen?

G1: Well, we've been drinking cognac and whisky a lot. We'd like to have a change, but we don't quite know what to drink today. Can you recommend some famous Chinese liquors?

B: What about Wu Liang Ye, one of the most famous liquors in China? It's made from five kinds of cereal. It's fragrant and it never goes to the head. Its alcoholic content varies from 38% to 46%, and up to 52%.

G1: All right, we'll have the 46% one.

B: May I remind you all the Chinese liquors are served by the bottle here?

G1: Any other brands of liquor?

B: Yes, Mao Tai, Fen Jiu, Yang He, Xi Feng, Lu Zhou, etc.

G2: I hear Great Wall Wine is a famous brand.

B: Yes, it is. Would you like to try one bottle?

G2: OK, bring me the white wine as well. Make sure it is well chilled.

B: Yes, sir. A bottle of well-chilled white wine. Have you ever heard about Shaoxing Wine? It's a kind of still wine made from rice, somewhat like Japanese sake. Some Shaoxing wine is just good for your health.

G1: I believe it is, but you see we've got enough, we'll drink it next time.

B: Yes, sir. So you've ordered one bottle of Wu Liang Ye with 46% alcoholic content and one bottle of Great Wall white wine. Just a moment, please.

3. Western Liquors and Wines

(Scene: The bartender is serving drinks for two guests in a bar. They are talking about western liquors.)

(B: Bartender, G1: Guest 1, G2: Guest 2)

B: Good evening, sir. What can I do for you?

G1: I'd like a drink.

G2: Me too. Give me a double whisky and soda.

B: We serve brandy, whisky, vodka and so on. What would you like? (To Guest 2)How would you like the whisky, straight or on the rocks?

G1: Without ice. Ice will spoil the taste.

B: Straight away, sir.

G2: I'm suffering from a cold.

B: Then I recommend the vodka swizzle. It is made from several liquors and mixed into vermouth.

G2: That sounds wonderful.

(One hour later.)

G1: We must be off now.

B: How about one for the road?

G2: Why not? The same again, please.

4. Western Liquors and Wines

(Scene: The bartender is serving drinks for several guests in a bar. They have different opinions on drinks.)

(B: Bartender, G1: Guest 1, G2: Guest 2, G3: Guest 3, G4: Guest 4)

B: What may I offer you, ladies and gentlemen?

G1: I don't know what I want. I'm not really a drinker.

B: An aperitif or some white wine?

G1: Um…a Qingdao Beer.

B: I don't believe we have that one. How about our special cocktail?

G1: That sounds good. How about you, Lily?

G2: I don't drink at all. Do you serve soft drinks?

B: Of course, madam. But how about a non-alcoholic cocktail?

G2: It sounds interesting. I'll take that one.

B: What would you like to drink, gentleman?

G3: Well, none of that stuff they're drinking, eh…Bob?

G4: No, Peter. We'll have the usual beer, I suppose.

G3: Yes, I'm very thirsty.

B: Any special brand, sir?

G4: What about your local brand? I hear it's good.

B: It is Five Star Beer. Bottled or draught?

G1:   Let's try the draught.

G4:   Yes, I want draught beer, not bottled beer.

B: Fine. One special cocktail and one non-alcoholic cocktail for the ladies and two draught Five Star Beer.

Words and Expressions

bartender	*n.*	酒保	Scotch	*n.*	苏格兰威士忌
cognac	*n.*	科尼亚克白兰地	chill	*v.*	使变冷
sake	*n.*	日本清酒	swizzle	*n.*	以甜酒为主的鸡尾酒的一种
vermouth	*n.*	苦艾酒	aperitif	*n.*	开胃酒
stuff	*n.*	东西，材料	draught	*adj.*	散装的
bartender	*n.*	酒保	barmaid	*n.*	女调酒师
aromatic	*adj.*	芳香的			

Learn by Heart

1. 酒吧的分类

主酒吧	main bar	服务酒吧	service bar
酒廊	lounge	宴会酒吧	banquet bar
多功能酒吧	grand bar	主题酒吧	theme bar
茶吧	tea bar	绅士酒吧	gentleman bar

2. 酒水服务常用语

"Mao Tai" is the best Chinese spirit.
茅台是中国最好的烈酒。

It's rather strong, but never goes to the head.

这酒度数很高，但是绝不会上头。

Which vintage would you prefer?

您喜欢哪一年的酒？

Would you like to try the dry sherry?

您要不要尝点干雪利酒？

Would you like to have cocktail or whisky on the rocks?

您要鸡尾酒还是要威士忌加冰？

Kahlua is a kind of liqueur.

甘露咖啡酒是一种利口酒。

We serve many kinds of drinks. Please help yourself.

我们供应很多种饮料，请自便。

Have you decided what you would like to drink?

您决定好喝什么了吗？

Would you like to have some snacks with your wine?

要不要来点小吃配酒呢？

How is the taste / color / bouquet / temperature /... of the wine?

这酒的味道/颜色/香味/温度……怎么样？

There is a lot of sediment in the bottle.

这瓶酒里有很多沉淀物。

Its alcohol content is very low. It's a fancy aperitif.

这种酒的酒精含量很低，是一种不错的餐前酒。

It's our self-brewed draught beer.

这是我们自酿的生啤。

Class Activity Role-Play

Scene One: The bartender recommends some Chinese wine to the guests and explains the difference between Chinese rice wine and Chinese white liquor.

Scene Two: The guest would like to bring her son who is 10 into the bar. The bartender says no to them by explaining the bar policy.

Further Reading

Bar Service

Beverage service, one of the most profitable service, is provided in different places such as restaurants, hotels, tea shops, coffee houses, etc. The most common place is a bar with a counter from which drinks are dispensed.

Based on different functions, bars can be classified into the following types.

Main bars with exquisite decoration, sufficient bar counters, chairs, and a full range of appliances for preparing and mixing drinks. The whole process of making and mixing drinks by the bartenders is open to the guests.

Lounges (e. g. music lounge) provide drinks and snacks but not staple foods. Customers prefer to be seated at tables instead of the counter here for leisure, meeting guests or chatting.

Grand bars are often located in entertainment venues. There are not only beverage services but also noisy song and dance shows here.

Banquet bars are temporarily and specially established for banquets.

Service bars are located in restaurants. Here, guests are attended by waiters or waitresses instead of by bartenders.

参考译文

酒 吧 服 务

酒水服务是最有利可图的服务之一。许多地方都有这项服务,如餐厅、酒店、茶楼和咖啡馆等。最常见的地方还是在酒吧,那里有一个吧台专门来分发酒水。

根据不同的功能,酒吧可以被分为以下几种:

主酒吧大多装修考究、别致,有足够的靠柜吧凳、酒水、调酒器具种类齐全。客人可以当面欣赏调酒师的全套操作过程。

酒廊(如音乐长廊)提供饮料和小吃,但不提供主食。客人喜欢坐在座位上而不是吧台旁来放松、会客或者闲聊。

多功能酒吧往往设在娱乐场所。这里不仅有酒水服务,还有热闹的歌曲和舞蹈表演。

宴会酒吧一般是临时专门为宴会设计的。

服务酒吧一般设在餐厅。在这里,客人由餐厅服务员来服务,而不是由酒保来服务。

Question

How to serve guest in different bars?

Unit 9   Banquet Service and Buffet

Listening Practice

【听力音频】

1. Listen to the dialogue and fill in the blanks.

A: Good morning, Mr. Smith. _____.

B: Glad to see you, too. Last Friday I ordered _____ for a group of
   20 people. I'd like to discuss some details with you. Have you got the arrangement
   ready?

A: I've reserved _____ for you in the Orchid Suite.

B: Very good.

A: Besides, we have two menus for you to choose from.

B: OK, show me the menus. (Reading the menus carefully.) Well, I will have this set
   of menu. But can I change some dishes?

A: Of course.

B: I'd like your specialties such as_____.

A: Certainly, sir. Do you need us to prepare a birthday cake?

B: Why not? It's for my daughter Lucy. She is 18 years old.

A: No problem. One more thing, could you pay _____?

B: Can I use my credit card to guarantee?

A: Certainly.

2. Listen and fill in the missing information.

Time of breakfast: _____   Time of lunch:_____

Place of afternoon coffee: _____

Number of vegetarians: _____

Situational Dialogues

1. Banquet Negotiation

(Scene: A guest negotiates with the clerk of the restaurant on a farewell party
arrangement.)

Guest: Hello, is this the Fisherman Wharf?

Clerk: Speaking. May I help you?

Guest: Yes. This is Jackson White from the ABC Auditing Firm. We'd like to have a
        farewell party banquet in your restaurant. Can you arrange it for us?

Clerk: Certainly, Mr. White. When would you like your banquet?

Guest: At 7:00 tomorrow evening.

Clerk: How many people will there be in your party?

Guest: There will be 50 altogether.

Clerk: Then I will arrange five tables for you. Could I recommend the Coco Beach—the newly decorated hall? It's well equipped and spacious. I'm sure it's suitable for a company banquet and you will take it.

Guest: That sounds great. We'll take it.

Clerk: Then how much would you like to spend for each table?

Guest: About 2,500 yuan and we want have the Cantonese cuisine. Besides, we'd like some special treatment or a pleasant surprise for our most important guest in the party.

Clerk: Certainly. How about "Good Fortune & Huge Luck"? It's the pig's knuckle roasted with our House Sauce.

Guest: Great. It will be perfect for our farewell banquet.

Clerk: That's fine. And how about drinks?

Guest: Please prepare some Great Wall Dry Wine, Qingdao Beer, Champagne, Coconut Milk and Carrot Juice.

Clerk: All right. What kind of fruit would you like?

Guest: Please prepare some watermelon, apples, oranges, pineapples and grapes.

Clerk: OK. So let me repeat what you've ordered: a farewell banquet in Coco Beach Hall at 7:00 tomorrow evening; fives tables for 50 people, each table about 2,500 yuan; drinks and fruit; a special dish of "Good Fortune & Huge Luck" for the special guest. Is that correct, Mr. White?

Guest: Yes. That's right.

Clerk: Thank you, Mr. White. We'll get everything ready before the banquet. I hope you'll enjoy it.

Guest: Thank you very much. Goodbye.

2. Serving the Western Style Banquet

(Scene: The waiter is serving a Western style banquet.)

(S: Staff, C: Customer)

S: You're at Table 18. Here we are. Take your seats, please.

C: I'm nearly late. Listen, our host is making the speech.

S: Yes. Let me fill brandy in your cup. The host is raising his cup for a toast.

(Host: Ladies and gentlemen, may I propose a toast to the health of you all? Cheers!)

C: Hey, this dish looks like a squirrel. What on earth is it?

S: This is the Squirrel-Shaped Mandarin Fish. Not only is it in the shape of a squirrel, it will sound like a squirrel crying when I pour the broth on it.

C: Is it that wonderful?

S: Yes. Please stay a little bit far away from the plate. When broth is poured, the broth might splash.

C: How does it taste?

S: It tastes crispy with sour and sweet flavors. Here is one portion for you. Would you try the flavors for yourself?

C: Hum, well, it is so soft inside.

S: May I take this plate away?

C: OK. What desserts do we have tonight?

S: Mango Pudding and Homemade Cheese Cake.

C: When will fruits come?

S: Just a minute, please. Here is your fruit knife. Do be careful.

(Host: Ladies and gentlemen, thank you for your coming this evening.)

S: Do you enjoy your meal this evening?

C: Yes, everything is fine.

S: I'm glad to hear it. This is your coat, sir. Good night.

3. Catering Service for Wedding Party

(Scene: Mr. and Mrs. Laurens have been working in China for two years. They want to order a wedding banquet in Xinhua Restaurant.)

Clerk:	Welcome to Xinhua Restaurant. May I help you?
Mr. Laurens:	We want to know if you could arrange the catering for wedding party.
Clerk:	Yes, sir. Take a seat please. As for catering, our Banquet Manager is in charge. I'd like to introduce to you. Just a moment please. Something to drink? We've got very fresh Chamomile Tea.
Mr. Laurens:	Oh, that's good. Thank you.
Clerk:	You're welcome.
Manager:	Good afternoon. I'm Chilly Yang, very glad to meet you. May I know your name please?
Mr. Laurens:	Jeff Laurens. And this is my wife.
Manager:	Well, Mr. and Mrs. Laurens, Would you like a banquet with Chinese style for your wedding party?
Mrs. Laurens:	Yes we do. In the party, we want to entertain our Chinese friends.
Manager:	Certainly, sir. When would you like your banquet?
Mr. Laurens:	Well, the wedding's on 12 June.
Manager:	And how many guests will there be, sir?
Mr. Laurens:	The guest list stands at around 80 at the moment.
Manager:	I see. Then our Raffles Room and Golden Dragon Room can accommodate approximately 100 people. However, I'll send you details of our various function rooms and you can choose.

Mrs. Laurens: I like the Raffles Room. It seems more capacious.

Mr. Laurens: It truly is. We'll take it.

Manager: OK. We are holding the Raffles Room for your wedding day. And what time will you want the reception to start, sir?

Mrs. Laurens: After the ceremony at about 1:10 p.m.

Manager: Very well. Were you thinking of having Chinese food, sir?

Mr. Laurens: Exactly.

Manager: Actually, we have four combination menus for banquet. Here they are. You see, several traditional Chinese dishes and drinks are included for each menu, discount already given. And we offer fruits for free.

Mr. Laurens: Well… sounds reasonable. I think set NO.1 looks fine, according with our budget. What do you think, honey?

Mrs. Laurens: You're the boss.

Manager: Well, let me repeat your order: Raffles Room at 1:10 p.m. on 12 June, NO.1 set meal. Is that right?

Mr. Laurens: Exactly. Thank you.

Manager: My pleasure. Everything would be ready for your wedding banquet then. I hope you would have an unforgivable wedding party.

4. The Orders for a Banquet

(Scene: A guest is booking a banquet for two tables in a Chinese restaurant with the banquet manager.)

(G: Guest, M: Manager)

G: Are you the banquet manager here?

M: Yes. Can I help you?

G: I'm going to invite some friends to dinner in the evening the day after tomorrow. Where should I order dinner?

M: What kind of dishes would you like?

G: Two tables of Chinese dishes.

M: Could I know your budget?

G: I'd like my banquet at one thousand yuan a table excluding drinks. How many courses are there altogether?

M: Two cold dishes, one soup, six dishes and two desserts. I will show you the menu later.

G: Please arrange a sitting room for us.

M: You have to pay extra fee for a sitting room.

G: Will the dishes be enough?

M: That's enough, I think. We ensure not only quantity but also quality. Will you please pay the deposit?

G: How much shall I pay now?

M: You may pay the whole amount or half of it. By the way, are there any drivers coming? We can provide special food for drivers. Is there anything else you want us to do for you?

G: Nothing else. It's very considerate of you.

M: You are welcome.

Words and Expressions

Fisherman Wharf		渔人码头	knuckle	*n.*	肘关节
toast	*n.*	祝酒词	squirrel	*n.*	松鼠
broth	*n.*	肉汤，清汤	portion	*n.*	份，部分
bottomless	*adj.*	无底的，无限的	turnip	*n.*	萝卜，大头菜
catering	*n. & v.*	承办酒席	chamomile tea		洋甘菊茶
capacious	*adj.*	宽敞的，大气的	set meal		套餐

Learn by Heart

1. 宴会的分类

国宴	state banquet	正式宴会	banquet
便宴	dinner	冷餐会	buffet dinner
鸡尾酒会	cocktail lounge	茶话会	tea party

2. 宴会服务常用语

Would you like a streamer and amplifier?
您要横幅和扩音器吗？

Shall we prepare a meal for the drivers?
我们需要为驾驶员准备饭菜吗？

Is it necessary for us to prepare a lounge for you?
需要我们替您准备休息室吗？

How much would you like to pay for each person?
每位的标准是多少？

The minimum charge for a 200-person dinner party is 10,000 yuan, excluding drinks.

200 人的宴会最低收费是 10000 元，不包括酒水。

I was hoping to pay about ¥ 40 a head. Will that be possible?

我预计人均 40 元左右，可以吗？

I am very glad you like it, do have more.

我很高兴你喜欢这菜，请多吃些。

This is a course of Chinese dish, help yourself.

这是一道中国菜，请慢用。

Anything special on the menu?

要什么特别的菜吗？

Do you need highchairs for babies?

您需要婴儿椅吗？

I hope you can pay 100 yuan as deposit.

我希望您能付 100 元作为订金。

I'm sure we can arrange that.

我保证我们可以安排好这个。

Here is one portion for you.

这是您的一份。

Do you enjoy your meal this evening?

您今晚用餐愉快吗？

Class Activity Role-Play

Scene One: A guest wants to have a wedding ceremony in your restaurant. There will be nearly 200 guests. The guest has many requirements such as the dishes and tables.

Scene Two: Mr. Kirk is checking through the arrangement for a three-day seminar to be held in the Lily Suite with the banquet manager.

Further Reading

Western Style Banquet

Banquet is very normal in nowadays society. There is much etiquette in the banquet especially in western style. For example, people have to wear evening dress for the banquet. The hotel staff also needs to maintain organization of banquet service areas. However, do you know how to eat western food?

Western-style food refers to the food or dinner cooked according to the customs of western countries. Western-style food is originated in Europe and the European cooking methods were conveyed by an Italian——Martin Polo to China. Later, after the Opium War, it was transferred from "residential dish" to "western restaurant" and then "western-style food restaurant" run by Chinese people. It was only served for some officials and business men.

In recent years, the number of foreign guests increased rapidly. More and more hotels have western-style food services. At the same time, more and more Chinese people have accustomed to the hobby of eating western-style food.

When eating western-style food, you can talk with others freely and lightly. But, when you talk with others, don't chew the food in your mouth. Generally speaking, clean your lips with napkins before talking or drinking.

When eating western-style food, you cannot hold the plate when eating; cannot stab the food while eating the large piece of food. You should cut the food into small pieces and then put them into your mouth.

When eating western-style food, the way of eating is similar to the way of eating Cantonese food. That is—drink soup first and then eat the dishes. When drinking the soup, and hold the spoon with right hand, the spoon should face the outer side to ladle out the soup, and then put it into the mouth. Don't make any sound while drinking the soup.

When eating western-style food, the bones and thorns should not be put into the mouth when you meet the dishes which have them. The food which already eaten into the mouth cannot be spit out. So you should know the food you eat when eating western-style food. For the food which you are not so sure or the food which you don't like, then you'd better not put them into your mouth.

When eating western-style food, if you leave the table without finishing the dinner, you should put the knife and fork crossed beside the plate, let the edge of the knife faces inside. If you have finished your meal, you should put the knife and fork side by side to show that the plate can be removed.

参考译文

西 餐 宴 会

宴会活动在如今社会非常普遍。参加宴会有许多礼仪,尤其是西餐宴会。例如,人们需要穿着礼服出席晚宴,酒店员工还需要维护宴会厅区域的整齐有序。但是,你知道如何吃西餐吗?

西餐是指根据西方国家的习俗烹调的食物或主餐。它起源于欧洲的烹调方法,是由意大利人马丁·波罗传到中国的。后来,鸦片战争后,它从"家常菜"转变到"西餐厅",然后到中国人经营的"西式餐厅"。这也只是为一些官员和商人服务的。

近年来,外国游客的数量迅速增加。越来越多的酒店有西餐服务。与此同时,越来越多的中国人已经习惯了吃西餐。

吃西餐时,你可以与他人轻松自由地交谈。但是,当你与别人交谈时,不要咀嚼食物。一般来说,谈话或喝水前请用餐巾纸清洁你的嘴唇。

吃西餐时,你不能按住盘子吃饭,有大块食物时也不能戳着食物吃。你应该把食物切成小块,然后再把它们放进嘴里。

吃西餐时，吃的方法与吃粤菜的方法相似。这就是先喝汤后吃菜。喝汤时，用右手持勺，勺子要向外侧舀出汤，然后把它放入口中。喝汤的时候不要发出任何声音。

吃西餐时，当你遇到有骨头和刺的菜时，不要把它们放入口中。已经吃进嘴里的食品不能吐出。所以吃西餐时你应该知道你吃的食物是什么。如果不是那么肯定的食品或不喜欢的食物，那么你最好不要把它们放进嘴里。

吃西餐时，如果你要离开没有吃完的餐桌，应该把刀叉相交放在盘子上，让刀刃向内。如果你吃完了这一顿，你应该把刀叉肩并肩地摆好来示意盘子可以被撤走了。

Question

How to serve guests in the western style banquet?

Unit 10　Dealing with Complaints

Listening Practice

【听力音频】

1. Listen to the dialogue and fill in the blanks.

A: Waiter!

B: Yes, sir?

A: I've been trying to _____ for the last 15 minutes.

B: I'm sorry, sir. I will _____ right now.

A: How much longer we're going to have to wait for our dinner?

B: I'm afraid the Beijing Roast Duck takes quite a while to prepare. I'll see about your
　 order._____?

A: No, thanks.

B: Please have some _____ now. It's free for you.

A: OK, but_____.

B: I see. I will urge the cook as soon as possible.

2. Listen and fill in the missing information.

Guest's mood: _____　　The food guest ordered:_____

Problem of the food: _____

Compensation for the mistake: _____

Situational Dialogues

【拓展音频】

1. Complaint about a Late Order and an Accident

(Scene: A guest is complaining about the late order. And he has even got a little angry
when found a tiny hair in his dish. The waiter is trying to solve the problem.)

(G: Guest, W: Waiter, M: Manager)

G: Waiter. I ordered my meal at least thirty minutes ago and it still hasn't come. Why
　 is it taking so long?

W: I'm very sorry, sir. I'll check your order with the chef. Would you like some
　 appetizer while you are waiting?

G: Fine. Please do any hurry up! I have to catch the plane at 3 p.m.

W: Just a moment, please. (The waiter brings the dishes after 10 minutes) Your meal,
　 sir. We're very sorry for the delay. Please enjoy your lunch.

G: (5minutes later) Waiter, waiter!

W: What's problem, sir? Can I be of assistance?

G: Look at my fruit salad! There is a tiny hair on the cabbage. You see? It's quite disgusting!

W: Oh, truly sorry sir. This is quite unusual. We'll look into the matter.

G: I waited for so long and then a hair in my salad! How awful. You really ruined my day! I have to speak to your manager.

W: Sorry sir, please calm yourself. I will get our manager.

M: I'm terribly sorry sir. There could have been some mistake. I do apologize. To express our regret for all the trouble, we offer you a 10% discount.

G: I do not think that's enough. How about my salad?

M: I will have them prepare another one. Would you like some drinks while you are waiting? The drinks will be on the house, of course.

G: I do not prefer cold drinks then.

M: Of course, sir. How about heated apple juice?

G: Well, all right.

M: Thank you, sir. We do apologize for the inconvenience again. We will soon bring you new salad and heated apple juice in a minute. I'm sure everything will be right again next time you come.

2. Cold Environment

(Scene: A guest feels cold in the restaurant. His friend is talking with the waiter and wants to turn up the heat.)

(G: Guest, W: Waiter)

G: Waiter. May I see you for a moment?

W: Yes, what can I do for you?

G: My friend is freezing.

W: I'm sorry, but I can't turn up the heat because we've had several complaints that it's too warm here.

G: I know. She arrived looking uncomfortable with hunger and cold.

W: Don't worry, sir. How about putting on your jacket?

G: All right. I don't particularly care for eating with my jacket on.

W: Perhaps you'd like to sit over there in the corner? There is less draught.

G: That's OK.

W: Besides, you may sit in our dining room. The room was furnished in warm reds and browns.

G: Good. I will tell you if we need.

3. Complaint about Food

(Scene: A guest is not satisfied with the steak. He thinks it is not very fresh.)

(W: Waiter, G: Guest)

W: Is everything to your satisfaction?

G: No, the steak was recommended, but it is not very fresh.

W: Oh. Sorry to hear that. This is quite unusual as we have fresh steak from the market every day. I'll look into the matter.

G: So what? It is not fresh and I'm not happy about it!

W: I'm sorry, sir. Do you wish to try something else? That would be on the house, of course, how about a delicious dessert, with our compliments?

G: No, I don't want to try something else, and find it's not fresh again! This is very annoying.

W: I see, sir. Just give us another chance, you will find this restaurant really lives up to its name. I'm sure everything will be all right next time you come.

G: All right. Maybe I'll come again.

W: Thank you very much, sir.

4. Complaint about the Dishes

(Scene: A guest wants to see the manager for he has a complaint about the dishes.)

(G: Guest, W: Waitress)

G: Excuse me, miss!

W: Can I help you, sir?

G: Yes. You may try the tenderloin. It's as tough as leather.

W: Excuse me, sir. But you wanted the steak to be cooked medium well.

G: So, you're telling me? Can I see the manager, please? I have a complaint.

M: Good evening, sir. I'm the manager of the restaurant and this is my business card.

G: Let me tell you something. I ordered the tenderloin medium well and it's not well done. And your waitress tried to put the blame on me. Is this the way you treat the guests?

M: (The manager asked the waitress to leave for some time.) I'm terribly sorry, sir. On behalf of the hotel, I apologize for what has happened. There might have been some misunderstanding. We should not blame any of our guests in any case. Shall I get another steak for you now? It'll be certainly on the house.

G: I don't think it will agree with my stomach.

M: Please be assured we'll look into the matter and our chef is very particular.

G: I'd rather not have any steak now.

M: Please try our smoked salmon if you don't mind.

G: All right, but I want it within 15 minutes.

M: Yes, sir. (10 minutes later) Sorry to have kept you waiting, sir. This is the salmon.

G: Well, the salmon doesn't taste good. There is an unusual flavour.

M: The salmon is smoked with coffee. It might taste of coffee.

G: Ah, I see. There is a coffee-like flavour in the fish. Sorry, I should not have said anything negative about the fish.

M: Never mind.

Words and Expressions

disgusting	*adj.*	恶心的		draught	*n.*	通风，气流
pray	*v.*	请求，恳求		splash	*v.*	泼溅
scald	*v.*	烫伤		freezing	*adj.*	冷的，冰冻的
draught	*n.*	通风，气流		compliment	*n.*	称赞，致意
annoying	*adj.*	讨厌的		tenderloin	*n.*	里脊肉
salmon	*n.*	大马哈鱼		negative	*adj.*	负面的，否定的

Learn by Heart

1. 餐饮投诉的分类

对设备的投诉	facilities	对菜肴的投诉	dishes
对服务态度的投诉	attitude	对服务质量的投诉	service quality
对突发事件的投诉	accident	对环境的投诉	environment

2. 餐饮投诉常用语

I'm very sorry, sir. I'll return your…to the chef.
非常对不起，先生。我会把您点的……退回给厨房。

I'm very sorry, sir. I'll bring you another one/bottle.
非常对不起，先生。我会替您送来另一份/瓶。

I'm sure the waiter didn't mean to be rude. Perhaps he didn't understand you correctly.
相信服务员并不是有意无礼，他只是可能没有听懂您的意思。

We might have overlooked some points.
我们可能忽略一些细节。

Our manager is not in town. Shall I get our assistant manager for you?
我们的经理不在本地。我帮您叫助理经理来好吗？

This is really the least we can do for you.
我们能为您做的非常有限。

I'm terribly sorry, but that is the situation. Please take a seat. I'll soon have something arranged for you.
很抱歉，但情况已是如此，请坐一会儿，我尽快为您做安排。

I'm very sorry, sir. I'll bring you some more.

非常对不起，先生。我会帮您多取一些来。

Is there anything wrong with your order, sir?

您点的菜有问题吗，先生？

What would you like me to do?

您需要我做些什么？

There will be no charge for this. This is a compliment of the manager.

这不用付费，它是经理赠送的。

I'm very sorry for my mistake/clumsiness.

我为我的错误/笨拙道歉。

I'm very sorry to have spoilt your evening.

我很抱歉破坏了您今晚的兴致。

I'd like to apologize for our carelessness. May I clean it up for you?

我为我们的粗心向您道歉。我可以替您清理吗？

We're very sorry for the delay. Please enjoy your lunch.

抱歉耽搁了，请享用您的午餐。

Please calm down, sir. I will try to help you.

先生请冷静，我会尽力帮助您的。

I will speak to the person in charge and ask him to take care of the problem.

我会对负责人讲，让他来处理这件事。

Class Activity Role-Play

Scene One: A guest has a complaint that he thinks sometimes he had to wait too long for dishes. And occasionally there were one or two pieces of tableware that didn't look so clean.

Scene Two: Mr. White personally prefers to dine in a quiet place. He found it was a bit noisy here. Besides, he saw some customers smoking in spite of the warning "No Smoking" on the wall. He would appreciate it if the waiter could deal with this.

Further Reading

Complaints

Hotel staff, like people working in other service businesses, is bound to receive complaints and criticisms as well as compliments and commendations. Some of the complaints and criticisms are well justified and very constructive. They are perfect reminders of the areas of a hotel service that still leaves something to be desired. Other complaints are just results of fastidious and difficult personalities. People who make complaints and criticism can be friendly and reasonable or they can also be rude and abusive. No matter how the person behaves, the hotel staff should always try and be nice to them. An argument with the guest is the most undesirable thing that can happen to a staff member and the hotel.

In handling complaints, the hotel staff should always be polite and helpful. He/she should always be ready to lend an attentive ear to what the guest has to say and always hear the guest out. He/she must not interrupt the guest unless necessary. It is advisable for him/her to jot down what the guest has said. He/she should then make a short apology and express his/her understanding of the guest's situation or sympathy with the guest. Only when he/she puts himself/herself in the guest's shoes can he/she look at the problem from other person's perspective. And only when the staff member can look at the guest's problem in the guest's way can he/she be ready to sympathize with the guest. After that the staff members should take actions quickly to remove the complaint, either by making polite, patient and detailed explanations, or making swift, effective corrections and remedies, or reporting the complaints to a superior. But whatever he/she intend to do, he/she must keep the guest informed of the measures or actions he/she plans to take and when he/she will carry them out. It is not at all easy to be always nice to the guest, especially when the guest is unfriendly and rude, even abusive. But the success of any business in the hospitality industry depends on people-pleasures.

参考译文

投　诉

酒店员工和其他服务企业的工作人员一样，可能会受到投诉和批评，以及赞美和表扬。有些投诉和批评是合理的，而且非常有建设性。它们是完美的提醒者，尤其是对酒店服务等领域不尽如人意的地方。其余的投诉则是过分苛刻和性格挑剔的结果。投诉和批评的人可能是友好的和合理的，也可能是粗鲁的和辱骂的。不管他们如何表现，员工都应该对他们友好。对于员工和酒店来说，与客人争论是最不可取的事情。

酒店员工在处理投诉时，应该总是彬彬有礼、乐于助人的。他/她应该随时准备倾听顾客的意见。不要打断客人的讲话，除非在必要情况下。可取的做法是酒店员工要记下客人的讲话，然后他/她要做一个简短的道歉，并表示他/她了解了客人的情况或表示同情。只有站在客人的立场，才能从客人的视角来看待问题。只有员工以客人的方式来看待客人的问题，他/她才会同情客人。之后，员工应采取行动，迅速解决投诉，或礼貌、耐心细致地解释，或做出迅速、有效的纠正和补救，或向上级报告投诉。但是无论他/她打算做什么，都要告知客人他/她采取的方法或行动，还有问题什么时候可以解决。总是友好地对待客人不是一件容易的事情，尤其当客人不友好和粗鲁，甚至破口大骂时。但在酒店餐饮业中任何业务的成功都取决于顾客的高兴和满意。

Question

How to serve a guest when he was rude and abusive?

Chapter 4

Health & Recreation

Unit 1　At the Health Center

【听力音频】

Listening Practice

1. **Listen to the dialogue and fill in the blanks.**

(A: Attendant, G: Guest)

A: Good evening, sir. Welcome to our_____.

G: Good evening. I'm looking for a place to do some exercises.

A: You've come to the right place. Ours is a well-equipped health center. We have all
　　the latest gymnasium apparatus: race apparatus, _____, _____,
　　rowing and jogging machines and other apparatus for body exercises.

G: Any other facilities?

A: We also have a billiard room, a bowling alley, _____and
　　three _____.

G: Is the swimming pool safe?

A: Yes, we have excellent _____ on duty from _____.

G: How much do you charge for the use of the facilities?

A: _____each time.

G: Can I play tennis now?

A: I'm sorry, sir. Tennis courts are fully occupied now. They should be booked a day in
　　advance.

G: I see. Thanks.

A: You are welcome.

2. **Listen and fill in the missing information.**

Claude Health Club

Number of tennis courts nearby_____

Name of the guest_____

Room number_____

Date and time_____

Cost of using tennis racquets_____

How to travel to the tennis court_____

Situational Dialogues

1. In the Health Club

【拓展音频】

(Scene: After dinner, Mr. and Mrs. Brown come to the Health Club. A clerk is showing them around.)

(C: Clerk, M: Mrs. Brown, B: Mr. Brown)

C: Good evening, sir and madam. May I help you?

M: We're really interested in your health club. Can you show us around?

C: Certainly, this way, please. We're proud of our health club. It is considered the best of its kind in our city.

B: I think it's very modern and well-equipped.

C: Let's start over here. There is our aerobics room. There's a class going on right now. Over here is our gymnasium. We have all the latest equipment.

M: But I haven't used exercising equipment before. Can you tell us some more details?

C: Certainly. We have the race apparatus, stationary bikes, rowing machines, muscle builder sets, chest-expanders, bar bells, dumb bells, spring-grips, wall bars and so on.

B: Working in the gymnasium is a very good way for overcoming a weight problem. What else do you have?

C: This way please. Besides the gym, we have a billiard room, a squash court. The chess room is on the second floor. Next to it is the dance hall. We hold dance at night every day. Bowling center and mini-golf on the third floor. They're all open from morning till midnight. Also, there are some sauna rooms and beauty saloon on the forth floor. All these are ready to serve you at your convenience. In addition, we have an indoor swimming pool on the top floor.

M: That's wonderful! I like swimming. How about outdoor activities?

C: We have a nine-hole golf course and four tennis courts. Here is another exercise room. You've probably heard of our traditional Chinese exercises: taijiquan and qigong.

B: Yes, of course. I've seen them on TV.

C: Mr. Zhang will give a qigong class this evening at 7 p.m. Why don't you go and have a look?

B: That's a good idea. We'll go there this evening.

C: You are welcome at any time.

2. At Sauna

(Scene: A guest comes to the hotel's sauna room, The recreation clerk is talking with her.)

(C: Clerk, G: Guest)

C: Good morning, sir. Here is the hotel's sauna room. What can I do for you?

G: Yes. This is the first time I've come here. Could you please tell me something about it?

C: Sure. Those who have heart disease or high blood pressure are not allowed to take sauna, for their sake.

G: Thank you for telling me about this. What should I do here?

C: First, change your shoes to slippers. Then walk up to the changing room to get prepared for a shower.

G: OK. How about after the shower?

C: After the shower, step into the washroom with birch switches, dip them in the warm water and briskly whisk them over your skin.

G: That sounds comfortable.

C: Yes, then enter the bathroom. There is a stove tired with wood in the room, and on the top of the stove, there is a pile of stones, which keep the heat. Throw some water on the stones, and dry steam is given off.

G: Thanks a lot. I'll have a try.

C: My pleasure.

3. At the Indoor Swimming Pool

(Scene: Mrs. Smith and her daughter come to the indoor swimming pool of the Atlantic Hotel. A clerk comes to greet them.)

Clerk: Welcome to our hotel's indoor swimming pool, madam. How may I help you?

Guest: Yes, I'm Mrs. Smith in Room 1102.

Clerk: Welcome! For registered guests, swimming is free of charge.

Guest: But my daughter is 6-year old. I'm wondering whether the water is too cool to swim in.

Clerk: Children under 12 are not allowed to use the pool unless accompanied by a parent. Will you be here with her, madam?

Guest: Yes, of course.

Clerk: That's OK. Don't worry, madam. Ours is a solar heated one with a temperature of some 28 degrees centigrade now.

Guest: Fantastic! You see, we are not good swimmers. Can you tell me how deep the pool is?

Clerk: Never mind, madam. We have full-time coaches to ensure your safety. The deepest place is 2.5 meters. You can swim in the shadow area, which is only one-meter in depth.

Guest: That's good.

Clerk: And we have separate locker rooms over there. You can use them free of charge. You can also have a shower there.

Guest: Thank you. I'll do that.

Clerk: Have fun. If you need something else, please don't hesitate to call me.

4. At the Billiard Room

(Scene: On Sunday afternoon, Mr. and Mrs. Smith come to the Billiard Room. A clerk comes to greet them.)

(C: Clerk, M: Mrs. Smith, S: Mr. smith)

C: Good afternoon, madam and sir. Welcome to our Billiard Room.

M: Good afternoon. Oh, it's crowded.

C: Yes, we are often fully occupied on Saturdays and Sundays. Please take your seats to wait for a few minutes.

(15 minutes later)

C: Sorry to have kept you waiting. Now this way, please.

S: The billiard room looks very spacious and has got four pool tables.

C: Yes, sir. We have snookers and pools, what would you like?

S: We'd like the pool. Lady is fit for it, I think.

C: Come this way, please. They are fifteen balls. The scoreboard is on the wall over there.

S: Thanks. What's the cost for it?

C: 40 yuan per hour. There is no fee for registered guests. Would you like some drinks?

S: Yes, two bottles of beer.

C: OK. I'll bring them right away. Please enjoy your time.

Words and Expressions

well-equipped	*adj.*	设备良好的，装备精良	stress	*n.*	压力；紧张
aerobics	*n.*	健美操	massage	*n.*	按摩
race apparatus		赛跑器械，跑步机	registered	*adj.*	注册的；登记过的
stationary bicycle		健身自行车	body massage		全身按摩
rowing machine		划式练力器	point massage		穴位按摩
muscle builder set		肌肉健壮器	foot massage		足底按摩
chest-expander	*n.*	拉力器	price list		价目表
bar bell		杠铃	indoor swimming pool		室内游泳馆
dumb bell		哑铃	centigrade	*n.*	摄氏度
spring-grips		弹簧握力器	fantastic	*adj.*	太棒了
wall bars		墙铃	accompany	*vt.*	陪同，伴随
gymnasium	*n.*	健身房	solar	*adj.*	利用太阳光的
billiard room		桌球室	coach	*n.*	体育教练，私人教练

squash court		壁球场	shadow area		浅水区
golf	*n.*	高尔夫球	locker	*n.*	衣物柜
chess room		棋室	separate locker room		单独的更衣室
sauna	*n.*	桑拿	pools	*n.*	美式台球
beauty saloon		美容美发中心	snookers	*n.*	英式台球
convenience	*n.*	方便	scoreboard	*n.*	记分板，记分牌
tennis court		网球场	slipper	*n.*	拖鞋
traditional	*adj.*	传统的	birch switches	*n.*	桦条
Taijiquan	*n.*	太极拳	briskly	*adj.*	轻快的
qigong	*n.*	气功	whisk	*vt.*	拂动
recreation	*n.*	消遣，娱乐，游戏	stove	*n.*	炉子
listless	*adj.*	无精打采的，倦怠的	dry steam		干蒸汽
relieve	*vt.*	缓和，减轻；解除			

Learn by Heart

1. 其他健身方式及设施器材

瑜伽	Yoga	热水浴池	hot tub
围棋	Go	踏车跑步机	treadmill
举重机	weight-lifting machine	跑步机	jogging machine
自由力量	free weights	保龄球馆	bowling alley

2. 健身常用语

Welcome to our Health Club.
欢迎来我们健身俱乐部。

There is no fee for registered guests.
我们对会员免费。

Besides the gym, we have the billiard room, a squash court, bowling center and mini-golf.
除了健身房，我们还有台球室、壁球场、保龄球中心和迷你高尔夫球场。

Don't worry, we have full-time coaches to insure your safety.
别担心，我们有专职教练保证您的安全。

This is our aerobics room. There is a class going on right now.

这是我们的健美操房，现在正在上课。

It is a popular system of exercises keeping your heart and lungs in top health as well as for overcoming a weight problem.

健美操是一种流行的体操，它可以保持心肺健康，还能减肥。

It's a complimentary service for club members.

我们对俱乐部成员的服务是免费的。

We have spring expanders, dumb-bells, a balancing bar, parallel bars, hand rings and many others.

我们有拉力器、哑铃、平衡木、双杠、吊环等。

The swimming pool is free of charge.

游泳池是免费的。

Class Activity Role-Play

Scene One: A registered guest enters the gym. The clerk comes to greet him and show him around.

Scene Two: A guest with a nine-year-old son wants to go to Yoga while dropping his/her son off for a swim. The pool attendant explains that children under twelve are not allowed to use the pool unless accompanied by a parent.

Further Reading

The Recreation Center

"All work and no play makes Jack a dull boy and work while you work, and play while you play. This is the way to make you happy and gay." These are popular sayings, which mean that all men need recreation. One can't work all the time if he is going to maintain good health and enjoy life.

As leisure time in people's lives increases, and health becomes people's first consideration, opportunities for recreation become more important and practical. Therefore, more and more hotels make entertainment and recreation programs and complete facilities. Guests of all ages with all degrees of emotional and physical health go to the Recreation Center to do exercises to relax them or to enjoy nightlife.

The Recreation Center organizes and conducts a variety of entertaining and recreational activities for guests. These things are focused on arts, fitness and sports. The recreation staff must be good at motivating guests and sensitive to their needs. Besides good healthy and physical stamina, they should know how to maintain recreational sports apparatus, supervise all exercises, and be able to make judgments.

参考译文

康 乐 中 心

"只工作，不玩耍，聪明小孩也变傻。工作时好好工作，玩耍时尽情玩耍。这才是让你幸福和快乐的生活方式。"这句时下最流行的说法说明了一个道理：所有人都需要娱乐。一个人如果要保持健康并享受生活，就不可能永远只工作不休息。

随着人们休闲时间增加，健康成为人们的第一考虑要素。娱乐机会变得更重要、更现实。因此，越来越多的酒店建立康乐中心，推出各种康乐活动，其设施设备一应俱全。那些有不同程度的心理或生理健康状况的各年龄层次的客人，都去康乐中心做运动，以放松身心，享受夜生活。

康乐中心为客人组织开展各种有关艺术、健身和体育等娱乐休闲活动。康乐服务人员必须善于激发客人的各种需求，并对他们的需求保持敏感。除了拥有良好的健康和体能，他们应该知道如何保养各种运动器材，监管所有的练习，并能在安全等方面做出正确的判断。

Question

Do you like to play in the recreation center?

Unit 2   In the Beauty Salon

Listening Practice

【听力音频】

1. Listen to the dialogue and fill in the blanks.

(B: Barber, G: Guest)

B: Good afternoon, sir. What can I do for you?

G: Can you tell me your _____, please?

B: We are open from _____. There is no break at the noon.

G: Good, I will come back later.

B: You won't have to wait long, sir. You're _____.

G: All right.

B: It's your turn, sir. Please sit in the chair. How would you like your _____?

G: Make it _____, please.

B: Certainly, sir. Do you want me to use to razor for the back and the sideburns?

G: Yes.

…

B: Yes, sir. How's that?

G: Very nice. Thanks.

B: And now for the _____?

G: Yes, but be careful, my beard is rather rough.

B: You needn't worry, sir. I will be more careful.

…

B: Now _____. How does it look?

G: Let me see. Very good, thank you.

2. Listen and fill in the missing information.

Biannual card price:_____   Annual card price:_____

Quarterly card price:_____   Off-peak time: _____

Reason for writing down the phone number:_____

Situational Dialogues

1. At the Beauty Salon

(Scene: Mrs. Graham is at the beauty parlor. The staff is talking with her and recommending a stylist to her.)

(S: Staff, G: Mrs. Graham, St: Stylist)

S: Good afternoon, madam. Welcome to our parlor.

G: Good afternoon. I'm Mrs. Graham. I have an appointment for a perm.

S: Oh yes，Mrs. Graham. Could you sit here，please？Do you have your own stylist?

G: No, I haven't.

S: May I recommend one of our best stylists?

G: Thank you.

S: Good afternoon，madam. I'm No.3 designer, glad to be at your service. How do you like your hair done?

G: I'd like it done in one of the latest styles. Could you show me some pictures of hair styles？

S: Certainly，Mrs. Graham. Here are some of the latest styles in fashion now: hair sweptback，chaplet，shoulder-length, horse-tail style，etc. Choose one, please.

G: Thank you. I prefer this one, but trim a little on the sides.

S: I think you would look cute with short hair. Perhaps you should go even shorter than in the picture. The short hair wave may right for you. It fits your face very well.

G: You are right. I would like to have a try. By the way, I also want my hair dyed.

S: What color do you like?

G: Light brown, how do you think about it?

S: Yellow is right for your skin.

G: OK, I'll take it.

S: Very well. Now let me explain what I'll do. I'll cut your hair to the middle of your back，have it curled inside at the ends. And then，I'll part it in the middle and make it wavy at the sides. First of all, Jack will give you a shampoo. I want to cut your hair wet.

…

S: Please have a look. How do you think of your new hairstyle?

G: Oh, you've done a beautiful job. I like it very much.

S: And it's easy to take care of.

G: Thank you.

2. Manicure

(Scene: Mrs. Green wants to have a manicure and a pedicure. The Manicurist is serving her.)

(M: Manicurist, G: Mrs. Green)

G: Hello. I want to know how much it costs to have a manicure and a pedicure?

M: Usually, it's 60 dollars for a manicure and 80 dollars for a pedicure. But with this special discount, the total for both is only 120 dollars. And you can get them painted as well for free.

G: That's nice. I'd like to give it a try. I think I'd like Passion Red please.

M: All right. Do you want your cuticles cut, too?

G: No.

M: Would you like the shape square or round?

G: Square, but with rounded edges, please.

(After a while)

M: All right, it's done. Please follow me to the drying section.

G: How long will it take to get them dry?

M: In about five minutes, you'll be all set.

G: I see. Thank you.

3. Facial Treatment

(Scene: It's Mrs. Black's first time to go to the beauty salon. She is asking the beautician some information about the facial treatment.)

(B: Beautician, M: Mrs. Black)

B: Good evening, madam. May I help you?

M: I want a facial. But this is the first time I've come here, can you tell me how you do it?

B: Sure. Most facials start with a thorough cleaning. Then we usually use a toner to invigorate the skin, followed by exfoliation treatment—a peeling mask or scrub that removes the dead cells which makes the skin look dull. After that, we'll massage your face and neck with oil or cream to improve the circulation and relieve the tension, followed by a mask to moisturize and soften the skin.

M: That's exactly what I want. How long does it take?

B: We have half-hour and one-hour treatments.

M: What's the regular price?

B: Well, the half hour facial costs 50 yuan and the one hour costs 80 yuan. If you want a make-up, another 30 yuan will do.

M: Good, I will take the one-hour facial with make-up.

B: That's fine, madam.

M: By the way, could you give me a manicure? Use a light nail polish, please.

B: Yes, madam.

Words and Expressions

beautician	*n.*	美容师	pedicure	*n.*	足部治疗；修脚
parlor	*n.*	美容院	cuticle	*n.*	表皮；角质层
perm	*n.& vt.*	烫发	square	*n.*	正方形 *adj.* 正方形的
stylist	*n.*	设计师	facial	*n.*	脸部按摩；美容 *adj.* 脸的；面部
sweptback	*adj.*	(头发)向后梳的	cleanse	*vt.*	使清洁，清洗
chaplet	*n.*	盘花冠式	toner	*n.*	化妆水，调色剂
bob	*n.*	短发 *vt.* 剪短(头发)	invigorate	*vt.*	滋补，滋润；使活跃

dye	vt.	染，把……染上颜色		exfoliation	n.	剥落；剥落物
trim	n.	修剪 vt. 修剪，修整，整理		peel	v.	剥(皮)；被剥(或削)去皮
curl	n.	卷发 vt. 使(头发)卷曲		scrub	n.	擦洗；擦净 vt. 用力擦洗；揉
part	vt.	将(头发)分线		circulation	n.	循环，环流；运行
wavy	adj.	呈波浪形的；起伏的		moisturize	vt.	给皮肤、空气等增加水分
shampoo	n.	洗发剂，洗头 vt. 洗(头发)		tonic	adj.	滋补的
manicure	n.	修指甲 vt. 修(指甲)		make-up		化妆
paint	vt.	涂色于……				

Learn by Heart

1. 基本发型

光头	bald head	马尾发型	pony-tail
发辫，辫子	pigtail	披肩发型	cape
中分头	central parting	娃娃头	pageboy style
爆炸头	afro hair	直发型	straight hair
平顶头	crop	大波浪型	wave hair
卷发型	curly hair		

2. 美容美发常用语

Nurse face or body?
您要做面部护理还是身体护理？

Hello, what about the strength?
您好，这样的力度可以吗？

Excuse me, would you like to nurse your eye?
打扰一下，今天要做一下眼部护理吗？

Hello, all is finished.
您好，整套护理已经完成了。

I'd like to have my hair cut.

我想理个发。

How do you want it?

您想理什么式样的?

Just a trim, and cut the sides fairly short, but not so much at the back.

两边剪短些,但后面不要剪得太多。

Nothing off the top?

顶上不要剪吗?

Well, a little off the top.

嗯,稍微剪一点。

Would you like a shave or shampoo?

您要不要修面或洗头?

Very well, and how would you like your hair cut, sir?

好的,您喜欢什么发式?

Do you want me to trim your moustache?

要我为您修剪一下胡子吗?

Well, could you cut a little more off the temple?

好,能不能把两边鬓角再剪短些?

Is that satisfactory?

您看这样满意吗?

I need a shampoo/conditioner/ blow dry/perm/haircut.

我要洗头/护发/吹发/烫发/剪发。

Class Activity Role-Play

Scene One: A middle-aged lady wants to have a manicure and facial treatment. You are serving her.

Scene Two: An old gentleman with gray hair wants to have a trim and a shave and also wants his hair dyed. You are receiving him.

Further Reading

Men's Hairstyles

In some countries, long hair has been in vogue for more than ten years now. The problem of distinguishing a man from a woman by hairstyle has become too familiar to be taken seriously. Among other things, people have learnt that hairstyles are a deceptive indicator of sex. A person's way of walking, the body shape and the clothing are more reliable in this respect. Worth mentioning is that very long hair for men is losing its popularity.

Indeed, if one pays close attention to hairstyles, one will discover men and women nowadays wear more or less identical hairstyles. This is not to say, of course, that the difference between a barber and a hairdresser no longer exists, but it does mean that similar services can be found in both establishments. Nowadays a man does not go to a barber only for a haircut. Instead, he might want a permanent wave, which makes his hair as wavy as any fair lady's. Even shaving, so masculine and regarded only as necessary for men, takes another form when it appears in a ladies' beauty-parlor. Although a delicate process is involved that is not easily comprehensible, electrolysis is just as efficient as any razor blade and shaving cream in removing women's facial hair.

There are people who still prefer the conventional hairstyles and women do look more natural with feminine styles. To pursue this end, hair stylists have invented more equipment than one can name. Hair clippers, and curlers appear very primitive in the company of recent innovations, which make use of new discoveries in other fields of knowledge such as biochemistry, electronics and psychology. For the first category, hairsprays, conditioners and hair-restorer are the products of the joint-efforts of fashion and chemistry. Convenient sets of dryers and blowers would not have come into being without knowledge of modern physics. As for psychology, it seems that it is used widely by hairdressers to convince their customers that "original" is another word for "bad-looking".

Men's hairstyles remain simpler by comparison, despite the efforts of stylists to compete with the women's in complexity. Perhaps, there is really a natural lack of concern over appearance in some men. Although a barber's now provides different kinds of services, a trip to a barber's still means a haircut, a shampoo and a shave to most men. Nevertheless, even simple operations like these work wonders for one's appearance. They can turn a dishevelled beggar into a successful businessman. Freshness, brightness and optimism are all conveyed by a proper hairstyle.

参考译文

男 士 发 型

在一些国家，长发已经流行了十多年了。因此，人们往往通过发型来区分性别，但现在人们已经认识到，通过发型来判断性别很容易出错，所以要谨慎使用发型来区分性别。通过一个人的走路方式、身材体形和着装来判断性别更可靠。值得一提的是，男性的长发正在逐渐受到冷落。

事实上，如果关注到发型，就会发现如今男性和女性留着大致相同的发型。当然，这并不是说，男性理发店和女士美容院之间的差异不再存在，但我们确实发现两种店都提供类似的服务。如今，一位男士进理发店不只为剪发，他也可能会想烫一个和任何窈窕淑女一样的波浪发型。甚至被认为是男子专利的剃须，也以另一种形式出现在女士美容厅。虽然整个精细过程不太容易理解，但电解作用在去除女士面部毛发方面与剃须刀及剃须霜修理男士胡须一样高效。

有些人还是喜欢传统的发型，认为这种风格更自然。为了改变人们的这种观念，发型师们发明了很多甚至我们都很难叫出名字的设备。其中，最有代表性的是理发剪和卷发器，这些发明运用了生化、电子和心理学等方面的知识。例如，发胶、护发素和生发剂是时尚和化学催生的产品；同样，如果没有现代物理学的知识，就没有各种各样使用方便的吹风机和烘发机等；至于心理学，这是理发师们使用最广泛的知识，他们运用各种心理学知识让客人相信"自然、原始"的发型是"丑"的代名词。

尽管发型师们竭尽所能让男士的发型和花样百出的女士发型相竞争，相比较而言，男士的发型仍然要简单得多。或许一些男性天生就不太关注自己外貌。虽然现在理发店提供不同种类的服务，但对于大多数男性来说，理发师的工作仍然是理发、洗发和剃须。但是，像这些简单操作的工作仍然能完全改变一个人的外貌。他们可以把一个披头散发的乞丐变成一个成功的商人。一个适当的发型不仅让人感受到你的生气勃勃、活泼愉快，还能感受到你的积极乐观。

Question

Why isn't it possible sometimes to distinguish a man from a woman by their hair style？

Unit 3 Recreation

Listening Practice

1. Listen to the dialogue and fill in the blanks.

S: Good evening. Welcome to _____. Can I help you?

G: Sure. Is there a discotheque in the hotel?

S: Yes, it's in _____, _____.

G: Is there any other entertainment? We want to relax a bit.

S: Yes, we have got Karaoke next to the _____.

G: How do you charge for it?

S: As for Karaoke, _____per hour for a medium room, _____per hour for a large room, and 180 yuan for a _____.

G: We'd like a private room from _____.

S: That's the _____. It's 200 yuan per hour.

G: OK. Thank you.

S: You are welcome and _____.

2. Listen and fill in the missing information.

Activity: _____

Arriving Time: _____

Room type:_____

Guest's name: _____

Guest's telephone number: _____

Situational Dialogues

1. At the Ball Room

(Scene: Mr. and Mrs. Black are walking to the nightclub. They stop in front of the ball room and ask for some information about it.)

(S: Staff, M: Mrs. Blaok, B: Mr. Black)

S: Good evening, sir and madam. Welcome to our Moon Star Club. What can I do for you?

M: Good evening. Would you give us some information about dancing hall?

S: Certainly, madam. Most young people like modern dances, such as rock & roll, the twist and the break dance. What dance do you like?

M: I like the old graceful style of dances as waltz, rumba, tango and fox trot.

S: I admire you! The waltz is available tonight.

B: Great. Do you have a discount for ladies?

S: Yes, we give ladies a 50 % discount.

B: Good. We'll have a try now.

S: OK, Would you please let me put your clothes at the cloak room?

B: Thank you.

S: Now follow me, please. Where would you like to sit, at a table or at the bar?

B: Well, I prefer to sit not far away from the bar.

S: This way, please.

M: I like it here.

M: The dance hall looks very nice and the music is wonderful.

S: I'm glad you like it. Would you like something to drink?

M: Yes, I'd like a glass of ginger ale with ice. Richard, what would you like?

B: Do you have a dry white wine?

S: How about a California Chablis?

B: Chablis will be fine.

S: Here are your drinks. Please enjoy them.

2. At Karaoke Bar

(Scene: After dinner, Mr. and Mrs. Steward go to the Karaoke bar. The staff is talking with them.)

(S: Staff, M: Mr. Steward, MS: Mrs. Steward, W: Waiter)

S: Good evening. Welcome to our Recreation center. How many persons do you have?

M: Two.

S: Yes, sir. Which do you prefer, VIP room or regular room?

MS: How do you charge?

S: For VIP room, 180 yuan per hour, not including the drinks. 80 yuan for regular room including the drinks. Are you staying in our hotel?

M: Yes, we are. We are in Room 1622.

S: Mr...?

M: Steward. Here is our room card.

S: OK, Mr. Steward. Since you are registered guests, you can have a 10% discount.

M: Oh, I see. VIP room, please.

S: Follow me, please. Is this room all right?

M: That's good.

W: Welcome to our bar, sir and madam. Here is a song list, song order slip and a pen. Just write down the songs you want on the slip. Our DJ will prepare the songs for you. By the way, what would you like to drink? Here is the drink list.

M: I'd like some soda water.

W: OK. What about you, madam?

MS: A glass of orange juice，please. Would you tell us what kinds of songs you have got here?

W: We have Mandarin，Cantonese and Taiwanese songs，English songs, Italian songs，Japanese songs, and French songs. You name it，and we have it. You may consult the song list. Take your time. I'll be with you shortly.

　　…

W: Here're your soda water and orange juice. Can I take your song order now?

M: Yes. I'd like to sing the English song "My Heart Stays with You".

W: Yes, sir. Please wait a moment. Your first song "My Heart Stays with You" will begin soon. Enjoy your time.

　　…

MS: (She waves to the waitress.) May we have the bill?

W: Yes, please sign your name here. The hotel will charge you when you leave.

MS: Thank you.

W: You're welcome. Goodbye.

3. At Chess and Card Room

(Scene: Mr. and Mrs. Green are walking to the Mahjong room. A staff is greeting them.)

(S: Staff, M: Mr. Green, G: Mrs. Green)

S: Good afternoon, sir and madam. Welcome to the Mahjong room.

M: Mahjong, what is it?

S: Mahjong, also known as Mah Jong, is a traditional Chinese recreational game. Mahjong is very similar to Rummy and is played with tiles.

M: Can we play mahjong now?

S: Certainly, yes, sir. But you still need two other persons to play together. It is somewhat like playing cards.

M: Really? Sounds interesting. Would you say something more?

S: OK. It needs four people to play mahjong. And if you are really interested in playing, we have a supervisor here who can teach you how to play with it and at the same time he'll tell you all the detailed regulations.

G: What's the price?

S: If it is in a single room，the price is 200 yuan till midnight, including small towels tea and a dish of peanuts. Of course, you can order drinks, but that will be charged. If one would like to play in the hall where there are many other tables together, the price is much cheaper, only 80yuan till midnight.

G: Richard, I don't think we can learn to play mahjong at once. Besides, it seems very time-consuming.

M: What a pity! Thank you very much. Maybe next time. Bye-bye.

S: Next time, please have a try. Bye-bye.

4. In the Tea Room

(Scene: Mrs. Green is at the tea room. A staff is serving her.)

(S: Staff, G: Mrs. Green)

S: Welcome to our tea room. What can I do for you, madam?

G: I'd like some tea, please.

S: We offer green tea, black tea, oolong tea, scented tea and compressed tea. Which tea do you prefer?

G: Green tea, please.

S: About green tea, we have got Dragon Well tea from Hangzhou and Bi Luo Chun from Jiangsu.

G: I've heard a lot about Dragon Well tea. So, Dragon Well tea, please. By the way, what kind of black tea do you have?

S: The most famous one is oolong. It's said that it can help people reduce weight.

G: Really? You mean I should drink some oolong, don't you?

S: No. I should say you're slim and green tea is the wisest choice, especially in summer.

G: Thank you. What's jasmine tea?

S: Oh, it's a kind of green tea with the smell of jasmine. Beijing people like it very much. They prefer a strong tasting tea.

G: I see.

S: Would you like to have your tea now, madam?

G: Yes, please.

S: A cup of Dragon Well tea for you.

G: That's right.

Words and Expressions

ball room		歌舞厅	DJ (disk jockey)	流行音乐节目主持人
rock & roll	n.	摇滚舞	mahjong	n. 麻将
twist	n.	扭摆舞	Rummy	n. 拉米(一种纸牌游戏)
rumba	n.	伦巴	tile	n. 瓦；瓷砖；墙砖；地砖
tango	n.	探戈	supervisor	n. 指导
cloak room		衣帽间；存衣处	regulation	n. 规章；规则，规定；条例
nightclub	n.	夜总会	peanut	n. 花生；花生果；花生米
waltz	n.	华尔兹	time-consuming adj. 费时的；旷日持久的
the break dance		霹雳舞	Dragon Well tea	龙井茶
fox trot	n.	狐步舞	black tea	红茶
available	adj.	可用的；可得到的	oolong tea	乌龙茶

ginger ale		姜味较淡的姜汁汽水	slim	*adj.*	苗条的，纤细的
Chablis	*n.*	夏布利白葡萄酒	scented tea		花茶
Mandarin	*n.*	普通话	compressed tea		茶砖或砖茶
Cantonese	*adj.*	广东的	jasmine	*n.*	茉莉花
Taiwanese	*adj.*	台湾的			

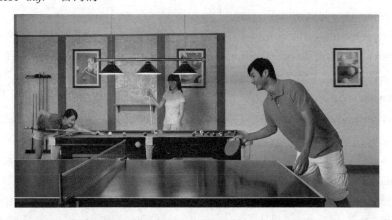

Learn by Heart

1. 一些游戏名称

扑克牌	playing card/squeezer	(5 人玩的)抢位置游戏	puss-in-the-corner
象棋	chess	排号码牌游戏	lotto
藏手帕	hunt-the-thimble	多米诺骨牌	domino
骰子游戏	ludo	桥牌	bridge
谜语	riddle	纵横拼字谜	crossword puzzle
凭动作猜字谜	charade		

2. 康乐服务常用语

The waltz is available tonight.
今晚我们有华尔兹舞曲。

Would you please let me put your clothes at the cloak room?
需要我帮您把衣服放到衣帽间吗？

Which do you prefer, VIP room or regular room?
您需要什么房间，VIP 房还是普通房？

For VIP room, 180 yuan per hour, not including the drinks.
VIP 房是每小时 180 元人民币，不包含酒水。

Since you are registered guests，you can have a 10% discount.
您是我们的住店客人，可以享受 9 折优惠。

You name it, and we have it.
您想要的我们这里都有。

Can I take your song order now?

现在您准备好点歌了吗？

If it is in a single room, the price is 200 yuan till midnight, including small towels, tea and a dish of peanuts.

单人间是 200 元，一直到午夜，包含小毛巾，茶水和一盘花生。

We offer green tea, black tea, oolong tea, scented tea and compressed tea.

我们这里有绿茶、红茶、乌龙茶、花茶和砖茶。

Class Activity Role-Play

Scene One: Tom White and his wife enter the ball room. They would like to enjoy themselves here. You，the waitress(or waiter)tell them some information about it.

Scene Two: You are receiving some American young people who enter your KTV room to celebrate one of their friends' birthday.

Further Reading

Health Spa

An ever-increasing emphasis on physical fitness and overall health has provided a new and major amenity which many resort hotels can offer——the health spa.

The original concept of spas was associated with springs producing mineral water containing various salts, such as carbonates, phosphates and sulphated metals, i. e. magnesium, calcium, lithium, potassium and sodium. It is a place where people come for cures of various diseases.

However, recently the popularity of the traditional mineral water destinations has decreased, and they have been replaced as destinations in demand by new modern-style spas offering a wide range of facilities and services.

Spa facilities can be best described as both recreational and exercise-oriented. Many of the more recreational facilities are commonly found as part of a hotel's guest facilities.

Swimming pools, tennis course, handball and racquetball courts are commonly used by spa activity participants but also by regular hotel guests.

Other spa facility programs can be jogging or running tracks, aerobic exercises, and various kinds of exercise machines. There are also some types of treatment offered in spas, such as the body or facial massage and other massages, the herbal wrap which is used to relax and soothe the muscles and detox the skin.

Where spa programs are offered as an option to hotel guests, the spa should be operated as an operation department of the hotel, however, the management of the department and the spa facility should be in the hands of a professional spa manager.

参考译文

健身温泉水疗

随着人们对体能和健康的日益重视，许多度假酒店开始提供一个新型舒适设施服务——健身温泉水疗。

对水疗最原始的概念来自于含有碳酸盐、磷酸盐和硫酸盐等多种盐类，以及富含镁、钙、锂、钾、钠等多种金属的矿泉水。它是人们治疗各种疾病的地方。

然而，最近传统矿泉水旅游景区的人气有所下降，它们已经被拥有新现代风格的，可提供各种设施和服务的水疗中心所替代。

各种水疗设施既可以是娱乐的也应该是以运动为导向的。许多康乐设施是酒店设施的一部分。

不仅泡温泉的客人经常光顾游泳池、网球、手球和壁球场，酒店常住客人也经常来玩。

其他水疗设施可以是慢跑或跑道、有氧运动，以及各种健身器材。也有一些温泉水疗提供如身体或面部等其他按摩，以及放松和舒缓肌肉和皮肤的排毒草药包等各方面的疗养。

酒店为客人提供水疗服务，水疗中心应作为酒店的一个部门经营，其运营和设施应由专业的水疗经理来管理。

Question

Do you like health spa?

Chapter

5

Business Center

Unit 1 At the Bank

【听力音频】

Listening Practice

1. Listen to the dialogue and fill in the blanks.

(C: Clerk, B: Mr. Bellow)

C: Good morning. Business Center. May I help you?

B: Good morning. This is Henry Bellow calling from_____. Would you mind giving me some information on your services?

C: Certainly not, Mr. Bellow. We have _____facilities and secretarial assistance _____ to the needs of all our business guests.

B: I have some documents to be typed at the moment and I hope they will be ready before_____ today.

C: How many pieces are they in all?

B: They will be about _____.

C: Well, it's rather a tough job, but we'll try our best, Mr. Bellow.

B: Good. I'd really appreciate if it could be arranged.

2. Listen and fill in the missing information.

How much to change:_____

What's the exchange rate _____

How to change_____

Reason to keep this exchange memo_____

Situational Dialogues

1. Opening a Bank Account

(Scene: Mrs. Green wants to open a checking-savings account in the bank. The clerk is receiving her.)

(C: Clerk, G: Mrs. Green)

C: Good morning，Mrs. Green. What can I do for you?

G: I want to open a checking-savings account in the bank. Will 50 US dollars' deposit be enough for opening an account?

C: Yes. Mrs. Green. Our minimum deposit for a savings account is US $50. Now please first fill in this form and then go to Window 3.

G: Thank you.

C: It's my pleasure.

2. Asking about Savings

(Scene: Grace wants to draw on her account to pay the things she bought in China, and the clerk is serving her.)

Clerk: Can I help you, Miss?

Grace: Yes. I want to pay for the things I bought in China. Can I draw on my account here?

Clerk: Of course. What do you want, US dollars or Euros?

Grace: Euros.

Clerk: How much do you want?

Grace: 500 Euros.

Clerk: According to today's rate, one Euro is equivalent to 7.11 yuan. Here is RMB 3555 yuan. Keep the exchange memo, please.

Grace: Thank you.

3. Asking about Deposit

(Scene: A customer wants to open an account and the clerk is receiving him.)

Clerk: Good morning, sir.

Customer: Good morning. I want to open an account here.

Clerk: What kind of account did you have in your hand? A deposit or a current account?

Customer: A current account.

Clerk: How much do you want to deposit with us?

Customer: 800 Euros.

Clerk: OK. Please fill in this form.

Customer: Thank you.

4. Currency Exchange

(Scene: A customer wants to exchange US dollar against RMB, and the clerk is serving him.)

(B: Bank clerk, C: Customer)

C: Excuse me, may I exchange foreign currency against RMB here?

B: Fill up the application form and sign your name, please.

C: OK.

B: Your sum, please?

C: 500 dollars.

B: The exchange rate fluctuates every day. Let me check. According to the list of exchange rate quotation today, 100 dollars can be exchanged for RMB 626 in cash, or for RMB 827 in traveler's cheque. Which dou you prefer, in cash, or in cheque?

C: The rate for cheque seems to be more favorable.

B: So you prefer traveler's cheque? Since the rate is RMB 827 against USD 100, USD 500 will be RMB 4135.

C: Yes.

B: But you need to pay a 0.75% commission for the exchange.

C: OK. Then i will get RMB 4104.

B: Correct. Any requirement for the face amount?

C: No requirement.

B: OK. Here you are.

Words and Expressions

checking account		支票账户	memo *n.*	水单
savings account		储蓄账户	deposit account	定期存款账户
deposit	*n.*	存款；保证金；押金；定金		
current account		活期存款账户	open an account	开户
exchange	*vt.*	交换；调换；兑换		
minimum	*adj.*	最小的，最少的，最低的		
cash	*n. & v.*	现金；兑现		
draw	*v.*	提取；领取	check *n.*	支票
Euro	*n.*	欧元	service charge	服务费
rate	*n.*	比例，率；比率	traveler's checks	旅行支票
be equivalent to		相等[当]于……，等(同)		

Learn by Heart

1. 各银行名称

中央银行 The Central Bank

中国人民银行 The People's Bank of China

中国银行 Bank of China

中国建设银行 China Construction Bank

中国农业银行 Agricultural Bank of China

中国工商银行 Industrial and Commercial Bank of China

中国民生银行 China Minsheng Bank

招商银行 China Merchants Bank

兴业银行 Industrial Bank

交通银行 Bank of Communications

中国光大银行 China Everbright Bank

中信银行 China CITIC Bank

广东发展银行 China Guangfa Bank

上海浦东发展银行 Shanghai Pudong Development Bank

平安银行 Ping an Bank

街道储蓄所 neighborhood savings bank

中国邮政储蓄银行 Postal Savings Bank of China

摩根大通银行 J. P. Morgan

花旗银行 Gitibank, N. A.

汇丰银行 HSBC Bank (China)

2. 银行服务常用语

I want to open a checking-savings account in the bank.
我想在银行里开个支票储蓄账户。

Will 50 US dollars' deposit be enough for opening an account?
最低存款 50 美元够了吗？

Now please first fill in this form and then go to Window 3.
请先填写这张表格，然后去 3 号窗。

Can I draw on my account here?
我可以在此提取存款吗？

Which do you want，US dollars or Euros?
您要哪种货币，美元还是欧元？

According to today's rate，one Euro is equivalent to 7.11 RMB yuan.
根据今天的汇率，1 欧元兑 7.11 元人民币。

Keep the exchange memo，please.
请保管好水单。

I want to open an account here.
我想在银行开个账户。

What kind of account did you have in your hand? A deposit or a current account?
您想要哪种账户？定期还是活期存款？

How much do you want to deposit with us?
您想在我们这儿存多少钱？

I'd like to cash this check, please.
请帮我兑现这张支票。

Do you want large or small bills?

您想要大额钞票还是小额的？

What do you want them?

要多大面额的？

Two fifties and some twenties would be fine.

两张 50 面值的，其余的要 20 面值的。

Do you want the whole amount in traveler's checks?

您想把您所有的钱都买成旅行支票吗？

Could you sign your name here on the bank?

可以麻烦您在支票背面签上您的名字吗？

I'd like to withdraw US $300 from my account.

我想取 300 美元。

I want to deposit US $ 200 in my account.

我想在我的账户中存 200 美元。

What kind of account would you like?

你想开什么账户？

Class Activity Role-Play

Scene One: Mr. Black likes to open a bank account. You give him some information about it.

Scene Two: You are working in the bank and now are talking to Mrs. Jones, who wants to change some money.

Further Reading

Foreign Exchange

Foreign exchange refers to currency and money claims, such as bank balances and bank drafts, which is expressed in the equivalent value in foreign money. Thus, a pound sterling note is money in Great Britain, but is foreign exchange in the USA. Deposit of US $1000 in an American bank to the account of a French company constitues that amount of foreign exchange in France. The term foreign exchange is also used to refer to transactions involving the conversion of money of one country into that of another or to the international transfer of money and credit instruments.

The use of foreign exchange arises because different nations have different monetary units, and the currency of one country cannot be used for making payments in another country. Because of trade, and other transactions between individuals and business enterprises of different countries, it becomes necessary to convert money into the currency of other countries in order to pay for goods or services in those countries.

参考译文

外　汇

外汇是指用等价外国货币形式表现出来的货币和货币债权，如银行往来余额和银行汇票。因此，一英镑钞票在英国是货币，而在美国就是外汇。存入美国银行的法国公司账户上的 1000 美元就成了同样金额的法国外汇。外汇一词同样用来表示涉及货币从一国向另一国转换的交易或涉及国际货币和信用票据的转换。

外汇之所以产生是因为不同国家采用不同货币单位，一个国家的货币不能用来对另一国家进行支付。由于不同国家之间的私人和公司企业进行贸易、旅游和其他不同的交易活动，有必要将一国的货币转换成别国货币以便支付这些国家所提供的商品或服务。

Question

Do you like coins?

Unit 2　At the Post Office

【听力音频】

Listening Practice

1. Listen to the dialogue and fill in the blanks.

(S: Mr. Smith, C: Clerk)

S: Good morning, Miss. I'd like you to help me. Is it all right?

C: Yes, of course, sir.

S: Just now I received an important call from my company. I'm leaving for Wuhan and will do business for a few days. You see, Christmas is coming, I'd like to send some _____ to my family members. Would you mail them for me?

C: No problem. How would you like to send them, by _____ or by_____?

S: How long does it take by surface mail?

C: At least_____.

S: It's too long. How long does it take by air?

C: As far as I know, about _____.

S: I prefer it by air. I really hope they will receive them before Christmas. What is the total postage?

C: Let me check…The total postage is _____.

S: OK, here is the money for the postage.

C: I'll see to it. Here are your change and the receipt. Have a pleasant journey.

2. Listen and fill in the missing information.

The guest needs: _____

Envelope types: _____

Mail types: _____

Mail time: _____

Postage altogether: _____

Situational Dialogues

1. Sending a Letter and Picking Up Package at the Post Office

(Scene: A customer goes to the post office and the clerk is serving him.)

Clerk:　　Next please…Hello, may I help you, sir?

Customer: Yes, I want to send a certified airmail letter to China.

Clerk:　　OK, it comes to US $ 3.45.

Customer: Here is US $5.

Clerk:　　Here is your change. Please wait for your receipt of the registered mail.

(After a while…)

Clerk:　　Here is your receipt. Anything else?

Customer: Yes, two aerograms, ten postcards, one roll of fifty 15-cent stamps and five airmail stamps.

Clerk:　　That's be US $11.60. Anything else?

Customer: I also want to pick up my package. This is the notice.

Clerk:　　Let me see…Hm…Just a minute. Here it is. We need your signature on this note.

Customer: OK. By the way, what is the size and weight limit for mailing a package?

Clerk:　　It is US $3 per kilo. The size is not more than 33 inches by 25 by 12. It also must be tied with string.

Customer: Can you write it down for me?

Clerk:　　Sure.

Customer: Oh, one more thing. Can I have this letter airmailed to New York?

Clerk:　　Well, we send all the first class mail by plane to the East Coast, so you don't need an airmail stamp.

Customer: I see. By the way, where can I mail this letter?

Clerk:　　Drop it in the mail box marked "Out Of Town" at the corner.

Customer: Thank you very much.

Clerk:　　You are welcome.

2. Sending a Letter

(Scene: Jack wants to send a letter, and he is asking the receptionist about the way to the post office.)

(J: Jack, R: Receptionist)

J: Excuse me, but could you please tell me where the nearest post office is? I'm going to mail a letter.

R: Do you wish to send it as an ordinary or registered letter?

J: What's the difference?

R: If you want to post an ordinary letter, you needn't go to the post office, you can drop it into the nearest pillar-box.

J: I want to send this letter by registered mail.

R: In that case, you'll have to go to the post office.

J: Thank you.

(Then Jack is now at the post office.)

J: Good afternoon. I want to send this letter to Beijing by registered mail. Is there enough postage on it?

C: The letter is rather heavy. You'd better have it weighed.

J: How much does it weigh? Is it overweight?

C: It's 6 grams overweight. You need 2 yuan stamps.

J: Can I catch the last post today?

C: Oh, certainly. The last mail goes out at 6:30.

J: Thank you.

3. Sending parcels

(Scene: A customer walks into the post office to send a parcel, and the clerk is giving him some information.)

(C: Customer, C1: Clerk 1, C2: Clerk 2)

C: Excuse me, is this the parcel post counter?

C1: No. It's at counter 6, right over there.

C: (At counter.) I'd like to send this parcel by post.

C2: What's in it, please?

C: Just a few shirts and blouses.

C2: OK. You may wrap it now. Please fill in this form and label it.

C: Will it do, then?

C2: Yes, sir. It's within the prescribed limit. Would you like to have it registered?

C: Yeah. Please weigh it, and would you tell me whether this parcel is too large for parcel post?

C2: Yes. And by air or ordinary mail?

C: I'd rather send it by ordinary mail. Then, what's the postage I have to pay?

C2: Five dollars and thirty cents.

C: Here you are.

C2: Here's the receipt.

C: Thank you so much.

C2: You're welcome.

4. Sending Money

(Scene: Bob wishes to send some money to London. The clerks are serving him.)

(C1: Clerk 1, B: Bob, C2: Clerk 2)

C1: Good morning. Can I help you?

B: Good morning. I wish to send a sum of 100 Euros to London. Would it be better to get a money order or send it in a registered letter?

C1: It depends.

B: Then I'd like to get a postal order.

C1: Postal orders are over there, at Counter No.5.

   …

B: Please give me a postal order for 100 Euros.

C2: Will you fill in the money order form? Please write down the names and addresses of both the sender and the recipient legibly and do not abbreviate or use initials. And don't forget the reverse side of the form. You can put down the sender's remarks here, if you like.

B: Is the form filled in properly?

C2: Yes.

B: Thank you very much.

C2: You are welcome.

Words and Expressions

certified airmail	航空挂号信	label	*n.&v.* 标签，贴标签于
registered mail	挂号信	prescribed	*adj.* 规定的
receipt	*n.* 收据，收条	ordinary mail	*n.* 平信
aerogram	*n.* 航空信件，航空邮简	money order	汇款单，汇票
roll	*n.* 名单，名册	postal order	邮政汇票
string	*n.* 绳子	sender	*n.* 寄件人
mail box	邮箱，信箱	recipient	*n.* 收信人
ordinary letter	平信	legibly	*ad.* 字迹清楚地
registered letter	挂号信	abbreviate	*v.* 缩写
pillar-box	邮筒	initial	*n.* (姓名或组织名称等)首字母
postage	*n.* 邮资		
parcel post counter	包裹邮寄台	reverse	*adj.* 背面的，反面的
wrap	*v.* 包，裹	remarks	*n.* 附言，备注

Learn by Heart

1. 邮局基本词汇

分拣台   sorting table   汇票，汇单   money order, postal order

快递信件	express delivery letter	电汇汇单	telegraphic money order
收信人	addressee	邮资已付	postage paid
收件人	consignee	附加邮资	extra postage
收款人	payee	货到付款	cash on deliver
发信人	sender		

2. 邮局常用语

I want to send a certified airmail letter to China.
我想寄一封去中国的航空挂号信。

Here is your change. Please wait for your receipt of the registered mail.
这是找您的钱，请等一下，还有挂号信回执。

Two aerograms, ten postcards, one roll of fifty 15-cent stamps and five airmail stamps.
还要两张航空邮简，10 张明信片，一本装有 50 张 15 美分邮票的邮票簿，5 张航空邮票。

I also want to pick up my package. This is the notice.
我还想提取包裹，这是取包裹单。

We need your signature on this note.
我们需要您在单上签名。

By the way, what is the size and weight limit for mailing a package?
顺便问一下，邮寄包裹的体积和重量有什么限制？

It is US $3 per kilo. The size is not more than 33 inches by 25 by 12. It also must be tied with string.
每公斤 3 美元。体积不超过 33 英寸长、25 英寸宽、12 英寸高。包裹还必须用绳子捆绑。

Can I have this letter airmailed to New York?
这封信可以用航空寄往纽约吗？

Drop it in the mail box marked "Out Of Town" at the corner.
在那个角上，把信投进标有"外地"的邮筒里。

Do you wish to send it as an ordinary or registered letter?
您要寄平信还是挂号信？

It's overweight. You'll have to pay extra.
它超重了。您得另付邮资。

I wish to send a sum of 100 Euros to London. Would it be better to get a money order or send it in a registered letter?
我想寄 100 欧元到伦敦去。用邮政汇票好还是用保价信寄钞票好？

Please write down the names and addresses of both the sender and the recipient legibly and do not abbreviate or use initials.
请填上汇款人与收款人的姓名、地址。字迹要清楚，不要缩写，要用全称。

And don't forget the reverse side of the form. You can put down the sender's remarks here, if you like.
别忘了汇票的反面也要填写。如果需要，您可以在这里写上汇款人的附言。

Class Activity Role-Play

Scene One: Mr. Black wants to send a package to Los Angeles, but it's the first time for him in China. Please help him.

Scene Two: A guest comes to mail some urgent letters to his business partners. You, the business clerk suggest that he could have express service.

Further Reading

U. S. Postal Service

Phone books have white, blue and yellow pages. The white pages list people with phones by last name. The blue pages contain numbers of city services, government services, and public schools. Business and professional services are listed in a special classified directory—the Yellow pages.

The area covered by one area code may be small or large. For example, New York City has one area code, but so does the whole state of Oregon. There is an area code map of the U. S. and Canada in the front of the white pages.

Pay phones have numbers in the U. S. This means you can arrange to call a friend at a phone booth. Or if you are making a long distance call and run out of money, give the number on your phone to the person you're talking to. Then hang up the receiver and he can call you back.

If you make a long distance call and get a wrong number, call the operator and explain what happened. This means that you can make the call again to the right number without having to pay more money; or you can have the phone company mail you a credit coupon that has the same value as the phone call.

Some companies advertise a service called WATS. You can dial a special number without a long distance charge. These are called "toll-free numbers" and the area code for all of them is 800. WATS means Wide Area Telephone Service.

The U. S. Postal Service has competitiors. Courier services send or transmit messages; parcels and freight are delivered by a number of companies. Check the Yellow Pages for details.

There are two ways of sending things safely through the post office: registered and certified mail. Certified is much cheaper. Ask at the post office for more information.

You can have mail sent to you through General Delivery in any town. It will be held ten days, or up to a month if the sender writes "Please hold 30 days" on the envelope. Using the zip code will speed up delivery.

Remember, you cannot usually send telegrams or make telephone calls from U. S. post offices.

参考译文

美国的邮政服务

电话簿有白页、蓝页和黄页。白页刊登用户个人的电话号码，是按姓氏排列的。蓝页刊登城市服务、政府机构和公立学校的电话号码。黄页是商业和专业机构的分类电话号码。

一个区号的范围可大可小。例如，纽约市有一个区号，但是整个俄勒冈州也只有一个区号。在电话簿白页前有一张美国和加拿大区号的地图。

美国的付费电话是有号码的。这就是说，你可以在电话亭给朋友打电话。如果你在打长途电话时钱用完了，那么你可以把你的电话号码告诉对方。然后，你挂上听筒，对方就能给你打电话。

如果你打长途时电话号码拨错了，那么请给接线员打电话解释一下情况，你就可以再打正确的号码而不用另外付费；你也可以让电话公司寄给你退回电话费用的付款凭证。

有些公司推荐人们使用叫做 WATS 的服务项目。你可以拨一个特定的电话号码而不用付长途电话费。这种电话叫做"免费长途电话"，其区号都是 800。WATS 的意思是"跨地区电话服务"。

美国的邮政服务是有竞争对手的。信使专递可以收发信函；许多公司也运送包裹和货物。欲知详情，请看电话簿的黄页。

通过邮局进行安全投递有两种方式：挂号邮件和保证邮件。保证邮件要便宜很多。要知道更多的情况，请到邮局了解。

你在任何城市都可以通过"存局候领"收到邮件。邮局将保留 10 天，如果发信人在信封上写上"请保留 30 天"，邮局将最多保留 1 个月。使用邮政编码能加快投递。

请记住，通常你不能在美国邮局发电报或打电话。

Question

How to post a letter in America?

Unit 3   Booking Tickets

Listening Practice

【听力音频】

1. Listen to the dialogue and fill in the blanks.

(S: Staff, P: Passenger)

S: Eastern Airline. How can I help you?

P: Is CAAC Flight 173 to New York on schedule?

S: Yes. They make good time. For which date, please?

P: _____. What time does it get there?

S: It's scheduled to arrive at _____.

P: What time will it depart?

S: Flight 173 will depart on schedule at 03:15.

P: Do I check in at least _____before the departure of the flight?

S: Yes, ma'am. Do you already have your ticket?

P: I've reserved one from the travel agency in Shanghai.

S: Very good. Which seat do you prefer, _____ or _____?

P: I'd like a window seat, please.

S: Smoking or non-smoking?

P: _____.

S: Fine._____. Enjoy your flight.

P: Thank you for your help.

2. Listen and fill in the missing information.

Leaving to Osaka on: _____

Seat: _____

Travelling members: _____   Name: _____

Room: _____   Payment: _____

Deposit: _____

Situational Dialogues

1. Booking Air Tickets

(Scene: Mr. Graham is leaving for Shanghai and he wants to book two air tickets, and the clerk is helping him.)

(G: Mr. Graham, C: Clerk)

G: Good afternoon. Could you do me a favor?

C: It's a pleasure, Mr. Graham. What is it?

G: I'm leaving for Shanghai the day after tomorrow.

C: That's August 8th, isn't it?

G: That's right.

C: Are you going there by train or by plane?

G: By plane, of course. Planes are much faster than trains. How many flights are there to Shanghai every day?

C: There are four flights every day. The planes take off at about 7:00 a.m., 10:00 a.m., 4:00 p.m. and10:00 p.m.

G: I'll take 10:00 a.m. plane，then that suits me perfectly. Will you kindly book two tickets for me?

C: Certainly, Mr. Graham. Would you please fill in this form?

G: All right. Shall I pay cash now?

C: Yes, please pay 800 yuan in advance.

G: Here you are. By the way, when can I get the tickets?

C: You can get them on the evening of August 7th.

G: That'll be fine. Thank you very much.

C: Don't mention it.

2. Ticketing Service

(Scene: A customer wants to buy two train tickets and the clerk is serving her.)

Clerk: Good morning, madam. Can I help you?

Guest: Yes, I'd like to buy two train tickets.

Clerk: Where to?

Guest: To Shanghai.

Clerk: For which date?

Guest: May 18.

Clerk: Which kind of sleeper would you prefer, hard or soft?

Guest: Can you tell me the prices of both?

Clerk: 280 yuan for a hard sleeper and 420 yuan for a soft sleeper, plus 40 yuan service charge for each.

Guest: OK，give me two soft.

Clerk: That's 920 yuan.

Guest: Here is 1,000 yuan.

Clerk: Thank you. Here are your tickets and change.

3. Confirming the Ticket by Call

(Scene: Ina Hopkins has ordered a ticket, but she wants to make a change and now she is calling the staff.)

(S: Staff, H: Ina Hopkins)

S: Reservation Centre, Global Airlines. Can I help you?

H: Yes. I'm coming to confirm my ticket.

S: May I have you name, please?

H: My name is Ina Hopkins. In fact, I have a reservation on Flight No. 916 for London, leaving New York at 2:00 p.m. tomorrow. Now I'd like to make a change of my travel schedule. Is it possible to change my booking to the day after tomorrow?

S: Certainly, madam.

H: Do you have a seat available on the same flight the day after tomorrow?

S: Could you hold the line for a few seconds? I'll check the computer.

(Later…)

S: Yes, madam. You are reconfirmed on Flight No.916 for London, leaving New York at 2:00 p.m. on December 23rd.

H: Thanks a lot.

S: You are welcome.

Words and Expressions

sleeper	n.	卧车，卧铺
soft sleeper		软卧
schedule	n.	日程安排表

Learn by Heart

1. 航空公司代码

中国国际航空公司	CA	山东航空公司	SC
中国南方航空公司	CZ	厦门航空公司	MF
中国东方航空公司	MU	上海航空公司	FM
四川航空公司	3U	鹰联航空公司	EU

| 深圳航空公司 | ZH | 春秋航空公司 | CH |
| 海南航空公司 | HU | 奥凯航空公司 | BK |

2. 票务预订常用语

Are you going there by train or by plane?
您想坐火车还是乘飞机？

How many flights are there to Shanghai every day?
每天去上海的航班有几趟？

There are four flights every day. The planes take off at about 7:00 a.m., 10:00 a.m., 4:00 p.m. and 10:00 p. m.
每天有 4 趟航班，起飞时间为上午 7 点和 10 点、下午 4 点和晚上 10 点。

Please pay a deposit of 2,500 yuan in advance.
请付 2500 元定金。

For which date?
哪一天？

Which kind of sleeper would you prefer, hard or soft?
您要什么样的座位，硬卧还是软卧？

Now I'd like to make a change of my travel schedule. Is it possible to change my booking to the day after tomorrow?
可现在我想改变一下旅行日程。能不能将我的票改到后天？

You are reconfirmed on Flight No.916 for London, leaving New York at 2:00 p.m. on December 23rd.
您已重新确认 12 月 23 日飞往伦敦的 916 航班机票，离开纽约的时间为下午 2:00。

Are you traveling alone? And will anyone be traveling with you?
您是一人旅行吗？有人和您同行吗？

Will this be one way or return?
您是要单程票还是双程票？

When would you like to depart?/ When would you like to leave, sir?
您打算什么时候起程？

When would you like to return?
您希望什么时候返回？

Do you mind a stopover? Or would you prefer direct?
您介意中途停留吗？还是要直飞？

Would you prefer economy, business, or first class?
经济舱、商务舱和头等舱，您需要哪个？

Will this be round trip or one way?
双程还是单程？

I would prefer evening flight.
我要晚上的航班。

Let me check whether there're seats available. I'm sorry we are all booked up for Flight 802 on that day.

让我查一下那天是否有座。非常抱歉 802 次航班机票已订完。

Class Activity Role-Play

Scene One: John comes to the business center to book a train ticket to Shanghai. The staff receives him.

Scene Two: Mr. & Mrs. Smith who are staying in the hotel want to book airplane tickets to Hongkong. The bell captain helps them to reserve the tickets and send the tickets to their room.

Further Reading

Railroads

Historically the railroads played a vital role in the winning of the West. In recent times, however, the high-class train service of the early 20th century has become to a rather dilapidated and neglected system which doesn't compare to European train transportation. In America a traveler is much more likely to hop on a plane than a train. Long distances automatically imply an airplane. whereas a car or a bus will do for a short trip. Originally railroads were private companies. Today, they have been grouped into a national network of passenger service called Amtrak providing first and second class accommodations. Special tours including hotels and side trips are also organized by Amtrak.

参考译文

铁　　路

在历史上，铁路为西部的崛起起了关键作用。然而，20 世纪初那种高级火车服务设施，近年来却被人忽视，已变得破旧不堪，难以与欧洲的铁路运输相比。在美国，旅行者基本上乘坐飞机而不坐火车。长距离旅行，自然要坐飞机。短距离旅行，就乘小汽车或公共汽车。起初的铁路是属于私人公司的。如今，它们重新组合成名叫 "美铁(美国全国铁路客运公司)" 的美国国家铁路客运公司的全国性服务网，提供头等座和二等座。"美铁" 还组织了特别旅行，其中包括旅馆和游览。

Question

How do you know the relation between railroads and tourism?

Unit 4　Telecommunications

【听力音频】

Listening Practice

1. Listen to the dialogue and fill in the blanks.

(T: Tourist, O: Operator)

T: Ah! This phone booth is so dark. I don't know if I dialed the number right.

O: This is_____. How can I help you?

T: Oh, great. Yes, I'd like to _____to Seoul, Korea, please.

O: What's the number you want to call?

T: The area code is 2, and the phone number there is_____.

O: May I have your name?

T: My name is_____.

O: I'm sorry. _____, please?

T: Sure. It's S like in Sally or Sherry, Y—L—V—I—A.

O: And whom would you like to talk to?

T: _____. It doesn't matter. It'll be either my mom or my dad.

O: OK. Please hold on and I'll connect you. Alright, go ahead, ma'am, your party is

_____.

T: Thank you so much.

2. Listen and fill in the missing information.

Booking:_____

To which country:_____

The guest wants to make a _____call.

The party's name:_____

The party's telephone number:_____

The guest's name:_____

The guest's room number:_____

Who will pay for the call:_____

Situational Dialogues

1. Making a Long Distance Call

(Scene: Jack is asking the operator some information about making a long distance call to England.)

(O: Operator, J: Jack)

O: Good morning. Can I help you?

J: Yes, I'd like to make a long distance call to England. Could you please tell me the rate for calling England?

O: Yes, of course. The standard rate for calling England is 0.7 yuan for every 5 seconds, excluding service charge.

J: What's your service charge, then?

O: It's 15%.

J: I see. Thank you.

2. Internet Service

(Scene: A guest is asking the clerk some information about the Internet service.)

(Guest, C: Clerk)

G: Do you have Internet service?

C: Yes, we do.

G: How much does it cost to use it?

C: It's 50 yuan an hour.

G: OK. I'd like to use it. I need to get some information.

C: All right. Let me open the line for you. There you are.

3. Talking about Telecommunications

(Scene: Mr. Black wants to fax his friend, and Zhang Hua, the staff of the hotel, gives him some suggestion.)

(Z: Zhang Hua, B: Mr. Black)

Z: Good morning. What can I do for you, Mr. Black?

B: I want to fax my friend in Britain.

Z: OK. Fax is better than telephone.

B: You are right. When you phone somebody, he may not in. But fax can be received by the fax machine even when no one is in the house.

Z: You are right. But fax is expensive. So nowadays people prefer to use the cheapest way to communicate with others—e-mail.

B: I'll try it next time. Goodbye.

Z: See you.

4. E-Commerce

(Scene: Mrs. Black encounters her friend Xiao Yang and they talks about the E-Commerce.)

(B: Mrs. Black, X: Xiao Yang)

B: Hi, Xiao Yang. What are you doing before the computer?

X: I'm choosing a new shirt.

B: What? A new shirt form the computer?

X: Yes. This form E-Commerce benefits from wideband access. Imagine going to a retail site and instead of seeing pictures and prices, looking through an interactive catalog. You can see a person demonstrate.

B: That's really interesting

X: Sure. Life is becoming more meaningful.

Words and Expressions

a long distance call		长途电话	wideband	*n.*	宽带
operator	*n.*	接线员	access	*n.*	通道，入口
Internet service		互联网服务	retail	*n.& adj.*	零售
telecommunication	*n.*	电传通信，远程通信	interactive	*a.*	互动的
fax	*n.& vt.*	传真	catalog	*n.*	目录
E-Commerce	*n.*	电子商务	demonstrate	*vt.*	展示
benefit	*vi.*	得益，受惠	meaningful	*adj.*	有意义的

Learn by Heart

1. 电话种类

叫人电话 person-to-person call

叫号电话 station-to-station call

对方付费电话 collect call

国内直拨电话 domestic direct dialing phone

国际直拨电话 international direct dialing phone

市内电话 local call

长途电话 long-distance call

会议电话 conference call

救援电话 assistance call

信用卡记账电话 credit card call

2. 电信服务常用语

I'd like to make a long distance call to England. Could you please tell me the rate for calling England?

我想打个长途去英国。您能告诉我打长途去英国的标准费用是多少吗？

The standard rate for calling England is 0.7 yuan, for every 5 seconds, excluding service charge.

打给英国的长途标准费用是每 6 秒钟 0.7 元，不包括服务费。

Do you have Internet service?

你们有互联网服务吗？

Let me open the line for you. There you are.

我给您开通。可以了。

I want to fax my friend in Britain.

我想给我的英国朋友发份传真。

But fax is expensive. So nowadays people prefer to use the cheapest way to communicate with others—e-mail.

但是发传真贵。因此，现在人们喜欢用电子邮件这种最便宜的方式进行交流。

Is it a collect call or a pay call?

是对方付费还是您自己付费？

Could you tell me the party's name and the telephone number, please?

您能告诉我对方的姓名和电话号码吗？

Do you like to make a person-to-person call or a station call?

您是打叫人电话还是叫号电话？

Please hold on and I'll connect you.

请稍等，我马上为您连接。

Class Activity Role-Play

Scene One: You are the hotel operator. Mr. Smith, a guest of the hotel, wants to make an international call.

Scene Two: Mr. Black need to send some faxes, one is the local domestic fax, and the other is international. You are the staff of the business center, tell him the price and help him.

Further Reading

Using the Telephone

Using the telephone is highly necessary while traveling. We use the telephone to tell our families, friends and other people how we getting on, to ask for information, to send messages, to ask for directions, and so on. When we are speaking on the phone, especially to someone we are not familiar with, politeness and clarity are probably the two most important things we should pay attention to. We must try our best to avoid any misunderstanding or confusion. At the same time, we must be certain to listen carefully and understand what is being said or asked of us. In simple terms, if we are calling, it is polite to offer a greeting, identify ourselves, and state our reason for calling. If we want to speak to someone in particular, ask for that person by name. If we are calling someone at a large company abroad, we might want to ask for the person's department first and then, when we are connected with someone in that department, ask for the person by name.

参考译文

使 用 电 话

在旅行期间，使用电话是十分必要的。我们打电话告诉家人和朋友自己过得怎样，还可以询问信息，传递信息，请求指示等等。当我们通电话时，特别是和不熟悉的人通电话时，礼貌与清楚可能是我们最应该注意的两件事。我们必须尽力避免误解与含混。同时，我们一定要仔细听，明白对方说什么或让我们做什么。简单地说，我们打电话时，应该先问候，然后自报家门，再说明打电话的原因，这才是礼貌的做法。如果想同某一指定的人说话，一定要说出他的名字。如果我们打电话给国外某一大公司中的某个人，我们应先找到此人的部门，接通之后，再说出所要找的人的姓名。

Question

How to telephone someone we are not familiar with?

Unit 5   Convention Services

Listening Practice

【听力音频】

1. Listen to the dialogue and fill in the blanks.

Staff: Good afternoon. _____, sir?

Guest: Hello, I need to send some faxes.

Staff: Would your fax be_____ or_____, sir?

Guest: Both, actually. I'm afraid I have to send several faxes today to both Europe and here in China. How much for, say, three pages?

Staff: An international three-page fax would cost about_____. A local domestic fax would cost around _____ for three pages.

Guest: OK. One to _____, one to_____, and two to Guangzhou. Here are the fax numbers.

Staff: Well, let me take care of them… Oh, they are_____.

Guest: Thanks._____?

Staff: That'll be_____. May I know your name and room number?

Guest: _____.

Staff: Just a minute, please. Yes, please sign the bill, Mr. Smith.

2. Listen and fill in the missing information.

Time of the conference: _____

Equipment to book: _____

Total rental: _____   Time to check the equipment: _____

Name of the tenant: _____

Situational Dialogues

1. Booking a Conference Room

(Scene: A company will hold a congress and the clerk of the business center is serving the manager of the company.)

Guest: We're going to have a congress next Monday. I'd like to book some facilities and personnel for it.

Clerk: No problem，sir. Here is the rate list.

Guest: Thank you.

Clerk: Welcome，sir. Next Monday…that's July 2nd, isn't it?

Guest: Yes. We need an auditorium for 40 people，a projector and a video-camera.

Clerk: 40 people…I suggest you rent a small auditorium. That'll be enough.

Guest: Good idea. I also need an interpreter and two messengers.

Clerk: I see. Could you please sign here? And also your telephone number, please.

Guest: OK.

Clerk: Thank you，sir. Everything will be ready by Friday afternoon. Could you come and check it?

Guest: Sure. Thanks.

Clerk: You're welcome, sir. We look forward to serving you.

2. At the Business Center

(Scene: Mrs. Bellow walks into the business center and the clerk comes to greet her.)

Clerk: Good morning, Business Center. Can I help you?

Guest: Good morning. I want two reports faxed. Would it be possible?

Clerk: Certainly, madam.

Guest: Here you are.

Clerk: It has 10 pages all together. Is that all right?

Guest: Yes.

Clerk: Could you fill in this form, please?

Guest: No problem. The fax number is 033—815—962—38—49. I have asked them to confirm the fax to me. Please send it back when you receive it.

Clerk: Fine. I'll send it back，together with your original copy to your room as soon as possible.

Guest: Does your hotel have interpreters?

Clerk: Yes. We have English and French interpreters.

Guest: The International Medical Research Conference will be held in the Easter Hall from the 12th of this month. Our English interpreter has fallen ill. We would like an interpreter who can speak good English and has some basic knowledge on medicine.

Clerk: I'll see what I can do. May I have your name and room number，please?

Guest: Mrs. Bellow，Room 1018.

Clerk: How long do you need this service，Mrs. Bellow?

Guest: I'm not quite sure. It depends on the progress of the meeting.

Clerk: Mrs. Bellow，we charge 500 yuan per day for interpreter's service. Is that all right?

Guest: OK.

Clerk: well，as soon as I have made the arrangement，I'll phone you and send a confirmation form for you to sign.

Guest: OK. It would be better if I can talk with the interpreter in advance before the conference.

Clerk: No problem. I'll arrange it. I will phone you later.

Guest: That would be nice. Thank you.

3. Arranging Catering for a Convention

(Scene: A conference planner and the hotel staff are checking up the catering plan for a convention.)

Staff: Good afternoon, Mr. Black. Nice to see you again.

Guest: Good afternoon, Nice to see you again, too.

Staff: Shall we start now?

Guest: Yes. I would like to check the meal times first.

Staff: Well, breakfast will be served in the dining room on the second floor from 7:00 a.m. till 8:00 a.m. May I know your any special requirements?

Guest: A lot of Americans are attending the conference, so please add some eggs and bacon.

Staff: No problem, sir. And lunch is at 12:30. What type of service would you require? How about the buffet lunch?

Guest: Great. But we prefer buffet with table and seat.

Staff: OK. The afternoon coffee will be served from 3:00 p.m. to 3:30 p.m. with fresh fruits and dim sum.

Guest: Good.

Staff: Do you have special wishes as regards the food?

Guest: Some delegates are Islamic, so pork and shrimps will be out for them.

Staff: I'll make a note of that. We'll satisfy all our guests whatever religious or state of health may be.

Guest: Now to accompany the meal, I think the Great Wall White Wine would be fine.

Staff: Very good, sir.

4. Convention Booking Service

(Scene: A guest would like to book some facilities and personnel for the convention.)

(G: Guest, C: Clerk)

G: We're going to have a convention next Monday. I'd like to book some facilities and personnel for it.

C: No problem, sir. Here is the rate list.

G: Thank you.

C: Welcome, sir. Next Monday... That's July 2nd, isn't it?

G: Yes. We need an auditorium for 40 people, a projector and a video-camera.

C: 40 people... I suggest you to rent a small auditorium, that'll be enough.

G: Good Idea. I also need an interpreter and two messengers.

C: I see. Could you please sign here? And also your telephone number, please.

G: OK.

C: Thank you, sir. Everything will be ready by Friday afternoon. Could you come and check it?

G: Sure. Thanks.

C: You're welcome, sir. We look forward to serving you.

Words and Expressions

congress	n.	(正式)会议，代表大会
personnel	n.	(总称)人员，员工
auditorium	n.	会堂，礼堂
projector	n.	放映机
video-camera		摄影机
interpreter	n.	口译员
conference	n.	(正式)会议；讨论会，协商会
recorder	n.	录音机
transparency	n.	透明

catering	n.	提供餐饮服务
convention	n.	会议，大会；全体与会者
dim sum		点心
delegate	n.	代表；会议代表
Islamic	adj.	伊斯兰教的
religious	adj.	宗教的，宗教上的
consecutive	adj.	连续的

Learn by Heart

1. 会议设备及服务词汇

麦克风	microphone	高射投影机	overhead projector
讲台	lectern	董事会会议室	boardroom
电视天线	satellite dish	舞厅	ballroom
活动挂图	flip chart	宴会厅	banqueting room
视频会议设备	video conferencing equipment	因特网接口	Internet access
幻灯片放映机	slide projector		

2. 会议预订常用语

I'd like to book some facilities and personnel for it.
我想预订一些设施和人员。

No problem, sir. Here is the rate list.
没问题，先生。这是价目表。

We need an auditorium for 40 people, a projector and a video-camera.

我们需要一个 40 人的大礼堂，投影机和摄像机。

40 people…I suggest you rent a small auditorium, that'll be enough.

40 人……我建议您租一间小礼堂，就足够了。

Everything will be ready by Friday afternoon. Could you come and check it?

一切都会在星期五下午准备好。您需要来确认吗？

I'll send it back，together with your original copy to your room as soon as possible.

我会尽快连同您的材料原件一起送回您的房间。

We charge 500 yuan per day for interpreter's service. Is that all right?

我们的口译人员费用是 500 元一天。您看可以吗？

Well, as soon as I have made the arrangement, I'll phone you and send a confirmation form for you to sign。

好的，我一安排好，就会给您打电话并发送确认表给您签名。

Breakfast will be served in the dining room on the second floor from 7:00 a.m. till 8:00 a.m.

早餐安排在餐厅二楼，从上午 7 点到 8 点。

May I know your any special requirements?

您还有其他要求吗？

What type of service would you require? How about the buffet lunch?

您需要什么类型的服务，自助午餐可以吗？

Do you have special wishes as regards the food?

关于食物您还有什么特别需求吗？

We'll satisfy all our guests whatever religious or state of health may be.

不管我们的客人有什么宗教习惯，或者健康状况如何，我们都将满足他们的需求。

Class Activity Role-Play

Scene one: Your company will have an annual meeting with 200 people. Call the convention manager to get information about the facilities and the services. You'll need a convention hall and a small meeting room.

Scene two: Mr. Scoot is calling the Convention Center to know some information of conference facilities in Grand Hotel.

Further Reading

Meeting

Some hotels provide the service for holding meetings for discussion or yearly party. For discussion meeting, sometimes there should be a reception at the entrance of the venue for registration and guidance. And for yearly party, some companies ask for cocktail party.

参考译文

会　议

　　一些酒店提供举办供讨论或年会用的会议服务。对于讨论会而言，有时会在举办地入口处设有一个供登记和引导用的接待处。对于年会而言，一些公司还要求举办鸡尾酒会。

Question

Do you know cocktail party?

Chapter
6

At the Hotel Store

Unit 1　At the Textile and knitwear Counter

Listening Practice

【听力音频】

1. Listen to the dialogue and fill in the blanks.

(A: Assistant, C: Clare)

A: Welcome, miss. May I help you?

C: Yes, I'd like to buy a cheongsam for myself. Are there any ready-made ones _____?

A: Yes, of course. You may choose the style you like first_____. I suggest you buy a sleeveless one. It would display your youth.

C: Really? I like this style. It's dark green, hand-embroidered, _____on the front.

A: Fine. _____? It's made from precious Suzhou silk and sells pretty very well.

C: Wow, terrific!_____?

A: Yes, the fitting box is over there.

(10 minutes later.)

C: What do you think of it on me? Do you think the slits 9 are_____?

A: No, not at all. You seem to have an excellent figure in it as if the dress were made specially for you.

C: That's most kind of you!_____.

2. Listen and fill in the missing information.

What does Mrs. Black want:_____	What size:_____
Is the color fast:_____	Do they shrink:_____;
The materials are:_____	How much is it:_____;

Situational Dialogues

【拓展音频】

1. At a Clothes Store

(Scene: On the last day of his tour in China, Tom is at the fashion shop to buy a coat for his girlfriend.)

(A: Shop Assistant, G: Guest)

At: Good morning, sir. May I help you?

G: I'd like to get a typical Chinese coat.

A: We have many types of coats with different designs. Please have a look.

G: That's great.

A: How about this one, with the mandarin duck and made of silk?

G: Well, this one is OK, but my girlfriend like the Chinese phoenix.

A: Oh, look at this pink coat. The background painting is the Chinese phoenix and flowers.

G: I like this one. The pink had a phoenix on, it would be perfect.

A: What size does she wear, sir?

G: Size 18. But I wonder if the color will fade in washing.

A: It's both colorfast and shrink-proof. And it is made of 100% silk.

G: OK. How much is it?

A: RMB 280 yuan.

G: I'll take it.

2. Casual Wear

(Scene: A guest is at the fashion shop to buy a overcoat, and the shop assistant is coming to her.)

(A: Shop Assistant, G: Guest)

A: Do you want some assistance, madam?

G: I'd like to see an overcoat for the autumn. Not too heavy and not too light.

A: How do you like this, madam?

G: It's much too light in color for the autumn. I'd rather have something darker, and a bit heavier.

A: What about this then? It's made of exceptionally good quality, pure wool, very soft.

G: Very good. May I try this on?

A: Please come with me to the fitting room.

G: I like this style, but I don't care for the color. It's loose at the waist, and it's a bit too large.

A: What about this one? We have this model in several sizes and colors, dark brown, light green, light yellow and crimson.

G: Let me see the crimson one, in my size, please.

A: Yes, madam. This is your size, it's a lovely dress and very smart. It's in fashion now. Would you like to try it?

G: All right, it just suits me. I'll take it. How much do I have to pay?

A: Three hundred yuan.

G: That's rather more than I thought of paying. I should have something cheaper.

A: Maybe a little expensive, but the quality is very good, madam. It's exceptionally good in material and the handicraft is more exquisite. It wears very well and keeps its shape.

G: All right, I'll take it. I expect it's worth it. Can I pay by Visa?

A: We don't accept Visa, you have to pay cash.

G: OK. Will you accept Master Card?

A: Yes, we do. Please go to the cash counter and pay for it. I'll wrap it up for you.

G: All right, thank you.

3. Buying Chinese Silk Fabrics

(Scene: An American guest is standing by the silk counter and looking around with great interest. A shop assistant comes with a smile.)

(A: Shop Assistant, G: Guest)

A: Good afternoon，madam. What can I do for you?

G: Good afternoon. Have you got any fabrics?

A: Certainly，madam. We have silk fabrics，woolen fabrics，cotton fabrics as well as synthetic ones.

G: Could you show me some silk fabrics?

A: Sure，Madam. We've got a good selection of them, such as sand-washed silk, figured silk，reeled pongee，georgette，satin，brocade and taffeta. You see, we have got it here. You know, Wuxi and Suzhou are famous for silk production. Which do you prefer?

G: Figured satin, please.

A: I see. This is tapestry satin, and that is changeable satin.

G: That one looks beautiful. Will you please let me have a close look at it? How nice! Ah, you see, I need an evening dress. How many yards do you think I should buy?

A: Sorry，we don't sell fabrics by the yard，but by the meter. May you allow me to take your size? (The shop assistant takes the customer's size.)Two meters will be enough.

G: Thank you. Hum, I wonder if the color will fade in washing.

A: It's colorfast. But please wash it in lukewarm water with certain amount of special detergent for silk washing and rinse it well. Don't rub or wring it. It needs ironing before wearing it.

G: Thanks. This is great. Besides, I want some taffeta for my blouse.

A: Which color do you prefer?

G: Prefer light colors.

A: Here's a light one. It's silver. Will this do?

G: Oh, silver doesn't agree to me. Do you have any other colors?

A: Yes, madam. What about ivory?

G: Ivory is my favorite. Please give me one meter.

A: Yes, madam. Anything else?

G: No. How much do I owe you then?

A: A moment, please. Two meters is 146 yuan，and one meter is 75 yuan. That will be 221 yuan altogether.

G: Can I pay with traveler's checks?

A: We don't accept traveler's checks, I'm afraid.

G: Will Master Card do?

A: Yes. May I have a print of your card?

(The shop assistant print the card and wraps up the fabrics.)

G: OK. Thank you.

4. Fashion

(Scene: A customer enters the shopping arcade, attracted by the beautiful dresses. A shop assistant is receiving her.)

(C: Customer, A: Shop Assistant)

C: I'd like to buy a dress closely related to Chinese culture as a reminder of my China trip. What do you think will be the most suitable for me?

A: Well, madam. You have an excellent figure. Chi-pao is so popular with young ladies nowadays in China, so I think a Chi-pao will fit you.

C: Chi-pao? Would you show me one，please?

A: Certainly. How do you like this one? It's made of velvet. Black is quite in fashion this year.

C: Ah，that's my favorite color. I like it very much. May I try it on?

A: Sure，madam. Please come with me to the fitting room.

C: It looks gorgeous，but it's a bit too tight at the waist. What a shame!

A: What do you think of this one?

C: It's really elegant，but I'm afraid it's still a little tight across the shoulders.

A: I see. Please try that pink one, madam. It's made of brocade.

C: I like the style very much and the size fits me nicely. But don't you think this pink is too bright for me?

A: Yes, it is a very bright pink. Try that dark green one then.

C: It looks terrific on me. I'll take it. But I wonder if it is colorfast.

A: Yes. All the garments here are colorfast.

C: How much do you charge for this?

A: 820 yuan.

C: My god, that's too expensive.

A: It might be a little expensive，but the material is of the best quality, and our workmanship is the best in this city. It's worth every penny of it.

C: All right.

Words and Expressions

textile	*n.*	纺织品；纺织原料	changeable satin		闪光缎
knitwear	*n.*	(总称)针织衣物	evening dress		晚礼服
dressing room		更衣室；化妆室	yard	*n.*	码
fade	*vi.*	(颜色)褪去	lukewarm water		温水

colorfast	adj.	不褪色的	detergent	n.	洗洁剂，洗衣粉；去垢剂
shrink-proof		不缩水的	rinse	v.	漂净
casual	adj.	不拘礼节的，非正式的			
rub	v.	擦，摩擦	casual wear		休闲服饰
wring	v.	绞，拧	overcoat	n.	外套，大衣
iron	v.	熨，烫平	fitting room		试衣间
blouse	n.	(妇女、儿童等的)短上衣，短衫			
crimson	n. & adj.	深红色(的)，绯红色(的)			
silver	n.	银色，银灰色	dear	adj.	昂贵的，高价的
ivory	n.	象牙色，乳白色	arcade	n.	长廊商场
exceptionally	adv.	例外地；异常地；特殊地			
exquisite	adj.	精美的；精致的；制作精良的			
reminder	n.	令人回忆的东西	fabrics	n.	织物，织品；布料
figure	n.	外形，体形	sand-washed silk		砂洗真丝
velvet	n.	天鹅绒，丝绒	figured silk		提花真丝
gorgeous	adj.	极好的	reeled pongee		纺绸
elegant	adj.	雅致的，优美的；精致的			
georgette	n.	乔其纱(一种极薄的透明细纱)			
terrific	adj.	棒极了，好极了	satin	n.	缎
garments	n.	服装，衣着	brocade	n.	织锦，锦缎
steep	adj.	(价格等)过高的，不合理的			
taffeta	n.	塔夫绸	workmanship	n.	手艺，工艺；做工
tapestry satin		织锦缎			

Learn by Heart

1. 常见服装词汇

正装	formal wear		睡衣	pajamas
羽绒服	down jackets		披风	cape

内衣	underwear	喇叭裙	flare skirt
童装	children's garments	背心裙	jumper skirt
婴儿装	infant's wear	灯笼裤	knickerbockers
女装	lady wear	斗篷	mantle
男装	man wear	超短裙	mini-skirt
冬装	winter clothes	背带裙	overalls
运动服	sportswear	连衣裤	jump suit
职业装	business suit	棉袄	cotton padded coat
风衣	trench coat	筒裙	barrel skirt, tube skirt
三件套	suit(3pcs)	裤子	pants
两件套	suit(2pcs)	袜子	shorts
毛衫	sweater	围巾	scarf
领带	tie		

2. 服装店用语

I like this one with the Great Wall.
我喜欢这件带长城图案的。

What size do you wear，sir?
先生，您穿什么尺寸？

The fitting room is over there.
试衣间在那里。

It's both colorfast and shrink-proof. And it is made 0f 100%cotton.
不会褪色也不会缩水，是 100%棉制的。

I'd like to see an overcoat for the autumn. Not too heavy and not too light.
我想要看看秋天穿的风衣，不要太厚也不要太薄。

It's loose at the waist, and it's a bit too large.
腰部有些松，而且还有点大。

We have this model in several sizes and colors, dark brown, light green, light yellow and crimson.
这种款式有好几种尺寸与颜色，有深褐色的、淡绿色的、淡黄色的、深红色的。

This is your size, it's a lovely dress and very smart. It's in fashion now. Would you like to try it?
这是您想要的尺寸，这件衣服很漂亮，非常时髦。您要试试吗？

That's rather more than I thought of paying. I should have something cheaper.
比我想象的贵多了，我应该买件便宜点的。

Maybe a little expensive dearer, but the quality is very good, madam. It's exceptionally good in material and the handicraft is more exquisite. It wears very well and keeps its shape.
可能是有点贵，不过质量非常好，夫人。特别是布料非常好，做工也精细，它穿起来特舒服，而且不变形。

We have silk fabrics，woolen fabrics，cotton fabrics as well as synthetic ones.

我们有丝、毛、棉的织物，还有人造织物。

We've got a good selection of them, such as sand-washed silk, figured silk, reeled pongee, georgette, satin, brocade and taffeta. You see, we have got it here.

我们有很多品种可供选择，比如，洗水真丝素绉缎、提花真丝、纺绸、乔其纱、缎子、提花缎和塔夫绸。您看，都在这儿。

But please wash it in lukewarm water with certain amount of special detergent for silk washing and rinse it well. Don't rub or wring it. It needs ironing before wearing it.

但是，请用温水洗涤，洗涤时加入一定量的专用洗涤剂，并且漂洗干净，不要摩擦或拧他，在穿之前需要烫。

Black is quite in fashion this year.

黑色是今年非常流行的颜色。

It's really elegant，but I'm afraid it's still a little tight across the shoulders.

确实不错，但是我担心肩膀的地方还是会有些紧。

It might be a little expensive，but the material is of the best quality, and our workmanship is the best in this city. It's worth every penny of it.

可能是有些贵，但是它是本市的顶级师傅用最好的原料做的，这个价钱很值。

Class Activity Role-Play

Scene One: Emily wants to buy a silk skirt, and she comes to a cloths shop. The shop assistant comes to serve her.

Scene Two: Linda wants to buy a cheongsam in a shop, and a salesclerk greets her and gives her some suggestions, at last she takes the one made from Suzhou silk.

Further Reading

Shopping(I)

When making a purchase in the United States, you should be aware that, in most cases, the price on the label is not the price you pay. You will have to pay tax also. Usually the tax is between five and ten percent of the price on the label.

Also, in buying clothes including shoes, you should know that the sizes are measured differently in the U. S. from the way they are measured in China where we use the metric system. In these cases, you can always ask the clerk for help.

If you are looking for an expensive item, it is advisable to check in more than one store to compare their prices. There is no "state price" in the United States. Smart shoppers often look for "sales", a time you can get the same thing with the same quality at a much lower price.

参考译文

购　物(一)

在美国购物的时候你应该注意，在大多数情况下，标签上的价格并不是你所需付的价钱，你还得交税。通常来说，税金是价钱的 5%～10%。

还有买衣服、买鞋的时候，中国用的是公制单位，而美国衡量大小的方法与中国完全不同。在这种情况下，你可以请求售货员帮助。

如果你想买贵重物品，建议你对比一下几家商店的价格。在美国没有"国家规定价格"。聪明的购物者可以寻找一些打折促销的机会，这时你可以买到质量相同，但价格低廉的商品。

Question

Do you know the differences of shopping in China and in America?

Unit 2 At the Jewelry and Crafts Counter

【听力音频】

Listening Practice

1. Listen to the dialogue and fill in the blanks.

(A: Assistant, G: Mr. Green)

A: Good morning, How can I help you?

G: Yes. I'm looking for_____for my son. Could you give me some advice?

A: It's my pleasure. How old is your son?

G: He's_____.

A: What about these picture puzzles, tangrams, picture cubes for spelling and transformers?

G: Let me have a look at the samples, please.

A: Here you are.

G: They're great. How much are the_____ and _____?

A: _____ for picture cubes for spelling and _____ for the Transformers.
   That comes to _____.

G: OK, here you are.

2. Listen and fill in the missing information.

Why does Mr. Black come to buy pearl necklaces:_____

The kind of the pearl necklaces:_____

What does Mr. Black take:_____

How much is it:_____

Situational Dialogues

1. Recommending Traditional Chinese Crafts

(Scene: Mrs. Green is interested in the traditional Chinese crafts, so she goes to the hotel's store to have a look. A shop assistant is receiving her.)

(S1: Shop Assistant 1, S2: Shop Assistant 2, G: Mrs. Green)

S1: Can I help you, madam?

G: Yes, please. May I take a look at the porcelain there?

S1: Those? They're not porcelain. They are cloisonné.

G: Oh, thanks for telling me. But they do look so similar.

S1: Yes, they do. The outside of cloisonné is covered with enamel but the body is actually made of a special type of copper. And the designs are also outlined by copper strips.

G: How wonderful! Is it for making tea? (Stop at the tea utensils counter)

S1: Yes, it is a teapot from Jingdezhen.

G: Jingdezhen? "The capital of porcelain," isn't it?

S1: Yes, it is. It produces the best quality porcelain in China. And the Jingdezhen is famous for its elegant modeling, beautiful figuration and lustrous color.

G: OK, I will buy this China tea set. How much is this?

S1: RMB 210 yuan. Perhaps you'd like to have the cloisonné set too. It's not expensive at all.

G: Yes, just the thing I need. Could you wrap them up carefully, please? I don't want to end up with a heap of broken vases when I get home.

S1: Certainly. We'll pack them carefully for you. Altogether RMB 380 yuan.

G: That's fine. Here is RMB 400 yuan.

S1: Here are the change and the receipt.

G: Thank you.

S1: Thank you for shopping. Wish you have fun in China.

(Mrs. Green turns to the embroidery counter.)

S2: Can I be of any assistance to you, madam?

G: Oh yes. I'd like to look at some of the embroidered table-cloths.

S2: Certainly. What size and shape do you want?

G: Let me see. I'd like one that's rectangular, and big enough for eight people.

S2: I see. We have several kinds over here. Would you come to look at them?

G: They're lovely. Simply exquisite! The design is beautiful. And it's very good material. Is it hand-made?

S2: Yes, it is. It's linen and made in Suzhou. Suzhou embroidery is considered the best among Chinese hand embroidery. It is exquisite in workmanship and multifarious in patterns.

G: Wonderful. I just can't decide which ones to buy. They're all so lovely. I'll just have to look through them slowly.

S2: That's all right. Take your time.

G: OK. I'll take this one. Besides table-cloths, do you have other embroidered articles?

S2: Yes. We have cushion-covers, curtains, pillow-cases, handkerchiefs and even 6-inch cup-holders.

G: I'd like to have a look at the handkerchiefs. They'll be good souvenirs.

S2: Here you are.

G: Well, I think I'll have these over here. How much are they?

S2: That's be 100 yuan for the whole set.

G: Oh, that's very steep for the handkerchiefs.

S2: But it's not expensive, considering their quality.

G: Anyhow, can you cut the price a bit?

S2: I'll offer you a special discount of 5%.

G: Well, I'll take them at your price.

2. Buying Jewelry

(Scene：A guest wants to buy some jewelry. A shop assistant is helping her.)

(G: Guest, A: Shop Assistant)

G: I want to buy some jewelry.

A: What kind of jewelry do you like to have?

G: I should like to look at some bracelets.

A: May I show you gold ones or platinum ones?

G: Gold ones.

A: Pure gold or Karat gold?

G: Pure gold ones, please.

A: Certainly, madam.

G: What's the price for this one?

A: Five hundred and fifty dollars.

G: How about five hundred dollars?

A: I'm sorry we only sell at fixed prices.

G: OK. I'll take it. I want to have my initials engraved on it.

A: Oh, that can be done.

G: I wish to buy a diamond ring, too.

A: How many carats would you like it to be?

G: I want three carats.

A: Is this one suitable for you?

G: No, it seems too old fashioned to me.

A: What about this?

G: Let me try it on. Oh, it's too small for me. Haven't you got any larger ones?

A: Then you may take that one. It's very nice and latest in style.

G: This fits me well. How much do you charge for it?

A: One thousand and two hundred dollars.

G: It's too expensive, I can only pay you one thousand dollars.

A: AS I told you before, madam, our shop doesn't ask two prices.

G: Is that a real string of pearls?

A: Yes，that's genuine.

G: Will you guarantee it?

A: You may take it on my word, if you find out it is an imitation you may return it to me.

G: What does it cost?

S: It costs three hundred dollars.

G: Good, I'll have it. Have you got any brooches?

A: With diamond, ruby or sapphire?

G: Sapphire, please, how much is it?

A: Four hundred dollars.

G: All right, how much will it be altogether? Please send it to my address, I'll pay the messenger on delivery.

3. Recommending Typical Chinese Toys

【拓展音频】

(Scene: A customer is leaving China and wants to buy some typical Chinese souvenirs for her relatives and friends. The shop assistant is recommending some typical Chinese toys and paper-cutting to her.)

(A: Shop Assistant, C: Customer)

A: Good morning, madam. Could I be of service to you?

C: Yes, I'd like to see some typical Chinese toys.

A: We have a great variety of toys. Here's a giant panda, which is very popular. Many foreign visitors like to buy this panda.

C: What a lovely panda! It is a very rare animal, isn't it?

A: Yes, it is. China is the homeland of giant pandas so it could be an ideal gift for your relatives or friends.

C: It's so adorable. I'll buy both of them.

A: Thank you, madam. Anything else you want?

C: Yes. I'd like to buy some gifts for my aunt and uncle. What else do you recommend?

A: There are some local products available here. These are Wuxi Clay Figurines. The artisans of Wuxi mould figurines with local fine clay and then paint them in an exaggerated way. They all look life-like, especially the dramatic figures. They are the best. Here's one figure most foreign visitors like to buy, "daafu."

C: Wow, what a lovely baby!

A: This lucky fatty is considered the symbol of fortune and happiness.

C: I'm sure my aunt and uncle will love it. I'll take four of them. Is there anything else you can recommend to me?

A: What do you think of the paper-cuts? They are made by artisans of Yangzhou Arts and Crafts Institute.

C: I was wondering how they make the cutting.

A: With a pair of scissors and a piece of paper the artisans can produce paper cuttings of various kinds, human figures, landscapes, flowers, birds, etc. Paper cutting of Yangzhou has created a unique artistic style and strong local features. And most important, they are very convenient to take.

C: This is sensational. Please give me two sets, one of landscapes, the other of birds. Can you pack up the other things and send them to the U. S.?

A: Sure. Would you put down your address?

(She writes down the address: 46 Linden Street, Riverdale, New York.)

A: Thank you, madam. The Postage, of course, will be extra.

C: How much will the postage come to?

A: About 50 yuan by surface mail. There is also an extra charge of 50 yuan for the packing. You know, we'll have to make a special wooden box.

C: That will be fine. Thank you.

A: You're welcome.

Words and Expressions

craft	n.	工艺，手艺品	platinum	n.	铂，白金
cloisonné	n.	景泰蓝	carat	n.	克拉
enamel	n.	瓷漆，亮漆；瓷釉			
initial	n.	(姓名或组织名称等的)首字母			
copper	n.	铜	engrave	vt.	雕刻，刻
outlined	v.	画出……的轮廓	string	n.	线；细绳；带子
strip	n.	条，带；细长片	genuine	adj.	真的，非伪造的
delicate	adj.	精美的，雅致的	guarantee	n.& v.	保证
lacquer-ware	n.	漆器	imitation	n.	仿制品，赝品
layer	n.	层	brooch	n.	女用胸针
lacquer	n.	亮漆，漆	ruby	n.&adj.	红宝石(的)
carve	v.	刻，雕刻	sapphire	n.	蓝宝石
polish	v.	磨光，擦亮	messenger	n.	(邮件的)信差，邮递员
compressed	adj.	压缩的	delivery	n.	投递，传送
mother-of-pearl	n.	珍珠层；珍珠母；青贝	variety	n.	种类
subdued	adj.	被制服的；顺从的	relative	n.	亲戚，亲属
glow	n.	色彩鲜艳；光辉	adorable	adj.	可爱的
heap	n.	大量，许多	Wuxi Clay Figurines		无锡泥人
embroidery	n.	刺绣	artisan	n.	工匠，技工
rectangular	adj.	矩形的，长方形的	mould	v.	用模子做，铸造
hand-made	adj.	手制的	exaggerated	adj.	夸张的
linen	adj.& n.	亚麻的	life-like		生动的
multifarious	adj.	多种的；繁杂的；多方面的			
dramatic figure		戏剧性的形象	article	n.	物品；商品
daafu		大阿福	cushion-cover	n.	套垫
paper-cut		剪纸	curtain	n.	帘；窗帘
Arts and Crafts Institute		工艺协会	pillow-case	n.	枕套
sensational	adj.	引起轰动的，轰动社会的			
cup-holder		杯垫	postage	n.	邮费

| souvenir | n. | 纪念品，纪念物 | packing | n. | 包裹；包装 |
| jewelry | n. | (总称)珠宝；首饰 | bracelet | n. | 手镯 |

Learn by Heart

1. 珠宝名称

翡翠	jadeite	锆石	zircon
玛瑙	agate	水晶	crystal
黄水晶	citrine	紫晶	amethyst
珊瑚	coral	琥珀	amber
孔雀石	malachite	绿宝石	beryl
祖母绿	emerald	血石	bloodstone
石榴石	garnet	K 金	Karat gold

2. 商店购物常用语

First of all, they cover the box with layers and layers of lacquer. When it is dry, they carve out of the designs. There are other ways, too, like first drawing the designs and polishing them with a surface of lacquer. And this one here is made of compressed mother-of-pearl. And the lacquer layers keep is from fading and give it a subdued glow.

首先，他们用一层一层的漆覆盖了这个盒子，干了之后，分隔成这些图案。也有其他的方式，比如，首先画出图案，然后表面抛光，这里的这个是压缩的珍珠贝制成的，漆层是为了保护它不褪色，减弱它的光辉。

Suzhou embroidery is considered the best among Chinese hand embroidery. It is exquisite in workmanship and multifarious in patterns.

苏州刺绣被认为是全国手工刺绣中最好的。做工讲究，图案也是五花八门。

We have cushion-covers, curtains, pillow-cases, handkerchiefs and even 6-inch cup-holders.

我们有椅垫套、窗帘、枕套、手绢和 6 英寸的杯垫。

But it's not expensive, considering their quality.

看一下它们的质量，不算贵。

I'll offer you a special discount of 5%.
我可以给您 5%的折扣。

May I show you gold ones or platinum ones?
您要看黄金的还是白金的？

I want to have my initials engraved on it.
我想把我姓名的第一个字母刻在上面。

How many carats would you like it to be?
您想要多少克拉的？

Then you may take that one. It's very nice and latest in style.
那您可以买那个。那个非常漂亮而且款式最新。

AS I told you before，madam，our shop doesn't ask two prices.
夫人，我对您说过，我们店不还价。

You may take it on my word，if you find out it is an imitation you may return it to me.
我能保证，如果发现它是假的，您可以退还给我。

With diamond，ruby or sapphire？
要带钻石的，红宝石的还是蓝宝石的？

These are Wuxi Clay Figurines. The artisans of Wuxi mould figurines with local fine clay and then paint them in an exaggerated way. They all look life-like, especially the dramatic figures. They are the best. Here's one figure most foreign visitors like to buy, "daafu."
这些是无锡泥人，无锡的工匠用上好的泥土铸制成泥人，然后用夸张的手法绘制而成。它们看起来都很生动，尤其是那些戏剧性的形象。这些是最好的。大多数外国游客喜欢买的一个泥人叫做"大阿福"。

This daafu is considered the symbol of fortune and happiness.
这个大阿福是幸运和快乐的象征。

With a pair of scissors and a piece of paper the artisans can produce paper cuttings of various kinds, human figures, landscapes, flowers, birds, etc. Paper cutting of Yangzhou has created a unique artistic style and strong local features. And most important, they are very convenient to take.
用一把剪刀和一张纸，手工艺人可以剪各种各样的剪纸，如人物形象、风景、花、鸟等。扬州剪纸具有一种独特的艺术风格和强烈的地方特色。最重要的是，它们很方便携带。

About 50 yuan by surface mail. There is also an extra charge of 50 yuan for the packing. You know, we'll have to make a special wooden box.
平邮是 50 元，包裹另外加收 50 元，您知道，我们必须做一个特别的木头盒子。

Class Activity Role-Play

Scene One: Ann wants to buy a present for her parents. But she doesn't know where to buy something that is typical Chinese, so she comes to you for help. You could offer some recommendations.

Scene Two: Work with your partners. Search information about typical Chinese gifts and the make a PPT to present in class.

Further Reading

Shopping (Ⅱ)

There are many "sales" in the U. S., and the stores will lower their prices. This may all be very confusing to the visitors. Which is the best product to buy out of hundreds to choose from? How are you going to know how to "get your money's worth" when you shop? Perhaps the best advice is: Don't hurry. Visit various stores and determine the quality of merchandise. Examine the goods carefully. Read the advertisements so that you can compare prices. Explore and examine before you buy. It is wise to be especially careful with products that are on sale, because many stores will not allow goods on sale to be exchanged. In most cases, however, sales are an excellent opportunity to buy quality products at reduced prices.

There is a great variety of shops in the U. S., ranging from very large stores called department stores, offering clothing, furniture, household goods and many other goods, to very small shops that specialize in just one kind of product. There are "discount houses" offering goods at low prices and "dime stores" specializing in a wide range of inexpensive items.

参考译文

购　物(二)

在美国有许多"降价甩卖"的机会，那时商店会降低商品价格。这也许会使旅游者困惑。有成百上千种选择，究竟买哪个最好？在买东西的时候，你怎么才能知道让自己的钱"花得值"？也许最好的建议是：别着急！逛一下各个商店，鉴别一下商品质量。仔细地查看物品。读一下广告以便比较价格。买之前仔细调查研究一下。对甩卖的商品仔细看一下是明智之举，因为许多商店都不允许退换甩卖商品。但是，绝大多数情况下，甩卖是购买物美价廉商品的好时机。

美国有各种各样的商店，大到百货商店，出售衣物、家具、居家用品和其他很多东西，小到专卖一种商品的小店。还有"折扣商店"，专卖价格低廉的货品，也有叫"一角店"的，专卖种类繁多的廉价物品。

Question

What's the "sales" in the U. S.?

Unit 3   At the Medicine and Foodstuff Department

Listening Practice

1. Listen to the dialogue and fill in the blanks.

The art of cooking in China dates back _____ and it is an integral part of Chinese civilization. Today, Chinese cuisine is ranked among _____ and Chinese restaurants can be found nearly _____.

Chinese cooking pays great attention to _____, fragrance, _____, _____ and nutrition of the food. It requires a technique of _____ and_____ control. By tough estimate, there are about_____ different local cooking styles in China.

According to the local flavors, Chinese cuisine is subdivided into a great number of schools, among which the most popular and well-known schools are Guangdong, Sichuan, Shandong and Huai'an-Yangzhou cuisines.

2. Listen and fill in the missing information.

The usual dose is_____

Ginseng grows in_____

While having ginseng, don't drink_____

The price of one kilo ginseng _____

Situational Dialogues

1. Chinese Tea

(Scene: A customer wants to buy some tea for his family, so the shop assistant is recommending the Chinese tea to him.)

(A: Shop Assistant, C: Customer)

A: Good afternoon, sir. Can I help you?

C: Yes, I'm looking for some tea. What do you recommend?

A: How about Longjing tea? It is a first-class green tea. And it is fresh green, aromatic, sweet and smooth in appearance.

C: Wonderful. I'll take two tins. I still need some other kinds of Chinese tea. You know, we're a big family; every one has his own taste.

A: We have a variety of Chinese teas. We have Qimen black tea, Wulong tea, and jasmine tea.

C: Jasmine tea? What is it?

A: It's a high quality green tea mixed with dried jasmine flowers. It has a wonderful fragrance.

C: What else have you mentioned? Qi, black tea?

A: Yes, Qimen black tea. It has a rich, sweet smell, fine both in appearance and in quality. It's one of the most famous black teas around the world.

C: I was told there's a sort of Chinese tea which has a reducing effect. Is that so?

A: Yes, that's Wulong tea. More and more foreign visitors, especially ladies, come to buy Wulong tea in order to keep fit. Wulong tea is very refreshing and helps you to get rid of tiredness.

C: It's very kind of you to tell me all about it. I'll take three tins of each. Should I pay in cash?

A: Not necessarily. Traveler's checks or Master Card will also do.

2. Chinese Medicine and Tonics

(Scene: A customer is asking some information about Chinese medicine and tonics to help his wife who is not healthy. A shop assistant is serving him.)

(A: Shop Assistant, C: Customer)

A: Good afternoon, sir. Are you being attended to?

C: No. Could you show me some highly nutritious tonics?

A: Yes, of course. We have wild ginseng, Korean ginseng, young pilose antler, pearl powder, pearl oral liquid, ass-skin glue, tortoise-shell glue, gyrophora, white fungus, bird's nest, cordyceps, chicken essence with cordyceps. Do you want it for yourself?

C: No, my wife has been suffering from a poor appetite and asthenia of the heart and lungs for years.

A: I'm sorry to hear that. Please tell your wife not to worry too much, sir. I suggest she take cordyceps. (He shows him the cordyceps.)

C: Ah, how queer it looks. What is it?

A: It's a tonic only available in China, which can cure such ailments as anaemia. Most important, it has no side-effects.

C: Good. I'll buy three boxes of it. Will you please tell me how to take it?

A: Yes, sir. You may fill 3 or 5 pieces of cordyceps into a cleaned and chopped open duck's head and cook with the whole ducks or stew cordyceps with chicken.

C: That sounds very interesting. I think I should suggest my wife to take it as a must for her daily diet.

A: Please remind your wife not to eat turnip and garlic when taking this medicine.

C: Thank you for your advice. How much is it?

A: 168 yuan a box.

3. Chinese Local Flavor Food

(Scene: A customer wants to buy some local flavor food for his journey to Xi'an, and the shop assistant is recommending them to him.)

(A: Shop Assistant, C: Customer)

A: Good morning, madam and sir. Are you being attended to?

C: No, can you recommend to us some Nanjing specialties?

A: Yes, sir. Will you try Nanjing Salted Duck? It's vacuum-packed and can be kept for a period of time. People here enjoy eating it and often buy Nanjing duck as presents to send to their relatives and friends.

C: That's great. I'll buy 2 bags.

A: Is there anything else you are interested in?

C: Yes. We're traveling to Xi'an tomorrow. We need some picked cucumber and some other specialties for our journey to Xi'an.

A: Oh, in that case, I recommend you Yangzhou pickles and five flavored beans. Yangzhou pickles are well-known in China while five-flavored beans, Wu Xiang Dou, are one of Shanghai's specialties made by Yu Yuan Garden Bazaar.

C: OK. Get me two bags of Wu Xiang Dou and two bottles of Yangzhou pickles.

A: Here you are. Now, let me put them in the plastic bag. Please check the goods in the package. Will that do?

C: That's very thoughtful of you.

A: My pleasure.

Words and Expressions

recommend	v.	推荐	chicken essence with cordyceps		虫草鸡精
Longjing tea		龙井茶	appetite	n.	食欲，胃口
first-class	adj.	一级的，第一流的	asthenia	n.	无力
green tea		绿茶	lung	n.	肺
aromatic	adj.	芳香的，馨香的	queer	adj.	奇怪的，古怪的
smooth	adj.	平滑的，光滑的	ailment	n.	病痛
tin	n.	罐	anaemia	n.	贫血(症)
Qimen black tea		祁门红茶	side-effect		副作用
Wulong tea		乌龙茶	chop	v.	砍，劈，斩
jasmine tea		茉莉花茶	stew	v.	(用文火)煮，炖，焖
fragrance	n.	芳香	diet	n.	饮食，食物
black tea		红茶	remind	v.	提醒
reducing	n.	减肥法	turnip	n.	芜菁甘蓝
keep fit		保持健康	garlic	n.	大蒜，蒜头

tonic	*n.*	补品	local flavor food		当地风味食品
nutritious	*adj.*	有营养的，滋养的	specialty	*n.*	特产，名产
pilose antler		鹿茸	Nanjing Salted Duck		南京清真板鸭
pearl powder		珍珠粉	vacuum-packed		真空包装
pearl oral liquid		珍珠口服液	pickled cucumber		酸黄瓜
ass-skin glue		阿胶	Yangzhou pickles		扬州酱菜
tortoise-shell glue		龟甲胶	five-flavored beans		五香豆
gyrophora		灵芝	Yu Yuan Garden Bazaar		豫园商场
white fungus		银耳	plastic	*adj.*	塑料的
bird's nest		燕窝	thoughtful	*adj.*	体贴的，考虑周到的
cordyceps		冬虫夏草			

Learn by Heart

1. 中国传统小吃

红豆糕	red bean cake	蛋饼	egg cake
绿豆糕	bean paste cake	皮蛋	preserved egg
糯米糕	glutinous rice cake	麻花	hemp flowers

2. 购物常用语

We have a variety of Chinese teas. We have Qimen black tea, Wulong tea, and jasmine tea.
我们有很多种类的中国茶选择，有祁门红茶、乌龙茶和茉莉花茶。

It's a high quality green tea mixed with dried jasmine flowers. It has a wonderful fragrance.
这是一种高品质的绿茶混合了干茉莉花制成，非常芳香。

Qimen black tea has a rich, sweet smell, fine both in appearance and in quality. It's one of the most famous black teas around the world.
祁门红茶既有非常清甜的芳香，又有上乘的外观和质量，是世界上最有名的红茶之一。

Wulong tea is very refreshing and helps you to get rid of tiredness.
乌龙茶很新鲜，可以帮您消除疲劳。

We have wild ginseng, Korean ginseng, young pilose antler, pearl powder, pearl oral liquid, ass-skin glue, tortoise-shell glue, gyrophora, white fungus, bird's nest, cordyceps, chicken essence with cordyceps.

我们有野人参、高丽参、鹿茸、珍珠粉、珍珠口服药、阿胶、龟甲胶、灵芝粉、银耳、燕窝、冬虫夏草、虫草鸡精。

It's a tonic only available in China, which can cure such ailments as anaemia. Most important, it has no side-effects.

这是只在中国才有的一种滋补品，可以治疗贫血等这样一些症状。而且重要的是，它没有副作用。

You may fill 3 or 5 pieces of cordyceps into a cleaned and chopped open duck's head and cook with the whole ducks or stew cordyceps with chicken.

您可以把 3～5 片冬虫夏草放到干净的切开的鸭子头里，或者跟整只鸭子一起炖，或者和鸡一起炖。

Please remind your wife not to eat turnip and garlic when taking this medicine.
请提醒您的妻子在吃这个药的时候不要吃芜菁和蒜。

Will you try Nanjing Salted Duck? It's vacuum-packed and can be kept for a period of time. People here enjoy eating it and often buy Nanjing duck as presents to send to their relatives and friends.

您想试一下南京清真板鸭吗？它是真空包装的，可以放一段时间。人们很喜欢吃这个，经常把它作为礼物送给亲戚朋友。

I recommend you Yangzhou pickles and five flavored beans. Yangzhou pickles are well-known in China while five-flavored beans, Wu Xiang Dou, are one of Shanghai's specialties made by Yu Yuan Garden Bazaar.

那样的话，我建议您带扬州酱菜和五香豆。扬州酱菜在中国非常驰名，五香豆是豫园商场的特产。

That's very thoughtful of you.
您考虑得太周到了。

Class Activity Role-Play

Scene One: Mr. Blair needs to buy some presents for his parents, wife and son at the hotel shop. Please offer some recommends for him.

Scene Two: Work with your partners. Search information about the Chinese tea and the make a PPT to present in class.

Further Reading

Returning the Purchased Goods

It is usually possible to exchange defective items, even if they are bought when they are on sale. Be sure to do it as soon as possible, within a day or two, and remember to bring the receipt with you.

If the store happens to have sold out the item you wish to exchange, the store assistant may offer to show you something similar. If it is more expensive, you have to pay the difference. But you can get your money back if you do not like any other kind.

参考译文

退　货

　　通常来说，如果商品有损坏，即使是在甩卖的时候买的，也可以换。但是要尽快，在一两天之内，并且记住要带收据。

　　如果商店碰巧已售罄了你所要换的商品，售货员会让你看一些类似的商品。如果更贵的话，你必须付差额。但如果你不喜欢其他样式，你可以要求退款。

Question

Can you exchange items if you lost the receipt?

Unit 4 At the Chinese Arts and Stationery Department

【听力音频】

Listening Practice

1. Listening to the dialogue and fill in the blanks.

(S: Staff, B: Mr. Blare)

S: May I help you, sir?

B: I'm interested in _____. Have you got any good ones?

S: Yes, we have a great variety of Chinese antiques. Are you looking for something special?

B: I want to see some _____.

S: Well, we have _____, _____ and flower and bird painting. Which do you like best?

B: I'd like _____.

S: Good. How about this picture of_____? It was painted by a famous painter of Qing Dynasty.

B: Oh, the crane looks like real. I like it very much.

S: And what's more, in traditional Chinese thinking, cranes and pine trees symbolize longevity.

B: That sounds very interesting. How much is it?

S: _____.

B: It's lot of money, but the picture is excellent. I'll take it.

2. Listen and fill in the missing information.

Sorts of chinaware:_____

Objects he wants to buy:_____

Place of production:_____ Use of the porcelain:_____

Discount:_____

Situational Dialogues

1. Chinese Seal Cutting, Calligraphy and Paintings

(Scene: A shop assistant is giving explanations about Chinese Seal Cutting, Calligraphy and Paintings to a customer who is puzzled about them.)

(A: Shop Assistant, C: Customer)

A: Good afternoon, sir and madam. What can I do for you?

C: Good afternoon. We feel puzzled about the use of so many little piece of hard and soft stones.

A: Engravers cut seals on them. Seal cutting, as one of the typical Chinese traditional arts, which also includes calligraphy and paintings, is very popular with the social elite. Nowadays, many foreign friends who are interested in Chinese culture are fond of having their own name-seals cut.

C: That sounds great. But I'm particularly interested in traditional Chinese paintings. People tell me that Chinese calligraphy and paintings are the gem of Chinese culture. But I wonder what's the difference between Western oil paintings and Chinese ink paintings.

A: Well, briefly speaking, Western oil paintings are created by colors and brush touches while traditional Chinese paintings are by lines and strokes. Traditional Chinese painting is a combination in the same picture of the arts of poetry, calligraphy, painting and seal engraving.

C: Thank you for your explanations. But are the pictures in your shop original or reproductions?

A: They're all reproductions. But they retain so well the vividness and charm of the original that it is difficult to tell which is the original and which is not.

(The customer is looking through the pictures.)

C: Good morning! I want to buy some traditional Chinese paintings.

A: OK, this way please. Here is an exhibition of Chinese traditional paintings. I hope you like it.

C: Marvelous!

A: Well, sir. I should say you've got artistic eyes. This is an imitation of the famous painting "Spring Outing" by Zhang Ziqian, a great artist of Sui Dynasty (581 A.D. -618 A. D.). Zhang's painting is the earliest painting of landscape we've discovered to this day. Would you like to buy it?

C: Yes. How much is it?

A: RMB 900 yuan.

C: That sounds reasonable. I'll take it. By the way, who painted this "Galloping Horse"?

A: Mr. Xu Beihong, one of the most famous painters of modern China. His paintings are characterized by typical Chinese features as well as certain techniques of oil paintings.

C: Wonderful. I'll take it too. Do you accept American Express credit cards?

A: Yes, we do……Here is your invoice. Please keep it well.

C: Thank you.

2. The Four Treasure of Study

(Scene: A shop assistant is recommending the "Four Treasure of the Study" to a customer who wants to buy something special.)

(A: Shop Assistant, C: Customer)

A: Good afternoon, sir. What can I do for you?

C: Good afternoon. I'm leaving for Chicago tomorrow. I'd like to buy something special. Can you give me some suggestions?

A: My pleasure, sir. I suggest you taking something closely related to our ancient civilization. You may have heard that Chinese paining is closely related to the art of calligraphy. Both Chinese painters and calligraphers use black ink that can produce different shades and write brushes that can make many kinds of lines.

C: I was told that they are the so-called "Four Treasure of the Study". What are they?

A: Look here, sir. They are rice paper (Xuan paper), ink-brush, ink-slab, and ink-stick. You may take them as typical souvenirs from China.

C: Sounds interesting. Would you please give me some more details?

A: Sure. The "Four Treasures of the Study" was originally named for the rice paper produced in Xuancheng, ink-slab in Duanzhou, ink-brush in Huzhou and ink-stick in Huizhou. Xuan paper, honored as the "king of paper" and favored by Chinese artists, is soft and absorbent. It can bring the characteristic styles of Chinese paintings into full play. Duanzhou ink-slabs, also called Duan ink-slabs are the best among all the ink-slabs produced in China. It bears a tinge of purple in color, with exquisite veins and smooth jade-like appearance.

C: How nice! How about the ink-brush and the ink-stick?

A: Huzhou ink-brushes are famous for their material selection and elaborate craftsmanship. The materials for the brushes can be the wool of goats, hair of yellow weasels, of hares of a mixture. Huizhou ink-sticks are known as being "clear, moist, even and neat". The ink can always "stay firm keep its original touches once on paper".

C: That's very kind of you to give me such detailed explanations. But I'm afraid I can't write and paint with a writing brush, let alone using them in painting and calligraphy.

A: It doesn't matter. You can learn how to use an ink-brush.

C: I even don't know how to use ink-slabs and ink-sticks. Maybe I'm too old to learn any new tricks. Never have I dreamed that I could use an ink-brush someday.

A: One is never too old to learn, you know.

(The shop assistant shows how to make ink, how to grip the ink-brush and how to write with the brush.)

C: Ah, you are so persuasive. Please give me a dozen Huzhou ink-brushes, a Duan ink-slab and 40 sheets of Xuan paper. How much do they come to in all?

A: Just a moment, please…Oh, 790 yuan in all. I'll wrap them up for you.

3. Packing and Shipping

(Scene: A customer wants to send a set of porcelain and some embroidery to his friend, and the shop assistant is receiving him.)

(C: Customer, A: Shop Assistant)

C: Where is the parcel counter please?

A: May I ask what you are sending?

C: A set of porcelain that I've bought for a friend.

A: Will you open it for inspection?

C: But I have just packed it up nicely. I don't want to spend the next hour repacking it.

A: I'm sorry, but it is a question of security. That is the rule. We will just look into the box and will be very careful with it.

C: OK, if that's the rule. In Rome, do as the Romans do, as they say.

A: There is some embroidery here as well as the porcelain set.

C: Right. They go with the set.

A: You'll have to put them both on the form… Do you want to send it by air or surface mail?

C: Airmail please. How much is it?

A: That will be 72 yuan. Anything else?

C: No, thank you.

Words and Expressions

stationery	n.	文具
seal cutting		篆刻
calligraphy	n.	书法
engraver	n.	雕刻师；雕刻匠
seal	n.& v.	印章，图章；盖章
elite	n.	精华，精英
gem	n.	宝物，珍品
Chinese ink paintings		中国水墨画
stroke	n.	笔触
combination	n.	结合(体)，联合(体)
poetry	n.	(总称)诗，诗歌，韵文
original	n.	原著；原画
reproduction	n.	复制品
retain	v.	保留，保持
vividness	n.	生动；逼真；清晰
charm	n.	魅力
Galloping Horse		奔马图
Artistic	adj.	有艺术鉴赏力的
Spring Outing		游春图
characterize	v.	具有……的特征，以……为特征

Four Treasure of Study		文房四宝
ancient	adj.	古老的
civilization	n.	文明
calligrapher	n.	书法家
rice paper (Xuan paper)		米纸(宣纸)
ink-brush		毛笔
ink-slab		砚台
ink-stick		墨
absorbent	adj.	能吸收(水、光等)的
characteristic	n.	特性，特征，特色
play	n.	发挥
tinge	n.	(较淡的)色调，色彩
veins	n.	(木，石等的)纹理，条纹
jade	n.	翡翠；硬玉；玉
elaborate	adj.	精心制作的，精巧的
weasel	n.	黄鼠狼，鼬鼠
trick	n.	把戏；特技
persuasive	adj.	有说服力的
inspection	n.	检查
nicely	adv.	令人满意地；令人愉快地
security	n.	安全

Learn by Heart

1. 中国民俗文化英语词汇

唐三彩	tri-colored glazed pottery of the Tang Dynasty	风车	pinwheel
蜡染	batik	杂技	acrobatics
双面秀	two-sided embroidery	拨浪鼓	shaking drum
挂毯	tapestry	竹苗	bamboo flute
蜡染	batik	皮影	shadow puppet
藤条制品	wickerwork	糖人	sugar-molded
烟嘴	cigarette holder	踩高跷	stilt walk
鼻烟壶	snuff bottle	说书	monologue story-telling
盆景	potted landscape	相声	cross talk
屏风	screen	中国结	Chinese knot
轿子	sedans		

2. 购物常用语

Seal cutting, as one of the typical Chinese traditional arts, which also includes calligraphy and paintings, is very popular with the social elite.

篆刻是中国的一项传统艺术，它与书法和绘画在社会精英当中很流行。

Well, briefly speaking, Western oil paintings are created by colors and brush touches while traditional Chinese paintings are by lines and strokes. Traditional Chinese painting is a combination in the same picture of the arts of poetry, calligraphy, painting and seal engraving.

嗯，概括来说，西方油画重色彩和润饰，而中国画则重线条和笔触。传统中国画是诗、书法、绘画和篆刻艺术的融合。

Are the pictures in your shop original or reproductions?

您店里的图画是原件还是仿制品？

Mr. Xu Beihong, one of the most famous painters of modern China. His paintings are characterized by typical Chinese features as well as certain techniques of oil paintings.

徐悲鸿先生是现代中国最著名的画家之一。他的画以典型的中国油画艺术特征为特色。

I suggest you take something closely related to our ancient civilization.

我建议您带一些跟我们中国的古老文明紧密相关的东西。

They are rice paper (Xuan paper), ink-brush, ink-slab and ink-stick. You may take them as typical souvenirs from China.

这是米纸(宣纸)、毛笔、砚台、墨。您可以把它们当作有中国特色的纪念品。

Sure. The "Four Treasures of the Study" was originally named for the rice paper produced in Xuancheng, ink-slab in Duanzhou, ink-brush in Huzhou and ink-stick in Huizhou. Xuan paper, honored as the "king of paper" and favored by Chinese artists, is soft and absorbent. It can bring the characteristic styles of Chinese paintings into full play. Duanzhou ink-slabs, also called Duan ink-slabs are the best among all the ink-slabs produced in China. It bears a tinge of purple in color, with exquisite veins and smooth jade-like appearance.

当然可以，"文房四宝"最早是来命名宣城的米纸、端州的砚台、湖州的毛笔和徽州的墨。宣纸被誉为"纸中之王"，非常受中国艺术家青睐，很软而且易吸墨。它可以让中国绘画艺术得到淋漓尽致的展现。端州的砚台又称"端砚"，它在中国生产的砚台当中是最好的。它外表呈现一种淡淡的紫色，纹理很优雅，看起来像光滑的玉。

Huzhou ink-brushes are famous for their material selection and elaborate craftsmanship. The materials for the brushes can be the wool of goats, hair of yellow weasels, of hares of a mixture. Huizhou ink-sticks are known as being "clear, moist, even and neat". The ink can always stay firm keep its original touches once on

徽州的毛笔以其原料的选择和复杂的工艺而著名。毛笔的原料可以是羊毛，黄鼠狼的毛发，或者兔毛的混合物。徽州的墨被认为是"干净、湿润、平滑、匀整"。墨总是很坚硬，可以保持其在纸上的原样。

Will you open it for inspection?

您打开检查一下吗？

I'm sorry, but it is a question of security. That is the rule. We will just look into the box and will be very careful.

对不起，但是这是个安全问题，是原则。我们只是看一下盒子，会很小心的。

Class Activity Role-Play

Scene One: Mr. Blair needs to buy some presents for his parents, wife and son at the hotel shop, please help him.

Scene Two: Mr. Green wants to buy a painting in a souvenir shop, and the shop assistant introduces Chinese painting to him.

Further Reading

Prices of Goods

Americans do not usually bargain over prices as is familiar in much of the world. What they do instead is to shop around to find the store which offers the item and quality they want at the lowest price. Almost everything sold in the United States varies in price according to the store and often the time of year. (just before Christmas the prices are often highest; lowest just after Christmas or during August when many stores have sales). Sometimes the price varies according to state or local taxes. Many people cross state lines to buy liquor, cigarettes, or automobiles, etc., because there are wide fluctuation in taxes in such items from state to state.

参考译文

商品的价格

世界上大多数国家的人都在买东西时讲价，但美国人却不这样。他们的做法是四处转转，找一家商品质量最好、价格最低的商店。几乎所有在美国出售的商品的价格都会因时间和商店的不同而不同。(圣诞节前夕价格最高；圣诞节过后或8月的众多商家打折期间价格最低)。有时，价格也因州税和地方税的差异而不同。许多人经常跨州去购买酒、烟和汽车等商品，因为这些商品的税金在州与州之间有很大差别。

Question

Do you like to bargain over prices when buying goods?

参 考 文 献

[1] 江波，李啟金. 酒店实用英语[M]. 天津：天津大学出版社，2011.

[2] 袁露，阮蓓，李飞. 酒店英语[M]. 天津：天津大学出版社，2010.

[3] 胡扬政. 现代酒店服务英语[M]. 北京：清华大学出版社，2009.

北京大学出版社高职高专旅游系列规划教材

序号	标准书号	书 名	主 编	定价	出版年份	配套情况
1	978-7-301-27467-5	客房运行与管理(第2版)	孙亮	36	2016	电子课件, 习题答案
2	978-7-301-19184-2	酒店情景英语	魏新民, 申延子	28	2011	电子课件
3	978-7-301-27611-2	餐饮运行与管理(第2版)	王敏	38	2016	电子课件, 习题答案
4	978-7-301-19306-8	景区导游	陆霞, 郭海胜	32	2011	电子课件
5	978-7-301-18986-3	导游英语	王堃	30	2011	电子课件, 光盘
6	978-7-301-19029-6	品牌酒店英语面试培训教程	王志玉	22	2011	电子课件
7	978-7-301-19955-8	酒店经济法律理论与实务	钱丽玲	32	2012	电子课件
8	978-7-301-19932-9	旅游法规案例教程	王志雄	36	2012	电子课件
9	978-7-301-20477-1	旅游资源与开发	冯小叶	37	2012	电子课件
10	978-7-301-20459-7	模拟导游实务	王延君	25	2012	电子课件
11	978-7-301-20478-8	酒店财务管理	左桂谔	41	2012	电子课件
12	978-7-301-20566-2	调酒与酒吧管理	单铭磊	43	2012	电子课件
13	978-7-301-20652-2	导游业务规程与技巧	叶娅丽	31	2012	电子课件
14	978-7-301-21137-3	旅游法规实用教程	周崴	31	2012	电子课件
15	978-7-301-21559-3	饭店管理实务	金丽娟	37	2013	电子课件
16	978-7-301-27841-3	酒店情景英语(第2版)	高文知	34	2017	电子课件
17	978-7-301-22187-7	会展概论	徐静	28	2013	电子课件, 习题答案
18	978-7-301-22316-1	旅行社经营实务	吴丽云, 刘洁	28	2013	电子课件
19	978-7-301-22349-9	会展英语	李世平	28	2013	电子课件, mp3
20	978-7-301-22777-0	酒店前厅经营与管理	李俊	28	2013	电子课件
21	978-7-301-22416-8	会展营销	谢红芹	25	2013	电子课件
22	978-7-301-22778-7	旅行社计调实务	叶娅丽, 陈学春	35	2013	电子课件
23	978-7-301-23013-8	中国旅游地理	于春雨	37	2013	电子课件
24	978-7-301-23072-5	旅游心理学	高跃	30	2013	电子课件
25	978-7-301-23210-1	旅游文学	吉凤娟	28	2013	电子课件
26	978-7-301-23143-2	餐饮经营与管理	钱丽换	38	2013	电子课件
27	978-7-301-23232-3	旅游景区管理	肖鸿燚	38	2014	电子课件
28	978-7-301-24102-8	中国旅游文化	崔益红, 韩宁	32	2014	电子课件
29	978-7-301-24396-1	会展策划	高 跃	28	2014	电子课件, 习题答案
30	978-7-301-24441-8	前厅客房部运行与管理	花立明, 张艳平	40	2014	电子课件, 习题答案
31	978-7-301-24436-4	饭店管理概论	李俊	33	2014	电子课件, 习题答案
32	978-7-301-24478-4	旅游行业礼仪实训教程(第2版)	李 丽	40	2014	电子课件
33	978-7-301-24481-4	酒店信息化与电子商务(第2版)	袁宇杰	26	2014	电子课件, 习题答案
34	978-7-301-24477-7	酒店市场营销(第2版)	赵伟丽, 魏新民	40	2014	电子课件
35	978-7-301-24629-0	旅游英语	张玉菲, 谷丽丽	30	2014	电子课件
36	978-7-301-24993-2	营养配餐与养生指导	卢亚萍	26	2014	电子课件
37	978-7-301-24883-6	旅游客源国概况	金丽娟	37	2015	电子课件
38	978-7-301-25226-0	中华美食与文化	刘居超	32	2015	电子课件
39	978-7-301-25563-6	现代酒店实用英语教程	张晓辉	28	2015	电子课件, 习题答案
40	978-7-301-25572-8	茶文化与茶艺(第2版)	王莎莎	38	2015	电子课件, 光盘
41	978-7-301-25720-3	旅游市场营销	刘长英	31	2015	电子课件, 习题答案
42	978-7-301-25898-9	会展概论(第2版)	崔益红	32	2015	电子课件
43	978-7-301-25845-3	康乐服务与管理	杨华	35	2015	电子课件
44	978-7-301-26074-6	前厅服务与管理(第2版)	黄志刚	28	2015	电子课件
45	978-7-301-26221-4	烹饪营养与配餐	程小华	41	2015	电子课件, 习题答案
46	978-7-301-27139-1	宴会设计与统筹	王敏	29	2016	电子课件

　　如您需要更多教学资源如电子课件、电子样章、习题答案等，请登录北京大学出版社第六事业部官网 www.pup6.cn 搜索下载。

　　如您需要浏览更多专业教材，请扫下面的二维码，关注北京大学出版社第六事业部官方微信（微信号：pup6book），随时查询专业教材、浏览教材目录、内容简介等信息，并可在线申请纸质样书用于教学。

　　感谢您使用我们的教材，欢迎您随时与我们联系，我们将及时做好全方位的服务。联系方式：010-62750667，37370364@qq.com，pup_6@163.com，lihu80@163.com，欢迎来电来信。客户服务 QQ 号：1292552107，欢迎随时咨询。